Gabriela Mistral

This series of publications on Africa, Latin America, Southeast Asia, and Global and Comparative Studies is designed to present significant research, translation, and opinion to area specialists and to a wide community of persons interested in world affairs. The editor seeks manuscripts of quality on any subject and can usually make a decision regarding publication within three months of receipt of the original work. Production methods generally permit a work to appear within one year of acceptance. The editor works closely with authors to produce a high-quality book. The series appears in a paperback format and is distributed worldwide. For more information, contact the executive editor at Ohio University Press, Scott Quadrangle, University Terrace, Athens, Ohio 45701.

Executive editor: Gillian Berchowitz
AREA CONSULTANTS
Africa: Diane M. Ciekawy
Latin America: Thomas Walker
Southeast Asia: William H. Frederick
Global and Comparative Studies: Ann R. Tickamyer

The Ohio University Research in International Studies series is published for the Center for International Studies by Ohio University Press. The views expressed in individual volumes are those of the authors and should not be considered to represent the policies or beliefs of the Center for International Studies, Ohio University Press, or Ohio University.

Gabriela Mistral

The Audacious Traveler

Edited by Marjorie Agosín

Ohio University Research in International Studies
Latin America Series No. 40
Ohio University Press
Athens

12 11 10 09 08 07 06 05 04 03   5 4 3 2 1

The books in the Ohio University Research in International Studies Series
are printed on acid-free paper ⊖

Library of Congress Cataloging-in-Publication Data

Gabriela Mistral : the audacious traveler / edited by Marjorie Agosín.
    p.   cm.   — (Research in international studies. Latin America series : no. 40)
Includes bibliographical references and index.
    ISBN 0-89680-230-2 (alk. paper)
    1. Mistral, Gabriela, 1889–1957—Political and social views. 2. Mistral, Gabriela,
1889–1957—Journeys. I. Agosín, Marjorie. II. Series.
    PQ8097.G6Z5633 2003
    861'.62—dc21

                                                2003054714

This book is dedicated to my mother, Frida Agosín.
When I was a child, she read me the poems
of Gabriela Mistral, and they rocked me
into a peaceful sleep.

Contents

Acknowledgments

IN SANTIAGO DE CHILE, where the poetry of Gabriela Mistral was sung and recited, her presence acquired mythical proportions in my imagination. Her poetry has become part of an American identity that continues to grow and inspire all those who read her. I am grateful that my schoolteachers encouraged me to read Mistral and understand her complex world. Among them, I thank Luis Alvarez and Marta Alvarado. I also thank the scholars who so generously contributed to this book and enthusiastically shared their passion for Mistral.

I extend my deepest gratitude to Gillian Berchowitz, Tom Walker, and Sharon Rose for their vision and support. I am also deeply grateful to the honorable consuls of Chile, the Garber brothers, for their constant support of my work and their nominating me for the 2002 Gabriela Mistral Medal of Honor, awarded by the Chilean government. I also thank Monica Bruno Galmozzi for her support and editorial assistance and Bob Furnish for his insightful copyediting.

Marie-Lise Gazarian-Gautier, "Recado para Gabriela Mistral," collage, 1989.

Introduction

Marjorie Agosín
Translated by Monica Bruno Galmozzi

GABRIELA MISTRAL'S PRESENCE in the vast landscape of Latin American literature is passionate and complex. Her name is perhaps best known to children in cosmopolitan centers of the Americas, such as Santiago, Buenos Aires, or Mexico City, as well as the rural villages and the distant territories of Patagonia. Most adults in Latin America grew up with an image of Mistral that changed continually depending on current interpretations of history or the memory of the people. Her image fluctuated from that of a devoted rural teacher to that of a passionate advocate for human rights.

She is a global mosaic of ambiguities and contradictions, but even more she is a figure of such mythical qualities in the history of Latin America that her presence continues to be pondered, examined, and revised as if she were still alive. It is difficult to outline the boundaries that surround Gabriela Mistral within the Latin American literary canon. She is the best-known writer in the twenty-three Latin American countries, but she is also one of the least understood. Mistral is read in school textbooks, particularly in Chile, where she is a constant cultural and official national icon. Her face is emblazoned on coins and postage stamps.

Mistral was a perpetual voyager, a courageous traveler. Her epistolary life, as well as the particularity of the landscapes and sites she visited, continues to define her image as a wanderer.

Mistral is one of the great poetic figures of Latin America, but she is more than that. Only in the last two decades has her presence and power over two continents, as well as her complex position within the culture of the Americas, been studied in depth. Mistral's commitment to human rights, women's rights, and the rights of indigenous peoples has recently surfaced, perhaps because the last traces of authoritarian and colonial discourses and sensibilities are ebbing. Her presence continues to have political, historical, and social dimensions, and her work goes beyond her literary production to include a vast array of letters, essays, and newspaper articles that were distributed throughout the Americas and Europe.

Mistral's home in Vicuña is now a museum. It has become a living monument where one must decode and imagine the flow and interruptions in one's own history, where one can understand, feel, and imagine the poet's inner life.

Like Mistral's home, the home of Pablo Neruda eventually became a museum. For many years, his home was closed to the public, off limits to numerous visitors who used to write his poems about peace and solidarity on the old wooden slats. Once it reopened, a visit to his home in Isla Negra became almost a requirement for local and foreign tourists. Pablo Neruda represents the coastal territory, the Pacific with all its plenitude and devastating force. He became part of Chile's history and the popular and political culture of Latin America, as would Frida Kahlo and Che Guevara years later. Mistral's experience was different, and this allows us to elaborate on her life, her birthplace, and where she chose to die. Mistral, regardless of her great public presence in the Americas and her iconization as Chile's teacher and the divine Gabriela, has occupied a minor place in Chile's popular culture, and it is still difficult to get the general public to read her works. I believe this has to do with our view of her as enigmatic, complex, and distant.

Very few people are able to visit the Mistral museum in Vicuña, approximately six hours outside Santiago. Perhaps this isolation is what keeps the museum from entering Chile's collective imagination. Mistral spent most of her childhood in the Elqui valley and the town of Montegrande. To reach the valley one has to travel by car or bus and then by foot. Once one leaves the highways, one enters a landscape that seems to become smaller and more sinuous, as if one were navigating through the mountain's interior. It is a mysterious valley bordered by dangerous cliffs. The curves in the road remind one of the body of a voluptuous woman, a vision of Mother Earth offering nature, pure and fertile. The Elqui area awes first-time visitors and beckons them to return. The valley is shrouded in mysticism and has become a place for pilgrimage and religious encounter. Many skilled artisans, tired of city life, have chosen Elqui as a place where they can create and find peace. Mistral's presence permeates the valley.

The landscape is biblical, filled with fig trees, olive trees, and a river that seems to sing or cry and is constantly mumbling. Mistral never left this landscape behind. She continued to write about it. The Chilean sky gave her the space to write. It is an immense, clear, and generous sky. Mistral nourished herself on this landscape, and a great part of her life was spent imagining this particular valley.

Very few tourists and only a few Mistral scholars go to the Elqui valley. Once one reaches the museum in Vicuña, one finds a few sporadically dated letters and a couple of editions of her early books. I think Mistral's life was a permanent flight. She was a poet who understood that travel had become both her poetic itinerary and her destination. The voyage itself was exemplified through years of travel and epistolary wanderings. She left few clues to her life other than those we can find in her poetry. Unlike Neruda, who collected objects to fill his house, Mistral lived sparsely. She got rid of her material possessions, had no permanent address, lived with others, and saved her money. Her material life occupied a precarious space and she seemed to inhabit a constant state of marginality. Her only way of staying in touch with the world was through imagination and memory. Her memories of Chile were the memories of her childhood but also the memories of grief, since a great part of her existence was spent questioning Chile and her presence in this conflicted and complex nation that she loved.

To reach Montegrande, where Mistral studied, one must follow a tortuous road through an amazing geography of hills and mountains where one hears only the roar of the wind. Montegrande is a poor village, and it seems that nothing has changed since Mistral lived there. It is as if distances have been erased and time has stopped. All that is left are the poet's footsteps in the dust. Her half sister, Emelina, used one of the bedrooms in their modest two-bedroom home as a small school where she taught the local children. The children had to walk miles to reach the school and would return home after dark. Here Mistral learned her ABCs and read the powerful stories of the Old Testament. These stories opened the door to a universe where imagination went hand in hand with mysticism, where poverty and desolation became the tools for survival and provided the motivation to visit other places and conquer other histories. Mistral's opportunity for a great journey came when she was thirty years old and the Mexican government invited her to help it institute educational reforms.

My trip to Montegrande and the Elqui valley in 2002 left me with a plethora of questions but also with the absolute certainty of Mistral's genius and of her enormous capacity to be someone else, to define herself through her literary work, and maybe to live on the margins of official literary canons and move in and out of them. The essays collected in this anthology once again prove this versatility, celebrating and vindicating Mistral as one of the most noteworthy Latin American figures with her poetry, prose, and political thought. Latin America must listen to her and understand how, from such a remote and impoverished locale as Montegrande, Mistral was able to become a voice that went beyond the valley, an audacious traveler of passion, conscience, and courage.

THIS ANTHOLOGY RESPONDS to the need to explore and revisit Mistral; to discover a Mistral whose multifaceted life, works, and often erratic trips remain virtually unknown; a Mistral who was not only a poet but also a human rights activist; a Mistral who lived in Mexico and Brazil and responded to the great political and cultural changes of those countries and of Latin America as a whole. The central concept

here—as well as inviting distinguished intellectuals to write about
Gabriela Mistral—is a desire to rediscover a Mistral who had been, for
many years, trapped within the homogeneous image of a rural teacher
made popular by the official literary discourse. This anthology aims
to address the presence of Gabriela Mistral as a world citizen, one
who belongs to the struggle of the American continents and the devastation of the world after World War II.

The essays in this anthology fill in various blanks in Mistral's biography, seeking to understand the aspects of her life that have not previously been explored in depth, such as her stays in Mexico and Brazil.
Here we have attempted to uncover and rethink her life in these countries and its relationship to her literary work.

The first two essays in this anthology, by Joseph Slaughter and
Jonathan Cohen, situate Gabriela Mistral as one of the key representa-
tives from Latin America in the creation and elaboration of international human rights documents. Slaughter's essay signals how, from
the beginning of her literary career, and especially in her prose, Mistral
focused on the desire to appeal to all nations to work toward peace and
prevent genocide. Mistral was preoccupied with the pursuit and recovery of dignity within indigenous cultures and she had deep ties to
the Holocaust and the devastation of civilization, which she had experienced firsthand while living in Spain and later in Brazil, where her
friend and fellow writer Stefan Zweig committed suicide in reaction to
the Nazi genocide. These preoccupations were central in Mistral's political essays, as well as her more mature poetry, inspired by folklore, a
field in which she was sure she would find the pulse and the authentic
voice of the people.

Cohen's essay pursues some of the same ideas that Slaughter proposes, and it attempts to deal with Mistral's humane and unifying global
vision. Cohen focuses on the importance of the United States in Mistral's cultural and political life, but he also analyzes her condemnation
of the U.S. government of the 1920s and 1930s, with its colonial and
militaristic policies toward Central America. These policies seemed

almost prophetic when, nearly forty years later, the CIA participated in the coup that overthrew Chile's Salvador Allende. Cohen clearly outlines Mistral's Pan-American ideology and the importance she gave not only to values such as fraternity among nations but also to the tolerance necessary to understanding the different cultures.

These two essays serve as the foundation for understanding Mistral's political and humanitarian vision as reflected particularly in her journalistic essays and brief *recados* (messages). In these works she managed to create an intimate collective and personal history—a history never fully personal but one that denoted her relationship to a nation that, in the most metaphorical and symbolic way, embodies the American continents.

Verónica Darer's essay ties into the two previous ones by exploring Gabriela Mistral in her role as teacher. More than a rural teacher, as she used to identify herself, Mistral was a great educational visionary. Darer's essay shows us how Mistral created a stage for proposing her educational ideology through pedagogical writings and university reforms. Her educational perspective was a democratic and global one. Darer manages to create a clear portrait of the rural teacher who became an international teacher, especially when she was invited by the Mexican government to develop an educational reform program there. Darer evidences the complexity of Mistral's vision in her evolution from teacher to instigator of the educational reforms that would revolutionize Latin America at the turn of the century. Mistral's vision of teaching and learning as ways to create a better world are comparable to the ideas of Paulo Freire in his books about educating the oppressed and the people of the developing world.

Patricia Varas's essay complements the visions presented by Cohen and Slaughter by analyzing three of Mistral's texts that are not well known. These texts, dedicated to Augusto Sandino, are about the U.S. invasion of Nicaragua. The three brief and lively essays reveal how Mistral participated in and influenced the great political and cultural movements of Latin America and how her literary work fit within those movements, from the global vision of a Pan-American society to the individual portraits of those who fought to achieve independence. In them Mistral moves from the universal to the individual and reveals her passion for social and economic justice.

The next group of essays in this volume focuses on specific works by Mistral, in particular her poetry. At the same time, the essays illuminate the revisions of the standard interpretations of Mistral's work. Eugenia Muñoz proposes an alternate view of the very traditional "Sonetos de la muerte," one of Mistral's most famous poem cycles, a view that emphasizes the poetry's great audacity and ferociousness. Muñoz offers an important revision of Mistral's most-discussed poems and the very modern way that the poet worked with a traditional form.

Doubt, ambivalence, and the possibility of re-creating one's identity have all been definitive aspects of Mistral's life and work. These essays steer away from ambiguity in order to redefine Mistral through her various historical immersions. Darrell Lockhart's essay presents an innovative and alternative perspective on Mistral's literary work by exploring her connection with Judaism. There is no attempt to speculate about her Jewish background; rather Lockhart explores her connection with Judaism and Judaism's relationship to the history of the West. To do this, Lockhart relies on the poetry that Mistral dedicated to the Jewish people, as well as her numerous relations with prominent figures of Jewish background, among them Stefan Zweig and his wife. Mistral's antifascist political awakening had been gestating since her involvement in Spain's Civil War. It culminated with her public denouncement of Nazism in Brazil as well as at the United Nations. Lockhart's essay bears witness to Mistral's understanding of the relationship between Jewish history and religious and racial discrimination. Lockhart's essay reveals much about Mistral's character and her position within the hermetic Catholicism of Chilean culture and about her deep understanding of and union with the Judeo-Christian tradition.

Ivonne Gordon Vailakis takes on the task of restoring what has generally been denied to Mistral: a place in the poetic vanguard of the early twentieth century. Vailakis stresses that Mistral did participate in avant-garde construction—in her choice of topics, in the ways in which she approached the processes of renewing language, and through the numerous poetic masks with which she subverted the poetic authority of the masculine traditions of her era. Like Muñoz, Vailakis assumes that reading Mistral requires the immediate interpretation of the masculine literary canons and the ways in which she participated in shifting them.

Although Mistral continued her poetic production and unending labor as a teacher, toward the end of her life, her gaze turned more toward her country, its history and nature. Mistral began to explore the ecology and geography of Chile, its fauna, flora, and vibrant indigenous culture. Santiago Daydí-Tolson's essay explores the process that Mistral underwent in order to create and re-create *Poema de Chile,* the work that became her obsessive artistic labor before she died. Through this essay we come to understand the new direction in which Mistral was heading, especially with regard to the environment and people's right to land.

Several chapters explore the idea of travel as a metaphor for both displacement and permanence in Mistral's literary work. For Mistral, traveling represented not only the constant crossing of borders or the feeling of living in perpetual exile, but a way to look in from the outside. Her nomadic condition went beyond her change of addresses—always being on the outside allowed her to explore in depth Chile or Brazil or Mexico or the Caribbean. The essay by Mexican poet and journalist Diana Anhalt examines a complex and often clouded subject. It tells the story of a well-loved yet repudiated Mistral during one of her initial voyages, a voyage that would have deep repercussions for her life as a rural teacher. Mistral's vision was that through education she would have the power and opportunities to transform political, social, and economic justice in the Americas. Anhalt dexterously guides us through the details of Mistral's conflicting experiences in Mexico, including her relationship with Palma Guillén, who would later become one of her most beloved friends. This essay is particularly significant because it manages to play with, revise, and reinvent what it meant for Mistral to always occupy the role of the stranger in foreign lands.

The chapter by Ana Pizarro explores in great detail Mistral's experiences in Brazil, where she was Chilean consul, and places her time there in its historical context. It is only in the last few decades that scholars have dedicated in-depth studies to Mistral's experiences in the Caribbean and Brazil, two regions that had been relegated to a secondary plane. During her stay in Brazil Mistral was awarded the Nobel prize in literature (1945). The period spent in Brazil forged important connections for the future of Mistral's thinking and writing. As Pizarro points out, Mistral lived in Brazil during the height of the Vargas dictatorship, from 1939 through 1945, dates that also coincided with the beginning and end of World War II. Pizarro and Anhalt are very perceptive about the social transformations these countries were undergoing, transformations they explore through Mistral's relationships with people such as Cecília Meireles, Stefan Zweig, or Palma Guillén in Mexico.

"Translating the Hidden Machine" by Randall Couch explores a diversity of histories surrounding Gabriela Mistral and the reception of translations of her works. He raises a series of questions about the ambiguity of her literary work and about how it has been received by the public. Mistral's reception in the English-speaking world has differed greatly from that of Neruda. Neruda achieved great popularity, both in academia and among the general public, and by the end of his life his books had acquired a massive readership. According to Couch, either Mistral's translated works assumed the traditional role ascribed to poetry written about children and the dispossessed, or she was used as a standard for human rights and the liberation of indigenous peoples. Translators such as Langston Hughes or Doris Dana, the executor of Mistral's estate, have also contributed to the exploration of these stereotypical visions of Mistral's work. Couch suggests that a new group of translators, especially the women among them, have managed to capture and transmit Mistral's sensibility, her position in the literary vanguard, and her poetic voice, which has no precedent in Latin America.

Mistral's writing evinces the ambiguity of her personal and political lives, the difficult synchronization of her ambivalent position with regard to her homeland, Chile, and the Mother Nation, Spain. The chapter by Patricia Rubio helps us understand, situate, and rethink Mistral through her letters. A great deal of her prose remains unexplored and uncollected. Her correspondence allows us to understand not only the times in which she lived but also her constant dialogue with a history of which she was so much a part, how she lived, and the color and texture of her passions. Rubio's essay is an enlightened interpretation of the symbolic relationships that Mistral held with her many correspondents. Rubio suggests the possibility of creating the self through letters. Just as Vailakis worked on the phenomenon of creating via the poetic voice, in Rubio's essay we see how Mistral takes shape through her letters.

Rubio helps us understand and imagine what I call the narrative of the self. The ideas Mistral discussed in her letters were preceded by historical or literary events, but oddly the letters do not mention everyday minutiae. However, Mistral offers enough details of her numerous illnesses that we assume that dealing with them took up a great part of her daily life.

Elizabeth Horan's essay treats Mistral's relationship with her native land. Although Mistral spent most of her adult life away from Chile, she returned twice: once after winning the Nobel prize and then when her body was returned to Chile after her death in 1957. In death she acquired enormous strength and presence. Her body was escorted back to Chile from Peru by a military escort, and Chile declared a national mourning period that lasted more than three days. Her funeral was as magnificent as that of a queen. The streets were covered in flower petals, and her body was escorted through the streets of Santiago to its final resting place.

Mistral's death and her triumphant funeral contradicted what her life had been all about. She had spent a great deal of her life living anonymously. We must then ask, How did Chile treat Gabriela Mistral after death? How was she read or not read? Was she ignored or persecuted? Horan's perceptive essay leads me to think about how nations identify or disqualify national heroes and female poets. In Mistral's case, death greatly speeded the process of canonization and made her part of the history of Chile, something she achieved only posthumously. As we observed, Mistral's relationship with Chile was incredibly sensitive. Many thought it bordered on paranoia. But after her death, Mistral and Chile were united. We must note, though, that in her posthumously published *Poema de Chile,* Mistral had recognized her relationship with her country and returned to it as a lyrical narrator represented by the ghost of a dead woman.

Horan's point of view is based on Mistral's death—that moment when the figure and the presence of Mistral become one and are canonized through her literature. Horan's article is almost a hagiography, showing us images of Mistral, from the rural teacher who was almost sanctified to the revolutionary woman living under the popular governments. A dead body fits the mold of any historical need or whim. Horan's text surprises us by recounting and reliving the relationship that Mistral had, not only with various Latin American nations but also with the masculinity of patriotism. Chile as a country has always retained a complex yet intimate relationship with its heroic male poets, including Neruda. As Horan points out, though, between Mistral's historical presence and her idolized persona there are incredible gaps that need to be filled in.

"Gabriela Mistral's Political Commentaries" by Emma Sepúlveda and "Gabriela Mistral and the United States of America" by Luis Vargas Saavedra examine Mistral's view of U.S. interventionist policies in Latin America. According to Sepúlveda, Mistral focused on supporting great Latin American leaders like Sandino and José Martí in numerous essays published throughout Latin America. Her anti-interventionist politics were the uniting vision of Latin American peoples.

Saavedra examines how important it was for Latin American peoples, especially Puerto Ricans, to maintain autonomy. Saavedra also states that in her writings Mistral stressed the importance of understanding the people of the United States as well as those of Latin America. He points out that Mistral's visionary writings are intended to globalize the experiences of our continents and not to privilege only U.S. experience and identity. Both Sepúlveda's and Saavedra's chapters speak of Mistral's extraordinary ability to express complex political ideas through her journalistic essays.

The last essay in this anthology, "The Walking Geography of Gabriela Mistral," paints a more intimate portrait of Gabriela Mistral. Marie-Lise Gazarian-Gautier met Mistral during her last stay at her home in Roslyn Harbor, Long Island. Through her words we are able to sense the complexities of Mistral's persona, her introspective spirit, and her enormous capacity for affection. In this picture of Mistral as human—more vulnerable and more sedentary after her travels throughout the Americas—Gazarian-Gautier helps us understand Mistral during what she considered to be one of her happiest times.

The essays that make up this anthology exemplify the many literary and social expressions that are the keys to Mistral's work. Hers was a voice that existed in different lyrical spaces; it is a skilled voice, born of peasant experience, immersed in oral history. One feels the need to read her poems out loud, as if they were songs. Teresa Kamenszain states that for centuries oral history has been a fundamental part of women's writing. The essays in this anthology show us Mistral as a historical character (a teacher who founded schools and achieved important education reforms in Mexico by the time she was in her early thirties), but also a Mistral who was raised in a rural village and who understood poetry to be a communal activity.

In her early love letters, we see Mistral as generous and vulnerable. I believe one particularly well illustrates her true self, the Mistral we see throughout these essays:

I have a great desire to rest. I want to read a lot and not be surrounded by people. I want to plant and water trees. It is a desire that sometimes feels like desperation and I want to carry it out soon . . . very soon. I live with very little. I do not eat the most expensive foods and I dress humbly. In four years I will try to have a plot of land with trees and I will go live far from any city with my mother, if she still lives, if not with my brother or with a child that I wish to raise. (*Cartas de amor*, 121)

This anthology aims to create, envision, and reveal—aims brilliantly achieved by each of the contributors. Mistral emerges more enigmatic than ever and more transcendental. At no time has Mistral been more important. She has always been seen as a pioneer in women's education and human rights. Her voice was heard in a period in which women's public voices were quiet and hidden. As we move into the twenty-first century, Mistral surprises us and allows us to meditate about so many preoccupations that now have singular importance in our American continents: her Americanist conscience and constant dialogue among the Latin American nations and her preoccupation with human rights vis-à-vis women's rights stand out as some of the defining ideas of the last century and the current one.

Provincial and cosmopolitan, private and public, Mistral was a visionary artist who transcended time and place. Anomalous and eccentric, a perpetual and audacious traveler, she represents a great advance in the self-understanding of postmodern culture. Gabriela Mistral is destined to be an imposing figure with the multiple sexual, religious, and philosophical ambiguities that forged her history and allowed the creation of one of the most monumental figures of the Americas. This anthology attempts to bring us closer to both the complexity of her work and the passions of her life.

Works Cited

Kamenszain, Teresa. *Bordado y costura del texto*. Buenos Aries: Editorial de Buenos Aires, 1992.

Mistral, Gabriela. *Cartas de amor y desamor*. Compiled by Sergio Fernández Larraín; prologue by Jaime Quezada. Santiago: Andrés Bello, 2002.

Chapter 1

Toward a Common Destiny on the American Continent
The Pan-Americanism of Gabriela Mistral

Jonathan Cohen

*My very flesh is permeated with
an infusion of the soil of this continent.*
—Mistral at the Pan American Union, 1946

WHEN GABRIELA MISTRAL DIED in 1957, she was living on Long Island, in the affluent north-shore village of Roslyn Harbor, close to New York City. She had been a resident there for the last few years of her life, in her retirement, far from the mineral mountains and fruitful desert of the Elqui valley, that oasis of northern Chile's arid mining country that had produced her. After the funeral service held in St. Patrick's Cathedral, her body was flown in a U.S. official plane to Lima, Peru, where it was met by a Chilean military transport that would return her to her homeland. Chilean president Carlos Ibáñez decreed three days of mourning, an honor previously accorded only to top army and government dignitaries. Half a million Chileans crowded the streets of Santiago to accompany her body in the funeral procession. The cortege ultimately made its way north to her final resting place in the mountain village of Montegrande, her childhood home in the Elqui valley, close to her birthplace; she was buried there at her request, so that the children of this poor and isolated village might never be forgotten by her country. An audacious traveler of the New World, Mistral had made her final journey: it took her from one corner of the Americas to another, across more than five thousand miles of what she pointedly called the American continent.

America—in the original sense of the word, signifying the entire hemisphere—was, of all the many places in the world that Mistral had known, the place closest to her heart. America, not simply Chile, was her true homeland. It defined her: the Basque mestiza, she somewhat proudly called herself, half European and half Indian (Incan). Not surprisingly, the Pan-Americanism that had begun to flourish during her youth—that is, the ideal of political and cultural unity between Latin America and Anglo America—appealed to her and moved her to champion this dream throughout her life.

Mistral's hopeful Pan-Americanism was tempered by a Christian and democratic humanism, as well as by her personal experiences with the United States. Her long relationship with this country began with the 1922 publication, in New York, of the first edition of her first book, *Desolación* (Desolation). Her frequent visits to the States starting in 1924; her long sojourns at northeastern colleges (Barnard, Vassar, and Middlebury), where she taught Latin American literature during the early 1930s; and her friendships with North Americans—Waldo Frank, Charles and Anne Lindbergh, Leo Rowe (director of the Pan American Union), Erna Fergusson, Margaret Bates, and Doris Dana, to name a few—all strengthened the friendly admiration she always had for the people of the United States. Indeed, the North American professors who had first published *Desolación* could never have guessed that Mistral's destiny, her glory, and her death would be so closely linked to the United States.

Mistral chose the United States as her home twice during the course of her life. The first time was in 1946, after having received the Nobel prize in literature in Sweden. Chile had just appointed her consul in

Los Angeles. Before moving there, the Union of American Women availed itself of her stay in Washington to confer upon her the title of Woman of the Americas. She then crossed the country to assume her new responsibilities and lived in Monrovia, California, near Pasadena. Not entirely happy with its climate, she moved to Santa Barbara, where she bought a house in which she lived until 1948. Then, stricken with diabetes, she left for Mexico to convalesce.

Finally, in 1953, after two years in Veracruz and two years in Naples, Italy, she returned to the United States to serve in New York as Chilean delegate to the United Nations. She lived in Roslyn Harbor, on Spruce Street, in the home of her long-time friend Doris Dana. When Mistral's failing health forced her to resign from her diplomatic post the following year, she retired to Roslyn Harbor and spent her final years on Long Island, Whitman's "fish-shaped Paumanok." It was a country refuge for her, but close enough to New York that friends and admirers could visit her.

At the start of Mistral's relationship with the United States in the early 1920s, the modern Pan-American movement was gaining popularity throughout the Americas. This movement, which aimed at promoting political, cultural, and economic ties among the independent nations of the Americas, had begun at the First International Conference of American States (also known as the First Pan-American Conference) held in Washington in 1889–90, sponsored by the United States. The Pan American Union was then established, with its headquarters in Washington. Participating nations looked for ways of solving their common problems, including the development of a united front for maintaining their rights and preserving peace throughout the Americas. Just over two decades later, the First World War would intensify relations between the United States and Latin American nations, in light of the wartime need for hemispheric solidarity of the Americas.

The early 1920s saw popular magazines dedicated to promoting the ideals of Pan-Americanism and facilitating cultural exchange, such as the monthly *Pan-American Magazine;* the monthly *Pan American Review* of the Pan American Society of the United States; and the bimonthly *Inter-America,* which offered English translations of articles published in the Latin American press, like its counterpart, *Inter-América,* which offered Spanish translations of articles published in the U.S. press. The monthly *Bulletin of the Pan American Union* was, in the early 1920s, publishing everything from agricultural assessments to poetry in translation.

Of course, there were serious problems facing Pan-American unity that had arisen from the recent intervention of the United States in the affairs of the small countries of the Caribbean and Central America, such as its illegal seizure of the Panama Canal Zone in 1903, its second intervention in Cuba from 1906 to 1909, its breaking of relations with Nicaragua and armed intervention there in 1909, and its ongoing intervention in the affairs of the Dominican Republic since 1916. As a result of the chronic interventionist behavior of the so-called Colossus of the North, intellectuals throughout Latin America voiced strong opposition to Pan-Americanism. For instance, the leading editorial in the September 1920 issue of *Nuestra América* (Our America), one of the most widely read magazines of Latin America, attacked the United States for threatening the independence of the Dominican Republic and concluded with this rallying cry: "Brethren of America, let us unite. Let us lift our arms in defense of the Latin republic whose honor is being wounded by the greedy Yankees" (in Inman, 333).

The so-called Gay Twenties that the United States was enjoying would show Mistral "the rampant materialism" that helped to crystallize her understanding of one of the fundamental differences between the cultural values of North and South America ("Gabriela Mistral and Interamerican Spiritual Understanding," 654). The 1920s were anything but "gay" in Latin America. In the United States they were years of rapid economic growth, of scandalous orgies under prohibition, of short-lived economic stability—the heyday of the movies, the Charleston, and the stock market. In Latin America, they were difficult years of foreign interventions, tyrannical governments, growing production of the foreign market, unfavorable terms of trade, and an increasing inflow of foreign capital, which entered neither to industrialize nor to modernize the economy of Latin America but rather to subjugate it more and more to U.S. domination.

This is how the continental stage of the Americas was set when, in 1924, Mistral entered it as an eloquent advocate of Pan-Americanism. The opportunity presented itself to her during her first visit to the United States, in the spring of that year. Already established as an important educator, poet, and humanist, she had just finished working for two years in Mexico in collaboration with that government's rural education program. Then, moved by the desire to get to know the States, she visited Washington and New York on her way to Europe.

The Pan American Union celebrated her in grand style at a reception attended by official, intellectual, and social Washington. There, in the stately Hall of Honor of the union's marble building (which had been designed to blend the architectural styles of North and South America by combining Aztec, Incan, Mayan, and European themes), Mistral delivered an address in which she laid out her concept of the value of "dissimilarity without inferiority" with respect to the Latin and Anglo-Saxon cultures of the Americas. "I do not believe that differentiation in nations is a world fatality. I believe that difference in the case of humanity, as well as in nature, is merely another form of enrichment. In this way what is Latin, even in its sharpest contrast, when face to face with Anglo-Saxonism, is a kind of strength through different virtues, through other modes of living, but in no sense the occasion of inevitable discord" ("Spiritual Understanding," 652).

Contemporary advocates of diversity and multiculturalism echo her wisdom. She argued that the "friendship of the different peoples sought by the Pan American Union would be easily attained if we were all imbued, to the farthest limit of consciousness, with the concept of *dissimilarity without inferiority*" (653; emphasis Mistral's). She explained: "Union will be entirely possible if those of the North, penetrating the unpleasing exterior to the fundamental nobility beneath, perceive that like a clear-running stream a deep, though confused, aspiration and longing for justice flows underneath all our sufferings; through the painful economic conditions afflicting our Chile, a country heroically poor, rich only in honor; through the long Mexican Revolution, holy in its aspirations; and through the lack of accord in Central America" (653).

In concluding her address, Mistral acknowledged the prevailing economic and intellectual approaches to continental unity, but asserted that a practical application of shared Christian faith and values was the "higher" path: "To stamp the relations between the countries of the North and South with the standard of Christianity, to place conscience, individual and national, above material and personal interests: That is the task" (654).

The July issue of the *Bulletin of the Pan American Union,* which celebrated Mistral's visit, noted that "from the purely intellectual and spiritual point of view [this occasion] constitutes one of the most significant manifestations of inter-American confraternity in the history of Washington" (655).

The United States would be a repeated theme in Mistral's prolific prose work. Between 1922 and 1948 she published numerous articles dealing with U.S. culture and policy that appeared in periodicals throughout the Americas, often in the daily press: *El Mercurio* of Chile, *La Nueva Democracia* of New York, *El Repertorio americano* of Costa Rica, *Puerto Rico ilustrado,* and the *Boletín* of the Pan American Union. Among her specific themes involving the United States were true Pan-Americanism and the relations between North and South America; agreements and disagreements between them; the moral and practical virtues of the North American people; Catholicism in the United States; the interest in Hispanic culture found among intellectuals. She also published glowing tributes to North American artists and writers, such as Isadora Duncan, Frances Horne, Alice Stone Blackwell, and Waldo Frank (whom she spoke of as a brother).

The occasion of the first Pan American Day, on 14 April 1931, provided Mistral with the opportunity to expound her view of continental unity and further promote Pan-Americanism. In early April she published a prose work titled "Voto de la juventud escolar en el día de las Américas" (for the complete English text, see "Students' Pledge on Pan American Day" at the end of this chapter). It appeared in Spanish in the Costa Rican paper *Repertorio americano,* and its publication there made it a powerful political statement, in view of the current four-year-long U.S. intervention that was taking place in Nicaragua, Costa Rica's northern neighbor. Also in April, the *Bulletin of the Pan American Union* published an English translation of the pledge, under the title "Message to American Youth on Pan American Day."

An expression of the popularity of Pan-Americanism in the first half of the twentieth century, the new holiday called Pan American Day was (and still is) observed throughout the Americas. It became an annual event celebrating the diverse cultures of the Americas and stressing inter-American goodwill. The date was chosen to commemorate 14 April, 1890, when the Pan American Union was established; this body subsequently evolved into the Organization of American States (OAS). In the United States, Pan American Day is now observed with ceremonies at OAS headquarters in Washington and with proclamations by the U.S. president and other government officials. On the same day, many cities hold concerts, festivals, and exhibits that celebrate Latin American culture.

Like many of her prose works, Mistral's pledge reads like a prose poem. Her compelling vision of Pan-American harmony and unity emerges in clear terms in this composition. Key to its rhetorical structure is Mistral's use and repetition of the first-person plural pronoun, which forms the collective voice of the youth, the future, of the Americas. The pledge begins: "We Americans of North and South America have accepted with our heritage of geographic unity a certain common destiny that should find a threefold fulfillment on our continent in an adequate standard of living, perfect democracy, and ample liberty."

Here the collective *we* is intended to affirm the entire American community. In the school setting, the recited pledge would be a didactic exercise meant to take students beyond the individual *I* and to challenge it. Mistral recognized the degeneration of the Whitmanian *I*, with its power of self-affirmation, which had given rise to the United States. She clearly rejected its transformation into imperial egoism that commodified Latin America, depriving South American nations of their autonomy.

A central theme of the pledge is that the American community shares "a common destiny" based on "our heritage of geographic unity" and the "common task" founded by our national heroes of American independence and democracy, Washington and Bolívar, Lincoln and San Martín. The governing national constitutions throughout the Americas are "the fruit of their insight," and have "the family resemblance of plants nurtured in the same soil." Having established the community of nations that resides on the American continent, the pledge reminds us that "our first duty is to our nearest neighbor," and instructs that "we have enough land so that no one need be envious of his neighbor."

Echoing her address delivered at the Pan American Union in 1924, Mistral wants America to appreciate through this pledge the concept of "dissimilarity without inferiority" that is essential to harmonious cultural diversity: "We must realize that the fact that two cultures differ outwardly does not imply that one is necessarily inferior to the other." And she emphasizes that "our very situation, between Europe and Asia, obliges us to comprehend conflicting viewpoints; even our coastline, looking both to the east and to the west like that of Greece, gives us the mission of welcoming different races [ethnic groups] with understanding" ("Message," 354).

Although the pledge does not explicitly use Christian language (as Mistral did at the Pan American Union), it expresses in fairly secular terms the Judeo-Christian values of human fellowship that she embraced. Not only does she tell us how we must treat our neighbors, the pledge establishes the ideal of "a republican sobriety to which vicious luxury is repugnant," as if to invoke the biblical condemnation of living for mammon. The golden rule of the Gospel is expressed in terms of an American virtue, that "unanimous religious and lay sentiment which considers fair dealing the only lasting basis for world relations."

Well aware of the inter-American political realities of her day and the challenges facing Pan-Americanism, Mistral concluded her pledge with an emphasis on the right of nations to self-determination:

> We Americans of North and South America have been nurtured on twenty-one constitutions, all of which proclaim respect for the independence of others as a basic principle of self-respect. Our republics were brought to life by Washington and Bolívar under the auspicious star of the rights of nations. From kindergarten through college we have been indoctrinated with a firm belief in the gospel of our national laws. Americans all, we affirm to the heroes from whom we are sprung our determination to hold the independence of all our homelands as sacred as our own. We renew our pledge that, in the intercourse between these twenty-one nations, we shall repudiate violence as treachery to the principles of eternal right and challenge injustice as a blot on that glorious honor by which we now and shall forever live. ("Message," 356)

Here Mistral indirectly registers her condemnation of the pattern of growing U.S. intervention in the affairs of Latin American nations (as in Nicaragua), while at the same time she affirms the high American ideal of liberty and justice for all. Thus, with "an adequate standard of living, perfect democracy, and ample liberty," North and South Americans can realize the full potential of the New World: "Together we shall give a new key, a new rhythm, a new democratic interpretation to European culture, European institutions, and European customs, art, education, and science, blending them all into a harmony of greater beauty and greater sweetness."

9

In February 1939, Mistral was again an honored guest at the Pan American Union, where she said she felt truly at home. This was her second visit to the union. In the stately Hall of Heroes, she gave a lecture titled "The Human Geography of Chile," taking her audience the length and breadth of her homeland and showing how poetry and beauty are found in its people and its landscape. Before her lecture she pointed out that in the fifteen years that had elapsed since her first visit she had noted with pleasure the increasing influence of the union and "the progress of an indisputable Pan American sentiment" ("Gabriela Mistral at the Pan American Union," 1939, 191).

Seven years later, in March 1946, having just come from a tour of Europe after receiving the Nobel prize, Mistral made her third celebrated visit to the Pan American Union. She had been appointed Chilean consul in Los Angeles and was on her way to assuming her new post there. The governing board had assembled to pay her the official tribute of the Americas for her literary achievement. Standing before its governing board, she stated:

> I declare my faith in this institution, and to it I entrust myself as to an entity sound and strong in storm or danger. . . . Your task, sirs—and you have never had a greater—is to keep the continent free from worldwide madness, from physical misery, and from the fatalistic and resigned depression that grows out of it. And while you are discharging this duty it is equally incumbent upon you, agents and interpreters of our spirit, not to slip on the treacherous stones of a certain zoological kind of nationalism which would station us here, would pin us in flesh and spirit to a single meridian, as if we were no more than the llama or the alpacaof the Aymaras. ("Gabriela Mistral at the Pan American Union," 1946, 303)

Reiterating the theme of continental community articulated in her 1931 Pan-American pledge, Mistral used the Lord's Prayer as an example of proper collective plurality, because it "begins and ends in a plural as round and unqualified as the blow of a hammer or the piercing phrases of the litanies" (303). She added that the "prayers which came later are for the most part entirely individual; perhaps for that reason they are more like counter-prayers, a perverse pagan about-face." Grave problems had arisen in the world because, as she asserted, "we left our course when we began to say that 'we' [of the Lord's Prayer] with a mind that was blank or wandering; when habit turned our prayers into a mere repetition, and their meaning went flat and stale."

She was driving home her point that both individuals and nations must learn to appreciate their place within, and their obligation to, the larger human community. A citizen of the collective Americas, she identified herself as American: "I have come to know almost the whole hemisphere, from Canada to Tierra del Fuego; I have eaten at the grandest and the humblest tables; my very flesh is permeated with an infusion of the soil of this continent" (303).

Mistral's address culminated with her call "to unify our countries from within by means of an education which shall grow into a national awareness . . . and also to unify those countries of ours in a harmonious rhythm that shall be almost Pythagorean, a rhythm in which those twenty spheres shall move freely, even gracefully, without ever colliding" (304). Freedom and democracy throughout the Americas, together with peace and social justice, were the ideals she invoked, in the face of what she called the world's "satanic postwar panorama" (302).

At every opportunity in the remaining decade of her life, as before, Mistral would speak out for Pan-American unity. Beyond that, the poetry she wrote during her sojourn in California would further express her embrace of the Americas. These were hard years for her personally— years of lingering personal grief in the shadow of the tragic deaths of people she loved. Nonetheless, the human and natural landscapes of North America moved her to compose new poems, such as "Amapola de California" (California poppy), "Ocotillo," and "Nacimiento de una casa" (Birth of a house). In the first poem, for instance, Mistral personifies California's state flower in a song. She identifies with it and reveals the common destiny that binds them:

> Your poor glory and mine
> (your poor soul, my poor soul)
> we burn without provocation
> and are equally urged to touch
> this shore of the world,
> descendants of Our Flame!
> (*Reader*, 120)

Like all of her poems that were born of an immediate and physical contact with the world around her, the poems that Mistral produced in the United States added a new dimension to her work rooted in North America. They would appear in *Lagar* (Wine press; 1954), the last book of poetry she published in her lifetime. Thus, an array of elements derived from the entire American hemisphere would distinguish the full body of her poetry, infusing it with her Pan-American spirit.

Commenting on Mistral's lifelong contributions to Pan-Americanism, her personal friend and biographer Margot Arce de Vázquez paints a noble picture:

> Few statesmen, few politicians worked as assiduously as Gabriela toward this beautiful goal [Pan-American unity]. She was moved by a proud and authentic Christian spirit based on justice and love. She considered herself *American*, in the broadest sense of the word; both the grandeur and misery of America were her innermost concerns. Her maternal inclinations sought to protect all the American countries as children of her spirit, and she watched over them with the prophetic and selfless view of a poet and of the most tender and far-seeing mother. (144; emphasis Arce de Vázquez's)

And concerning Mistral's high-minded response to the realities of the United States and its anti-American behavior, Arce de Vázquez explains:

> As a Hispanic American, she deeply regretted what seemed to her the errors of official North American policy in its relations with the peoples to the south; she was hurt by the economic exploitation, by the armed interventions, by the moral and material support of dictators, by the almost complete ignorance of the Hispanic spirit, culture, customs, and idiosyncrasies. But this critical view never caused hate or resentment on her part. She adopted, on the contrary, a free and creative attitude of love, with faith in men and nations and with firm confidence in the final triumph of reason, truth, and goodness. (140)

Similar praise had been expressed by Leo Rowe at the Pan American Union, when he introduced her there in 1939, at the height of her career: "She has dreamed of our nations united, loving each other, teaching each other and mutually protecting each other and has set an example of what true Pan-American friendship and cooperation are" (in Arce de Vázquez 142).

To the end, Pan-Americanism was close to Mistral's heart. The first Latin American to win the Nobel prize in literature, she had become not only one of the leading writers in the Spanish language but a prominent voice of the Americas that transcended language barriers and national borders. Her very diction expressed her Pan-American spirit. In her prose publications and her public addresses, as in her Nobel acceptance speech, she referred to the Americas as "the American continent." Mistral had long embraced the old idea that the American lands formed a single continent, and this phrase would underscore her belief that the geographical unity of the Americas formed the basis of their common destiny. In a tribute published soon after she had died, Waldo Frank celebrated the continental dimension of her voice: "She was the bard of mothers and children; but she was also the laureate of her vast American earth: of the mountains, ice and burning valley" (84). Two months after her death, *Américas* (formerly the *Bulletin of the Pan American Union*) reprinted her Pan-American pledge under the title "Pan American Manifesto," a piece that remains a full expression of her Pan-Americanism. Moreover, it stands as an enduring, hopeful vision of multicultural harmony and unity for America—in the sense of that word so much a vibrant part of her.

Students' Pledge on Pan American Day

GABRIELA MISTRAL

We Americans of North and South America have accepted with our heritage of geographic unity a certain common destiny that should find a threefold fulfillment on our continent in an adequate standard of living, perfect democracy, and ample liberty.

We whom Providence has favored by giving us an immense territory for our home had first to take possession of this mighty land. Our second task was to secure from the wilderness that we had tamed that social well-being promised by democracies to their citizens. Our present duty is to create a culture worthy of our racial [ethnic] inheritances and our geographic endowment.

We have enough land so that no one need be envious of his neighbor, a republican sobriety to which vicious luxury is repugnant, a unanimous religious and lay sentiment that considers fair dealing the only lasting basis for world relations, and scenic beauty such that peace appears the natural state for the Americas.

Throughout our 105 degrees of latitude, the earth seems to be more ready, more eager, and quicker than elsewhere to fulfill its mission of bestowing happiness on mankind.[1] Perhaps because American earth has been less exhausted by a long succession of generations, or because it is more richly blessed with the generative elements of heat and moisture and less burdened with population, it lends itself more readily than other lands to the men who, moved by the ideal of justice, strive for the equitable distribution of wealth and for a civilization woven in a shining pattern of good will on the warp and weft of the social virtues.

Heirs of the Old World and of at least two native cultures, we are endeavoring to outstrip both Europe and our indigenous empires in the perfection of a democracy that shall express the broadest possible concept of human liberty. Our very situation, between Europe and Asia, obliges us to comprehend conflicting viewpoints; even our coastline, looking both to the east and to the west like that of Greece, gives us the mission of welcoming different races with understanding.

We must realize that the fact that two cultures differ outwardly does not imply that one is necessarily inferior to the other, and that the expression which human groups give to the same idea is sometimes simple and touching, sometimes nobly beautiful. We should begin on this very continent, with a loyal interpretation of North by South America, or South by North America; our first duty is to our nearest neighbor. A better understanding of the rest of the world will come later and be as natural for us as following a well-known path down which habit leads us.

Latin culture has found in the nations of South America, a realm vaster than the classic Mediterranean Basin for the government of men according to its own high standard, while all cultures are trying to achieve in Anglo-Saxon America, so far without misadventure, the ideal of universal brotherhood in a single land. And until today no attempt to realize this goal had met with success anywhere in the world.

Our heroes of North and South America, Washington and Bolívar, Lincoln and San Martín, might all have been fashioned in a single hour, in the same mold; they were laborers in a common task. Our constitutions, the fruit of their insight, were inspired by equal vision and have the family resemblance of plants nurtured in the same soil.

Anglo-Saxon America, sprung wholly from Europe, has succeeded, more or less easily, in its task of amalgamating in new surroundings the great cultures of Europe. Latin America has effected, and is still effecting, with greater difficulty and therefore with more suffering, the fusion of European and Indian, two races of distinct physical endowments and even more distinct emotional temperaments; the triumph over such obstacles is more significant than anything hitherto accomplished by man.

North Americans and South Americans, together we shall give a new key, a new rhythm, a new democratic interpretation to European culture, European institutions, and European customs, art, education, and science, blending them all into a harmony of greater beauty and greater sweetness.

We have summoned people from the four corners of the earth with an utter lack of prejudice and with the hospitality of our far-flung shores, creating on our continent races in whose features may be traced their heritage from all the world—races capable of enlarging the older, classic view of life, and capable, too, of living the epic of the future.

In American stock and American ideals, both formed in an environment of vast spaces and little hampered by tradition, unprejudiced observers have noted a splendid assurance in the face of our high enterprise, and a happy confidence in the future. We believe that war will seem to the next generations of America like an illustration in a musty tome, an ancient order belonging to times forever gone, thanks to the wisdom of our lawgivers and our educators. The effect of war in America would be to devastate our entire continent, despoiling its natural beauty and depraving the collective conscience so that we should once more have to lay the foundation and laboriously reconstruct the edifice of society. The memory of the building of America is too recent for us to be willing thus to jeopardize the work of our forebears.

We Americans of North and South America have been nurtured on twenty-one constitutions, all of which proclaim respect for the independence of others as a basic principle of self-respect. Our republics were brought to life by Washington and Bolívar under the auspicious star of the rights of nations. From kindergarten through college we have been indoctrinated with a firm belief in the gospel of our national laws. Americans all, we affirm to the heroes from whom we are sprung our determination to hold the independence of all our homelands as sacred as our own. We renew our pledge that, in the intercourse between these twenty-one nations, we shall repudiate violence as treachery to the principles of eternal right and challenge injustice as a blot on that glorious honor by which we now and shall forever live.[2]

Notes

1. Canada was not at the time a member of the Pan American Union (after 1948 the Organization of American States), which is why Mistral's America here spans only 105 degrees of latitude, since the audience of her pledge was limited to the member nations that observed Pan American Day.
2. This anonymous translation was originally published in April 1931 in the *Bulletin of the Pan American Union* and subsequently revised by Jonathan Cohen.

Works Cited

Arce de Vázquez, Margot. *Gabriela Mistral: The Poet and Her Work.* Trans. Helene Masslo Anderson. New York: New York University Press, 1964.

Frank, Waldo. "Gabriela Mistral." *Nation* 184 (26 January 1957): 84.

"Gabriela Mistral and Interamerican Spiritual Understanding." *Bulletin of the Pan American Union* 58 (1924): 647–61.

"Gabriela Mistral at the Pan American Union." *Bulletin of the Pan American Union* 73 (1939): 189–203.

"Gabriela Mistral at the Pan American Union." *Bulletin of the Pan American Union* 80 (1946): 301–7.

Inman, Samuel Guy. *Problems in Pan Americanism.* New York: George H. Doran, 1921.

Mistral, Gabriela. *A Gabriela Mistral Reader.* Trans. Maria Giachetti. Ed. Marjorie Agosín. Fredonia, N.Y.: White Pine Press, 1993.

―――. "Message to American Youth on Pan American Day." *Bulletin of the Pan American Union* 65 (1931): 354–56.

―――. "Pan American Manifesto." *Américas* 9 (1957): 26–28.

―――. "Voto de la juventud escolar en el día de las Américas." In *Magisterio y niño*, 77–79. Santiago: Editorial Andres Bello, 1979.

Chapter 2

"A Wor[l]d Full of Xs and Ks"
Parables of Human Rights in the
Prose of Gabriela Mistral

Joseph R. Slaughter

FROM THE PAGES OF THE *United Nations Review* in 1956, Gabriela Mistral made what she called "An Appeal to World Conscience": "Despite all advances in our civilization the twentieth century must unfortunately be considered as one of those most guilty of the crime of genocide" (17). Although she notes that "genocide is a new name for an old evil," her remarks are directed more toward the future than the past, finding in the repugnance of genocide a universality with a capacity to reshape the world: "the word genocide carries in itself a moral judgment over an evil in which every feeling man and woman concurs" (16–17). As one of the few human rights documents about which Mistral writes explicitly, the Convention on the Prevention and Punishment of the Crime of Genocide—adopted by the United Nations General Assembly on 9 December 1948, one day before adoption of the Universal Declaration of Human Rights (UDHR)—presents a compendium of her lifelong concerns. Contemporary international human rights law, particularly those documents drafted at the end of the 1940s and throughout the 1950s, were part of the immediate aftermath of World War II and the revelations of the extent of the Holocaust. The documents were, then, intended as measures to prevent, and expressions of contempt for, acts that have "outraged the conscience of mankind" (UDHR). Mistral's appeal to that world conscience stresses more than a sense of repugnance at the loss of human life; rather, for Mistral, those lives and the collective that have been destroyed are measured in terms that attest to her sense of the value of the individual within the collective: "Losses in life and culture have been staggering" (17).

Genocide is conventionally understood to be a crime against a collective, and in her appeal Mistral makes reference to the convention's definition, where genocide is "the intentional destruction in whole or in part of national, racial, religious or ethnic groups" (17). The document itself makes explicit the Manichean nature of the conflict between the individual and the collective when it declares in Article IV that "Persons committing genocide or any other acts enumerated in Article III shall be punished, whether they are constitutionally responsible rulers, public officials or private individuals." Beyond the definitions cited by Mistral, the document elaborates its commitment to the collective in the enumeration of acts that constitute the crime of genocide: "killing members of the group"; "deliberately inflicting on the group conditions of life calculated to bring about its physical destruction in whole or in part"; "imposing measures intended to prevent births within the group"; and "forcibly transferring children of the group to another group." Genocide is, then, the act of an individual, sometimes working in the name of a collective as a public official, against a group.

Mistral's encomium on the convention does not treat the individual, or the collective, human toll of genocide as solely a matter of the suffocation of breathing beings; rather, her appeal focuses on the cultural casualties of the crime. For Mistral the individual is, when morally poised, an instantiation of a collective cultural consciousness. That collective is not simply, in Mistral's writing, another name for the state, which in fact is often a false collective in her work, but rather a complex of collective engagements in which the individual is constituted. Universal human dignity, which is the theoretical and natural-law rationale underpinning contemporary human rights, is, for Mistral, tied to culture, and she finds in the Anglo-European Enlightenment tradition of individualism a bankruptcy that threatens to undermine that culture. In her 1938 article "En el día de la cultura americana" (In the time of American culture), she characterizes the trajectory of post-Enlightenment "civilization" as retrograde, arguing that "man has devalued himself in his dignity since classical times, to such an extreme that our tears well up and we cry for him" (284). For Mistral, it is the course of contemporary civilization that has proceeded to devalue the "genuine" collectivities of family, language, culture, religion, and even economics and that has supplanted them with an internationally framed set of nationalist collectivities interested only in sovereignty and suzerainty. For Mistral, as I will show in this article, a "genuine" collectivity—whether the family, a linguistic group, or a "race"—emerges from a sense of shared culture; that is, collective sensibility arises from common cultural experience, and reciprocally, cultural sensitivity, which for her is the recognition and respect of difference, develops out of a collective consciousness where each individual feels that something is commonly at stake through the shared culture. The term *race* is a complex one in Mistral's writing. Sometimes it appears to be used as it is popularly used today; at other times it seems to stand conceptually for either a linguistic, ethnic, or national collective.

Mistral lauds the internationalization of a culture, rather than a dogma, of human rights as a remarkable achievement of the United Nations, though this internationalization is not a fait accompli but an aspirational process of growth, education, and elaboration. She heralds the internationalization of the definition and punishment of genocide but also, and more important, the internationalization of its prevention. Because for her the crime targets not only human bodies but people as instantiations of culture as well, Mistral underscores the importance of prevention, which, she argues, enters the field of sociology. Although the convention is itself rather mute on the details and methods of prevention, Mistral's encomium focuses precisely on this aspect: "Prevention is . . . obviously linked to education as well as to the development and growth of sensitivity in human society" ("An Appeal to World Conscience," 17). Here the cultural work of the artist and the teacher becomes part of the international promotion and protection of human rights: "Therefore the concept of genocide should be made part of the cultural consciousness of every nation, hence it should also be made the subject matter of literature, music, and the fine arts" (17). It might not be apparent how her own creative writing engages with the issues of genocide, but to recognize this aspect of her work one must understand that for her culture and enculturation are the meeting grounds between the international and the domestic.

During the 1920s, Mistral served as the director of the Section on Hispanic-American Letters in the League of Nations' International Institute of Intellectual Cooperation (IIIC). Responding to questions submitted by the editors of *Revue de l'Amérique Latine* in 1926, Mistral employed a series of rhetorical questions to express her belief that the IIIC had a cultural role to play in international peace and cooperation: "Did we not see, during the war, the results of the systematic and inspired organization of, shall we say, hate? Why should we not try to adapt these methods to organize the spirit of love?" ("L'Institut International," 14). Mistral's sociopolitical proposals often work according to principles of appropriation and conversion, in this case appropriating corrupt forms of collectivism and converting them to the purposes of her genuine collectivity. Beyond her hope that the kinds of effort that went into World War I in the name of hate can be reenlisted in the name of love, Mistral argues that the task of international intellectual cooperation must supplement the League of Nations' more explicitly political contraction of treaties and must reassert its cultural energies toward the goals of *fraternité*, not fratricide: "All of the League of Nations' efforts are directed at a single goal: beyond the conclusion of official governmental agreements, to reach out to the masses and infuse them with the idea of brotherhood" (13). Mistral envisions an internationality that manifests and makes genuine a spirit of cooperation, of equality, and of "universality." The notion that culture can overcome difference, not through its elision but through its enlistment in a larger collective, underpins much of her thinking on human rights and equality. Mistral's activities and attitudes in support of human rights demonstrate a commitment not to a vacated sense of individual humanity and fundamental dignity, but to a culturally inflected sense of the humane that grounds the individual in terms of a collective.

A similar sense of collectivity, this time gone bad, models her thinking on feminism and women's suffrage. Often disparaged in her time as antifeminist, Mistral's critiques of feminism and her insistence on the importance of institutional recognition of the differences between masculine and feminine emerge from her sense that many of the early twentieth-century feminist arguments in Europe and the Americas were not interested in women as a collective but only in a minority of upper-class women. In her 1925 article on the women's movement in Chile, "Organización de las mujeres" (Organization of women), Mistral recalls a provocative response she gave to an invitation to join the Consejo Nacional de Mujeres (Women's National Council): "[I will accept] with pleasure, when groups of working women take part in the council, and it truly is national; that is, when it shows in relief all three of Chile's social classes" (67). In her assessment, the rhetorical cloak of collectivity masks the limited and narrowly self-interested nature of this women's movement, threatening to foreclose the possibility of true collectivity. Mistral consistently demonstrates a suspicion of work and organizing done *in the name of* a collective that is not genuinely collective, and she identifies this "misrepresentation" as endemic to contemporary society: "Today's confused arrangement in which no one represents anyone does not interest me, even when half of it is made up of women" ("El voto feminino" [The female vote], 266). Such an arrangement works, in her assessment, at a superficial level, not touching the "*entrañas nacionales*" (inner workings of the nation), and thus not returning to the elemental foundations of society.

Mistral's sense of patriotism and nationalism is also inflected by a sense that genuine collectivity must form the basis of social and civic commonality. In "Pasión agraria" (Agrarian passion), her 1928 article on land reform in the Americas, Mistral contrasts what she identifies as the persistence of the feudal *latifundio* in Latin America with the French peasant's access to land, arguing that national collectivity can come only from below, and sketching her sense of the expansion of the individual into the collective: "The most concrete and immediate thing . . . is one's native land. The land of childhood and of the orchards that sustain the child; later, the land of history . . . , and after that, the collective sensibility" (271). For Mistral, genuine collectivity begins at home, springing from the individual's relationship to the land, from the child's relationship to the home, and from the family's relationship to society in an ever-expanding series of filiative engagements.

That genuine collectivity comes from below, that it must be a culture rather than a dogma, implicitly informs much of Mistral's 1956 "Mensaje sobre los derechos humanos" (Message on human rights), delivered on the eighth anniversary of the UDHR in the UN General Assembly: "We celebrate the universality of your civil feat, but there still remains in us a sad countenance. We take a look around the world and remain pensive. . . . I would be delighted if your noble efforts to achieve human rights were adopted with total fidelity by the nations of the world" (143). While the aspirations of universality merit her praise, the perceived shortcomings of the legal documents on human rights can be accounted for by their imposition of rhetorical equality from the top down, once again jeopardizing to some extent the emergence of genuine common interest through cultural development. Mistral sees collectivism, the basis of any human rights program, as a process and not as a declamation, and in her 1928 article "Los derechos del niño" (The rights of the child), she offers pedagogy as a tool to cultivate a cultural collectivism in the individual: "I detest education in mass, and I have an aversion to the brutal and brutalizing masses. . . . I always say, 'the greatest substance of individualism within the principles of collectivism.'" (278). Mistral's collectivism, at once spiritual, intellectual, and cultural, grounds her sense of the commonality of being human and the human experience; it is fostered, learned, and developed. That is, for Mistral one must always return to the core of the matter, and so to achieve genuine international collectivity the individual must first be grounded locally, and through education and cultural engagement that individual will find natural and fundamental filiative commonality through the acquisition of a cultural conscience.

Mistral's appeal to world conscience provides a sort of compendium of her concerns: she opposes what she sees as the rise and enshrinement of the individual at the cost of the collective; she insists upon the importance of mothers and children, but more especially of motherhood and childhood as cultural and moral training grounds; she entrusts pedagogy with the development of social sensitivity; and she fears the escalation of a conflict between the domestic and the international. Mistral's thinking is complex and nuanced, even at times contradictory, and I cannot exhaust the elaborate interrelationships between writing and human rights that her work evidences; I will, however, attempt to show that her prose work structures a coherent critique of what she sees as the shortcomings of the international political climate of her times. In comparison to her poetry, Mistral's prose has been traditionally underexamined, and yet for many years it was her primary source of financial support and it, as much as her poetry, helped to establish her as an international public voice of social conscience, a strategic deployment of an international and national image, as Licia Fiol-Matta has argued in *A Queer Mother for the Nation.* I want to suggest that these critiques of contemporary social structures and this ideological commitment to sensitization function according to parabolic processes of comparison and substitution. Suspicion of disingenuous collectivity, or the name of the collective, underpins much of her work. As can be seen in her identification of the horrors of the two world wars, the cloak of collectivism is the rhetorical ally of power and oppression, and it is her belief that the processes of genuine collective formation may be instituted by reennobling the familiar, the everyday, and the domestic. Her prose work, taken as a piece, attempts to describe the mechanisms by which this genuine collective sensibility may be constituted through culture and may, simultaneously, return culture to its valid role as social, political, and personal mediator between the individual and various filiative collectivities.

Raising the Domestic to Dominion: Culture and Collective Consciousness

Mistral's reading of the Genocide Convention in her "Appeal to World Conscience" stresses the role that culture has to play in the international promotion and protection of human rights. While culture is, for her, grounded in the domestic and the familiar, it is in no way parochial. In fact, it is precisely against a mercenary, locally individuated culture that Mistral posits her sense of the development of collectivity. Much of Mistral's most pointed criticism is directed at a revelation of the nonrepresentational, disingenuous aspects of contemporary collectivity that have emerged as part of an Enlightenment teleology of civilization. In "En el día de la cultura americana" (In the time of American culture), she explicitly yokes culture to civilization, warning against the insidious deployment of culture for individualist interests: "Civilization without a guiding collective conscience has become a Manichean enterprise of good and evil, . . . that with one generous hand cures our children as it could never cure before and days later kills entire populations with grenades and fetid gas" (283). For Mistral, women, in part because of a natural collective sensibility and in part because they have been relegated to a devalued sphere of domestic concerns, have played little part in the development of what she calls this "rabid culture of individualism" (282); in her writing, this individualism is the neopagan product of the Renaissance's and the Enlightenment's promotion of a cult of personality to the detriment of a natural social sensibility.

Although literary modernism, which she sees as the logical product of "rabid individualism," is similarly repugnant to Mistral, her own writings express anxieties about alienation that appear to concur with its critiques of "civilization" and its characterization of Africa as a primordial Europe: "The century of humanitarian positivism bequeathed to its successor an impulse to cruelty that has no cause to be jealous of the African jungle" (283). Mistral's sense that civilization has come undone issues from her profound commitments to difference, commitments that upon first glance appear to conflict with her sense of collectivism. It could be argued that her disdain for contemporary society, even her distaste for much of the early-twentieth-century women's movements, emerges from her conviction that rhetorical forms of equality—that is, equality cloaked in the language of progress and uniformity—are really elisions of these essential differences.

As a lifelong teacher, Mistral sees education as, at least in part, capable of cutting through the individualist bias to move toward collectivism in the development of a cultural sensibility. Education is not, then, selfishly directed toward the advancement of the individual except in as much as that advancement moves toward the goal of collective cultural consciousness, a cultivation that compares favorably in her writing with the role of motherhood. In her prose poem "La oración de la maestra" (The teacher's prayer) she explicitly analogizes the occupation of teacher to that of mother: "Allow me to be more mother than their mothers, to love and defend like they do what is not flesh of my flesh" (*Desolación*, 217). The roles of teacher and mother are so closely aligned in her work that she argues in her controversial 1927 article "Una nueva organización del trabajo (I)" (A new organization of labor) that, while guidance of the state should be left to men, the profession of teaching children should be reserved for women. Her sense of the feminine might seem to replicate the patronizing notion that the hand that rocks the cradle rules the world, but it re-visions that formulation, investing it with radical social potential. Mistral conceives of the moral and intellectual difference between women and men as essential to the well-being of society and to the formation of a truly representative cultural collective that respects difference and that does not cynically deploy difference to maintain the inequities of power.

In 1946 Mistral was appointed to the United Nations Commission on the Status of Women, whose mandate was to produce a document enumerating rights particular to women. Although she recused herself from the commission because she felt that the project of bifurcating human rights into masculine and feminine risked institutionalizing difference as a means of exclusion, she returned to the commission as the official Chilean delegate in 1954. Her attendance was erratic over the next two years of service, but her contributions to the discussions were consistent. She expounded on the importance of motherhood and the need for the protection of childhood in terms of the moral bases of cultural education, but she most often took the floor to speak about the economic inequities suffered by women and the obstacles to their education. In particular, Mistral argued for the capacity of cultural education to surmount the hatred of difference that she saw in the world; the secretary of the commission records her speech on one such occasion: "Miss Mistral (Chile) stressed the important part played by education in overcoming racial and other group prejudice, and prejudices against foreigners. . . . [She] deplored the fact that the various continents knew so little about each other. Lasting peace was possible only if the East and West learned to understand one another's mentality. To that end, children in schools should be given more information about distant lands, preferably by means of illustrated books, since pictures were worth many words, and should not grow up in the provincial belief that their country is the center of the world" (UN, E/CN.6/SR.137, 5, 11–12).

It is typical of her political pronouncements that she commits what the English literary critic John Ruskin would call the pathetic fallacy; she attributes to continents and to the abstractions of East and West the prejudices held by the peoples who live there. These processes of poetic substitution, rather than representing fallacious thinking, should be understood in the context of her poetic sense of organic collectivity. That is, in her sense of the moral development of cultural consciousness, the individual is tied to the earth, to the family, and to community, and thus, at each level of these collective filiations, the substantive collective comes to occupy the place of the individual in a narrower collective. Each expansion of the collective stands in parabolic relation to that which precedes it, and each can be understood as an allegorical representation of the others.

In 1922 the Mexican secretary of public education invited Mistral to consult in the country's attempts to reform the school system. Part of her contribution consisted of an anthology of primary school readings entitled *Lecturas para mujeres,* intended to serve as a textbook for the students in the school that bore her name, La Escuela Hogar Gabriela Mistral. In the introduction to her anthology, Mistral laments that culture in primary school consists mostly of stories about national heroes and historic battles, that it ignores the "domestic" and everyday, and she hopes that her scholastic reader will correct the masculine focus of those books by inculcating "generations with a moral sensibility," to produce "pure and vigorous citizens and women, and individuals in whom culture becomes militant" (15). Her sense of "feminine patriotism" asserts a sentimentality that evokes a love of country grounded in the familiar and that circulates from "the customs that the woman creates and conducts" (13). To that end, her anthology provides vignettes on quotidian events and objects as well as on the "great human affairs" of social justice, work, and nature. Her inclusion of readings about the "ordinary" begins to suggest the sense of the intimate connections between the quotidian and the political, between the home and international social justice. Mistral asserts the value of this focus by comparing it to a favorite example of hers: "we need pages of true art in which, like Dutch paintings of interiors, the ordinary is raised to a level of beauty" (11). She envisions her primary school reader as a practical intervention not only into the devalued arena of primary school pedagogy but also into the formation and institution of a moral culture in order to, after the verse of Eduardo Marquina, "raise the domestic to dominion"

(9). Mistral's sense of the quotidian and the domestic is not limited to conceptions of childhood and motherhood; it is, rather, more broadly conceived as the intimate relations between an individual and his or her everyday surroundings. It might be better to imagine Mistral's realm of the domestic as the (re)humanization of things: the world, the international social order, politics, art, science, history, and so on.

Folktales: The Syllabaries and Alphabets of Culture

Mistral's sense of the benefits of motherhood and education depends on her belief in the capacity of the domestic to develop a moral sensibility. She fears for the child whose mother and pedagogical surrogates have been replaced by the street and a culturally bankrupt social order, and she argues to the Commission on the Status of Women in 1954 that "Everyone was aware of the moral distress of children who were separated from their mothers, . . . [and] suffered profoundly from moral loneliness. . . . In the modern world, where, despite what was customarily called progress, greed and selfishness were still all too common, children who could not find refuge with their mothers fell prey to bitter thoughts which might have the most serious effects on their psychological development" (UN, E/CN.6/SR.143, n.p.). For Mistral, moral distress comes from distance from the mother, from the familiar and the domestic, but it is not confined to the separation from a literal mother; it is also, by parabolic extension, the result of distance from a motherland and a mother tongue. Language is the medium of moral accompaniment for Mistral, and she argues in "Sobre cuatro sorbos de agua" (On four sips of water) that, while initially experienced as a "catastrophe," immersion in a foreign language produces a rediscovery of the ordinary that emulates the intensity and exuberance of the mind in childhood.

If distance from the familiar measures alienation, Mistral conceives of language as having the capacity to refamiliarize the foreign, and she speaks of learning foreign languages and teaching children as similar processes of developing the soul. Nothing in the world is more beautiful, she observes in her 1923 "Pensamientos pedagógicos" (Thoughts on pedagogy), than "the conquest of souls" (61). Though her words ring with the resonance of the Spanish conquest of Latin America, Mistral sees in language a beneficial form of conversion, a form of participative exchange and interaction that itself converts the conquistador's impulse into something moral. In "La aventura de la lengua" (The adventure of language), delivered to a group of university students in California in 1947, Mistral praised the possibilities of language learning as a proper form of international collectivism:

> The conquest of foreign lands and bodies continues in the world today; the old, brutal, and greedy form of conquest has not ended . . . and it continues to be hateful, even when it is cloaked in the language of rights and benefits. To these eternal and violent operations on lands and bodies, I prefer the business of winning souls, which is the spread of every language. This paschal action of sharing the foreign spirit . . . does not represent invasion but a just and good appropriation. Its potential gives me joy, almost to the point of making me dance. (74)

Mistral sees language as intimately connected to the cultural consciousness of a people, as a key for revamping the predatory forms of conquest through the exchange of languages, of students, and, in the vein of nineteenth-century comparative literary studies, of the essences of a people: "That which is called the search for knowledge . . . requires subtle instruments. The first of these is learning languages" (75). But this is the "conquest" of foreign souls, and in Mistral's vision of the world the conquest must begin at home, with the native language, passed "naturally" from mother to child, capturing the soul of the child.

Part of the moral accompaniment that she seeks for the psychological development of children is found in the substance of culture, education, and motherhood. For Mistral, one such basic element is the folktale, which she identifies as particularly appropriate for children: "The child's first readings should be those that approximate most closely the oral tale, those, that is, that come from the stories of the elders and those about local events" ("Pasión de leer" [Passion for reading], 327). In "Algunos elementos del folklore chileno" (Elements of Chilean folklore), a lecture delivered at a summer exchange program to students in Montevideo in 1938, Mistral makes explicit her sense of the relationship between folklore and the education of children, arguing that "children's literature is the folklore of any country" (324). Folklore is, however, more than the essence of a domesticated moral sensibility, Mistral also valorizes it as the cultural repository, free of artifice, of a people: "There is a mystery in folklore, which is the mystery of the genuine voice of a race, of the true and direct voice, and in which the race speaks for itself. It does not speak in that form of suspicious amplification, like the poet or the novelist. Folklore resembles the viscera.... Entrails are not pretty, they are rather ugly; but they are the principal qualities of the organism. Everything else exists as adornment" (324).

If folklore represents the foundations of culture, of a moral education, and the growth of a collective sensibility, its destruction rises to the level of genocide—both because it contains the cultural residue of a "race" and because it provides the starting point for future collectivist cultural consciousness. In Mistral it is a medium through which the past becomes present and is directed toward the future, and it is precisely the loss of indigenous American folklore that she blames for part of a Latin American modernist alienation: "I believe that the best that we could have acquired after the language was the poetic folklore.... but they killed it, above all, with the horror of the heretic" (326). The colonial destruction of indigenous folklore leads her to condemn the Spanish conquest, particularly for the kinds of intolerance it demonstrated but also for the consequences of the loss of the fundamental grounds of future cultural identity and tolerance: "I'm certain that the missionary, when he destroyed, burnt, and cursed the texts—because he also cursed the texts—did so in his horror at heresy, at the possibility that one little drop of paganism might seep out of those precious texts that he consigned to oblivion. This operation of making a 'race' forget its folklore seems to me one of those that the theologians call a 'sin against the Divine Spirit'" (326). Mistral argues that despite this project of forced forgetting, indigenous folklore remains the common denominator, "the syllabary and alphabet," of a Latin American mestizo cultural collective because "[t]he Indian is not outside ourselves: we swallowed him, and we carry him within us" (330, 329). The project of cultural recovery is part of the work of the Latin American writer and teacher, and Mistral identifies it as crucial to a revalorization of the familiar and the renovation of the genuinely moral and collective cultural consciousness.

Mistral's sense of the importance of culture, education, and folklore expresses itself as a nostalgia for a past that is best exemplified in her valorization of the Greek classical golden age of democracy. The modern demonization of native folklore is, in her estimate, a symptom of social degradation and is analogous to a contemporary devaluation of the ordinary, particularly since folklore for her becomes the narrative equivalent of the literary familiar. Her condemnation of the missionary's attempts to make the people forget the fabric of their own culture might well apply to her identification of the century's devaluation of the domestic: "It is terrible to submerge in oblivion the memory of a people; it's like suicide" (326). For Mistral, while folklore represents the factual past "memory of a people," the individual's intimacy with the familiar represents the contemporary repository of a similar memory, one that can be collectivized through cultural sensitization.

Imagining Collectivity: Parables and the Poetic Mind

If folklore represents the fundamental matter of a cultural collective conscience, parables represent the work of the artist and teacher on those elemental materials. In "Pensamientos pedagógicos," Mistral,

33

with characteristic religious emphasis, explains that parables are the proper genre of storytelling for the teacher: "The parables of Jesus are the eternal model of teaching: use images, be simple and, under the guise of that simplicity, offer the most profound thoughts" (60). Much of Mistral's creative prose takes the form of parables or allegories; even her *recados* often suggest themselves as concealing a profundity of thought on complicated topics presented simply that seem to illustrate much more than a geographic portrait of Chile or a physiognomic portrait of the American Indian. In *Desolación,* Mistral includes under the heading "prosa escolar" a number of stories that clearly take the parabolic form as their model of instruction. In "Por qué las cañas son huecas" (Why the canes are hollow), she explicitly thematizes the issues of rights and equality that are her avocation and passion.

The parable has it that long ago, "one day, the social revolution came to the world of plants" (311). The caudillos of this revolution were the canes, who, with the help of the propagandizing wind, whipped the plant world into a frenzy over equality. Equality, however, was narrowly defined, and the pursuit consisted only in all plants growing to the same height: "To lift their heads to a uniform height was the ideal" (311). The dangers of an equality of such limited scope are suggested early in the story when it is revealed that the corn had no interest in becoming strong like the oak and the roses no intention of becoming useful, like the rubber trees. One night all the plants achieved their goal, with the help of the vital breath of monstrous spirits of the earth. The disastrous effects of the overnight growth spurt manifested first among the peasants who, along with their livestock, became lost in the obscure jungles of wheat and clover. But, while the canes rejoiced in their victorious revolution, "decadence" set in among the plants. The timid violets suffered early, drying out with their "purple heads in full sunlight" (315). The lilies then broke under their own weight, and the lemon trees lost their frail flowers to the violent winds; the clover was scorched, twisting in the heat; the weight of the corn's ears bowed the stalks to the ground, and the potatoes were stunted, putting all their energies into their stems and none into their tubers.

The narrator tells us, "It doesn't need to be said that there was no bread or fruit for man, no forage for the animals; there was hunger; there was suffering on the earth" (316). The situation had become serious, and even the canes began to fret. They self-destructed last, "signaling the total disaster of the theory of leveling, their roots rotting in the humid soil" (317). When the canes fell, it could be seen that in order to achieve such height, "their marrow had been emptied, and they were now like marionettes or rubber figurines" (317). After the great fall and the failure of the revolution, nature repaired the damage within six months, "returning the ridiculous plants to their natural states," except for the canes, who were left with their hollow stigmata (317).

There were of course dissenters; the violets for example spoke of divine law and a poet with a beard like the Nile condemned the project, declaiming "wise things about uniformity" (312). After nature's generous restoration, the poet composes verses on the affair: "Better like this, my loved ones. Beautiful every one as God made it: the oak strong and the barley fragile" (317). The poet lifts the quotidian to the divine in his role as reverent appreciator of beauty, as the creature capable of recognizing the extraordinary in the ordinary.

Mistral's parable was published just after the First World War and the Russian Revolution; it also appeared in the midst of numerous suffragist movements around Europe and the Americas. Given these multiple contexts, it would be difficult to isolate a particular "social revolution" as the parabolic reference in her story. While initially appearing to criticize in general a desire and drive for equality, the parable's abstract object of ridicule is rather more narrowly described. It is not, strictly speaking, a project of equal rights that the plants undertake (in fact, the narrator explicitly excludes "right to good water" as a motive for this revolution) (311); rather, the story warns against the dangers of uniformity (as opposed to equality) even, or especially, when it is cloaked in the language of social justice and rights. The *"teoría*

niveladora" is based on a flawed concept of collectivity whose affilia-
tions are not to be found in the natural qualities of individual plants or
in the divine order of things. Instead, this is a uniformity whose collectivism is imposed from a disconnected theory concocted by the vain-
glorious canes. In her parable, equality emerges as a project not of
equalization but of sensitization to equality through difference.

Writing in 1928 Mistral argues that women's suffrage "is something
to debate in the language of rights" and that she has always taken for
granted that voting rights belong universally to the "human gender"
("El voto feminino" [The women's vote], 261). This collective, defined
in terms of generic rights of human beings, seeks not to elide the essential differences that Mistral so cherishes; instead, it recognizes distinctions within a collective, whose members might themselves constitute
smaller collectives, without grounding the claim to equal rights in
equivalence. Mistral similarly identifies in some of the early-twentieth-
century women's demands for equal rights a project of uniformity,
choosing as objects of her derision examples that she finds particularly
distasteful: "mandatory military service, suppression of women's
dress, and even suppression of gender in language" ("Nueva organización," 254). These projects are akin, in Mistral's thinking, to that of the
plants' misplaced desire for equal heights. The risks of misguidance in
a set of rights framed not from a sense of experientially grounded collectivism but from theoretical principle are characterized in her writing
on women's suffrage where she states, "There are rights that I do not
care to exercise because they will leave me as poor as I was before" ("El
voto feminino," 265).

It is, of course, no coincidence that the figure in the parable that
takes stock of the situation, who recognizes the beauty in differentiation and the natural order, is the poet, whose spiritually inflected verse
appreciates the supreme in the ordinary. This is in itself a parabolic/
poetic move that through comparison reveals the interrelatedness and
interdependence of diversity in the recognition of a genuine collectivity. In "Sobre cuatro sorbos de agua," Mistral explains, "We poets, my

friends, are collectors, not only of broad images but of minute expressions" (198). She further suggests that it is through this function as a collector of images and human expressions that the poet has access to the cultural recesses of a people, that those very people are comprehended through the poetic processes. It is in the process of collection, not in the process of organization but appreciation, not through invention but conversion, that the poetic mind becomes parabolic itself, recognizing the intrinsic qualities that form collective relationships. This is part of the pragmatics of her political engagements as well, involving the methods of appropriation and conversion that underpin her arguments for the institution of genuine collectivity. In fact, Mistral perceives the entrance of women into literature as a corrective to the cultural, individualist sensibilities of poetry that have predominated since the Enlightenment: "Thanks to the return of poetry from Romanticism to everyday life, . . . it is possible to write about four sips of water. . . . I was always certain that if we women insisted upon recounting all our little nothings, if we spun into writing what we live inside, seated amid the living constellation of our objects, and speaking what we know of 'nourishment,' earthly and familiar, making us see the ordinary table, we might humanize this world" (197).

The domestic and the everyday are, for Mistral, gendered as feminine, but perhaps we ought to understand this gendering as a strategic deployment of the binary divisions that have been perpetuated by Enlightenment, dualistic thinking. In Mistral, the poetic mind, with its domestic sensitivities, can reintegrate the world by seeing behind the theoretical and rhetorical civilizing projects to recognize the innate unity and beauty of the natural order of things, to elevate the ordinary to the supreme. In an international climate euphoric with the notion of progress, Mistral's imaginative project is traditionalist, in her formulation of that concept: "Traditionalists begin and end everything with their own" ("Sobre cuatro sorbos," 199). Mistral laments the loss of one's own, particularly in the case of folklore in the Americas, and she seeks to reassert the recognition of one's own through a return to the domestic and the familiar, to the elements and substance of culture, that will lead ultimately to the development of a genuine moral collectivity.

Parabolic Institutions: Universities, Anthologies, and Libraries as Cultural Collectives

Mistral's sense of the value of the parable as an elemental form of moral instruction is not confined to the stories she writes for students; many of her pieces in praise of political and social institutions take advantage of its form. Among the institutions she singles out for eulogy are international organizations of cooperation, including the League of Nations, the United Nations, and the IIIC; but she also finds the more ordinary (though in her writing abstracted) institutions of the university, the anthology, and the library particularly deserving. These last three become allegorical for Mistral's ideal collective cultural consciousness, standing as parabolic exempla of her social ideals and in stark contrast to the state, which she holds primarily responsible for the devaluation of the familiar and for the disruption of genuine collectivism. In "La unidad de la cultura" (The unity of culture), delivered to an assembly of university students in Guatemala in 1931, Mistral laments the "tragedy" of civilization's "fatal separation" of "body and soul, of State and University," which has resulted in a fundamental antagonism between "power and thought, realization and conception" (71). For Mistral, this lamentable separation grows out of Enlightenment individualist and statist thinking that fails to recognize the interdependence and interrelatedness of all spheres of human activity, training, and thought, and in "Organización de las mujeres," she argues that a true social revolution would set about to reunite these "hemispheres." The enterprises of Mistral's collective-minded vision of the state range from pragmatic, if socially progressive, projects—of social security, welfare, and the extension of credit to rural farmers—to the more idealistic: "bring all of the social classes together through common interests and sentiments" (69). Mistral's state reenters the realm of the cultural to construct a nationalist ("racial") consciousness through projects intended to: "democratize culture, spreading the library of the people like a generous river, from one side of the country to the other; to humanize the State, and to create that network of interests and love that constitutes a race" (69). Mistral finds these institutions especially important for the working and rural classes, and she understands this moral collectivizing of the cultural sensibility as a process of extending "dignity to the citizen, in the houses of the workers" (69). Her article laments that the Chilean state in 1925 is a long way from attempting, not to mention achieving, this ideal, and she blames the separation of the cultural and the moral from the civic and the political for the current climate of individualism.

Having identified the self-interest of the state as the effect and agent of dualistic thinking and the devaluation of cultural collectivity, Mistral discovers in the university an allegorical embodiment of her ideal because it occupies itself with "the entire spiritual business of a race": "with respect to a country, it represents something like what the Egyptians called the double of the human body; that is, an ethereal body that contains all the factions and members of the material body. For me the university would be the moral double of a territory and it would have direct influence over everything from agriculture and mines to adult night schools, including in its jurisdiction the schools of fine arts and music" (69). Thus, in its social, moral, and cultural purview, the university becomes allegorical for the kinds of collectivity and cultural sensibility that Mistral values. It is exemplary not merely as an institution of learning, but more precisely in its assemblage and its role in facilitating a sense of common cultural destiny. Her praise for the university as a moral double of a territory is, however, qualified by her regret that its cultural influence and operation have been divorced from the political arena and have been removed from the social experience of many.

Like the university, anthologies, including her *Lecturas para mujeres* and the collections of Chilean folklore that she saw published while working with the IIIC, are also invested with allegorical social significance in their ability to comprehend contrasting opinions and authors within a single volume. But she reserves her most lavish praise for the library. In 1950, Mexican president Alemán invited Mistral to inaugurate the new Biblioteca Popular in Veracruz. Her encomium in "¿Qué es una biblioteca?" (What is a library?) focuses on the qualities that make the library an ideal of social collectivity and cultural consciousness. Similar to the integrative faculty of the poetic mind, Mistral's library represents collectivity through diversity, and she compares its vitality to the gifts of the natural world: "A library is a nursery of fruiting plants" (63). But this collectivity depends on the unique potential of each volume in the collection, both in its individual value and in its relationship to the collective: "each one becomes a true 'tree of life,' where all come to learn to season and consume its goodness" (63). The library is thus a microcosm of the international, national, and local order, each book possessed of the capacity to unify the separate registers.

For Mistral, the library is particularly praiseworthy for its capacity to house contrasting and contradictory ideas and instantiations of culture that in the world of politics have provided the impetus for conflict: "Lope and Quevedo, who often fought with each other, will here rub elbows, and our father Dante, the exile, will converse with his fellow Florentines" (63). But if international culture and cooperation are a product of exchange, like her sense of learning foreign languages, a library represents that process and product by means of domestication through the diverse contents of its shelves, where side by side sit "the strong and the meek, the wise and the delirious, the serious and the playful, the conformists and the rebels" (63). A library exemplifies the project of overcoming difference while learning to respect it: "Here one can learn tolerance for the ideas that most contrast with our own" (64). And, in Mistral's sociocultural allegory, it is also the proper battleground for ideological conflict: "a library, despite its silence, is like a small guerilla camp: ideas fight here at their pleasure. We . . . insinuate ourselves into the fray without blood" (64). I should note here that in actual practice, Mistral's library may not have been "bloodless." As Fiol-Matta demonstrated in *Queer Mother*, her private practice and public politics did not always coincide, and Marie-Lise Gazarian-Gautier reports that as the Latin American cultural broker for the IIIC, Mistral was known to compost books without "moral or literary value" in a well behind her house. It might be argued that her prose writings structure an aspirational and poetical politics (Gautier, 48).

Each of Mistral's allegorical institutions is doubly parabolic; they are both a means and an ends to sensitive cultural collectivity. That is, in their elaboration they represent the ideal of collectivity that promotes cooperation through respect and tolerance of difference, but they are also part of the processes of developing the collective cultural consciousness. They institute Mistral's sense of the moral ground of the movement out from the maternally domestic to an internationality that brings dominion to the intimacy of the domestic. Mistral's encomium for the library offers a vision of cooperation and cultural collectivism that parallels her engagements with the United Nations, UNICEF, UNESCO, and her work with the League of Nations' IIIC. In her article on the IIIC, Mistral argues that World War I, whose organizational efforts in the name of collective hate she hopes to reenlist in the name of collective love and tolerance, was instrumental in bringing Latin America and Asia out of their "isolation." She further argues that in the context of the internationalizing projects of the League of Nations and the IIIC, it is incumbent upon the European and other Western powers to come to know the differences they have thus far ignored, suppressed, and oppressed: "Europe, who profited from their material aid, has concluded a sort of moral contract, that of coming to know their soul" ("L'Institut International," 17). While idealistic, Mistral's promotion of intellectual cooperation through cultural interchange rings with the rationale adopted in the UDHR that proposes human rights as an antidote to violence: "it is essential,

if man is not to be compelled to have recourse, as a last resort, to rebellion against tyranny and oppression, that human rights should be
promoted by the rule of law." The individualist focus of the UDHR
might not reflect Mistral's sense of the importance of collectivity, but
it does, even if only to a limited extent, recognize the value of education and culture in the promotion and protection of human rights.

"A Wor[l]d Full of Xs and Ks": Liberty, Equality, Fraternity

Mistral's proposals for the development of genuine collectivity reflect
her cautious attitude toward the "progress" of civilization. I have not
intended in this synthesis of her social thinking to argue whether her
ideas are conservative or progressive (they are some mixture of the
two), only to organize those ideas and to suggest that they function according to parabolic, poetic principles of analogy and substitution. It
should be noted that most contemporary institutionalized commitments to human rights have not developed along the lines of her
thinking, and have tended to enshrine the individual at the cost of the
collective. Mistral's warning in her "Nueva organización del trabajo,"
remains as important and controversial today as it was at the beginning of the twentieth century: "Before celebrating the opening of
doors," it is necessary to examine "which doors have opened, and before putting a foot into the new universe" to take a look "behind us
and see what we are abandoning" (253).

Mistral's faith in the capacity of culture—both cultural collectivism
and cultural sensibility—is too unproblematic given the history of the
twentieth century and the deployment of culture in new forms of imperialism, and there is a lurking suggestion, in her condemnation of
genocide, for example, that the value of the human being arises from
the value of the culture instantiated in being human. And yet, perhaps
this permits her another way to make the case for human rights, not

according to the logic of what she sees as a debased individualism but according to the logic of human culture. In her published prose, the conditions of fundamental human value emerge from a sense of the individual constituted through culture and collectivist engagements. Her sense of the role of culture, from its moral grounding in the familiar, the everyday, and the domestic to its analogical elaboration in the national and international appears to foreshadow poststructuralist arguments about subjectivity, recognizing as the nexus of social, political, and cultural combinations that which we call the individual in all its visceral and psychological complexity. Her stress on returning the domestic to a valued category of human experience and foundation may be traditionalist, but it imagines the individual and the grounds of human rights as processes, not declamations, of dignification, sensitization, and filiative engagement achieved through education and cultural participation. It should be acknowledged that her versions of the feminine and the masculine have fallen out of critical favor, and her ideas about the "Orient" and Africa, when she records them, subscribe to the prejudices of her day, even when she recasts them for the purposes of valorization rather than denigration. But perhaps these blindnesses underscore rather than undermine her sense of the important task assigned to education in overcoming intolerance and establishing the bases of genuine cultural collectivity.

I end this essay with a final example of Mistral's poetic and parabolic conception of the bases of human rights. I have already elaborated the nature of her sense of equality and fraternity, but there is, of course, a third term in the Enlightenment triumvirate of human rights discourse: liberty. For Mistral, moral malformation of the child, and, by extension, society, is located in the distance imposed between mother and child, between the domestic and the social, between the local and the international. Liberty, too, is a casualty of that alienation. In her prose poem "El elogio del niño" (Elegy for the child), she declares that prior to their desire for physical sustenance, children are maintained above all by their innate love of liberty. Liberty is, in much of her work but most especially in her 1945 essay "La pobre libertad" (Poor liberty), attributed to youth and is young itself. Mistral argues that when we take a hard look at the trajectory of modern civilization, from the Spanish conquest to the present, we should be struck with the degradation of the natural qualities of the human being to the point that the word *liberty* itself sticks in our throats, "like an Aztec or Quechua word full of Xs and Ks" (144). Mistral's cultural collectivity imagines a world where cultural sensibility will teach tolerance for difference, appreciating rather than disparaging a cultural consciousness created from below, from that which has been devalued and suppressed; such a cultural collective spirit might make it possible for a Spanish mouth to relish the articulation of a refamiliarized wor(l)d full of Xs and Ks without swallowing it.

Note

Unless otherwise indicated, all translations are mine.

Works Cited

Fiol-Matta, Licia. *A Queer Mother for the Nation: The State and Gabriela Mistral.* Minneapolis: University of Minnesota Press, 2002.

Gazarian-Gautier, Marie-Lise. *Gabriela Mistral: The Teacher from the Valley of Elqui.* Chicago: Franciscan Herald Press, 1975.

Mistral, Gabriela. "Algunos elementos del folklore chileno." Lecture, Montevideo, January 1938. Rpt. in *Gabriela anda por el mundo,* ed. Roque Esteban Scarpa, 307–30. Santiago: Editorial Andres Bello, 1978.

———. "An Appeal to World Conscience." In *United Nations Review,* 16–17. New York: United Nations Publications, June 1956.

———. "La aventura de la lengua." *La Nación* (Buenos Aires), 9 March 1947. Rpt. in *Páginas en prosa: Gabriela Mistral,* ed. José Pereira Rodríguez, 74–79. Buenos Aires: Editorial Kapelusz, 1962.

———. "Los derechos del niño." *Repertorio Americano* (San José, Costa Rica), 18 August 1928. Rpt. in *Gabriela Mistral: Escritos políticos,* 277–80.

———. "El elogio del niño." *El Mercurio* (Santiago), 13 February 1944. Rpt. in *Antología de poesía y prosa de Gabriela Mistral,* 325–26.

———. "En el día de la cultura americana." *América.* (Havana), January 1939. Rpt. in *Gabriela Mistral: Escritos políticos,* 281–87.

———. "L'Institut International de Coopération Intellectuelle: Ce qu'il est; ce qu'il peut faire." *Revue de L'Amérique Latine,* 1 July 1926, 12–18.

———. Introduction to *Lecturas para mujeres.* Ed. Gabriela Mistral. Mexico City, Secretaría de Educación, 1924.

———. "Mensaje sobre los derechos humanos." 1956. Rpt. in *Gabriela Mistral: Escritos políticos,* 143.

———. "Una nueva organización del trabajo (I)." *El Mercurio* (Santiago), 12 June 1927. Rpt. in *Gabriela Mistral: Escritos políticos,* 253–56.

———. "La oración de la maestra." In *Desolación.* 3d ed. Santiago: Editorial Nacimiento, 1926.

———. "Organización de las mujeres." *El Mercurio* (Santiago), 5 July 1925. Rpt. in *Gabriela Mistral: Escritos políticos,* 66–74.

———. "Pasión agraria." *El Mercurio* (Santiago), 11 March 1928. Rpt. in *Gabriela Mistral: Escritos políticos,* 267–71.

———. "Pasión de leer." Madrid 1935. Rpt. in *Antología de poesía y prosa de Gabriela Mistral,* 327–30.

———. "Pensamientos pedagógicos." *Pegaso* (Montevideo), June 1923. Rpt. in *Páginas en prosa.*

———. "La pobre Libertad." *Política y espíritu* (Santiago), November 1945. Rpt. in *Gabriela Mistral: Escritos políticos,* 144–46.

———. "Por qué las cañas son huecas." In *Desolación.* 3d ed. Santiago: Editorial Nacimiento, 1926.

———. "¿Qué es una biblioteca?" *Repertorio americano.* (San José), 10 May 1950. Rpt. in *Páginas en prosa,* 63–67.

———. "Sobre cuatro sorbos de agua." *La Nación* (Santiago), 19 October 1947. Rpt. in *Prosa de Gabriela Mistral,* ed. Alfonso Calderón, 195–99. Santiago: Editorial Universitaria, 1989.

———. "La unidad de la cultura." *Repertorio americano.* (San José), 30 January 1932. Rpt. in *Páginas en prosa,* 68–73.

———. "El voto femenino." *El Mercurio* (Santiago), 17 June 1928. Rpt. in *Gabriela Mistral: Escritos políticos,* 261–66.

United Nations. Commission on the Status of Women. Economic and Social Council. Summary record, 9 April 1953. E/CN.6/SR.137.

———. Summary record, 13 April 1953. E/CN.6/SR.143.

United Nations. Convention on the Prevention and Punishment of the Crime of Genocide. 1948.

United Nations. Universal Declaration of Human Rights. 1948.

Other Sources

Mistral, Gabriela. "Contar." *Repertorio americano* (San José), 20 April 1929. Rpt. in *Antología de poesía y prosa de Gabriela Mistral,* ed. Jaime Quezada, 334–37. Santiago: Fondo de Cultura Económica, 1997.

———. "Cristianismo con sentido social." *Atenea,* November 1925. Rpt. in *Gabriela Mistral: Escritos políticos,* ed. Jaime Quezada, 272–76. Mexico City: Fondo de Cultura Económica, 1994.

———. "Jean Bruhnes y la geografía humana." November 1930. Rpt. in *Gabriela anda por el mundo, 33–38.*

United Nations. Commission on the Status of Women. Economic and Social Council. Summary record, 2 April 1953. E/CN.6/SR.128.

———. Summary record, 8 April 1953. E/CN.6/SR.133.

———. Summary record, 8 April 1953. E/CN.6/SR.135.

———. Summary record, 13 April 1953. E/CN.6/SR.139.

———. Summary record, 16 April 1953. E/CN.6/SR.147.

———. Summary record, 13 April 1954. E/CN.6/SR.156.

———. Summary record, 3 May 1954. E/CN.6/SR.163.

Chapter 3

Gabriela Mistral as Teacher
Revisiting Lucila Godoy Alcayaga's
Pedagogical Assumptions

Verónica Darer

THE PEDAGOGICAL MESSAGE OF Gabriela Mistral is as valid and prevalent now, at the beginning of the twenty-first century, as it was when
she was a literary and educational icon in the early 1900s. Known as
Lucila Godoy Alcayaga during most of her teaching career, Mistral's
educational philosophy regarding teachers, teaching, and schools
still offers an inspirational call to actively reform social and educational inequities and inequalities that plague many nations, including
those in Latin America.

Lucila Godoy Alcayaga was one of the first voices in Latin America
to propose democratic education for all, with no differentiation for students' gender, ethnicity, or socioeconomic status. Contemporary educational thinkers, especially those working from the perspective of
critical theory, would echo many of Lucila's pedagogical ideas. Critical
theorists view schooling as a crucial political tool used by those in positions of power to help or hinder others' paths to social justice. In a
similar way, Lucila Godoy Alcayaga utilized her persona as teacher to
decry the powerlessness of women, poor people, and indigenous populations, in order to obtain quality education (Horan, 56–58). Today,

Latin American educators such as Paulo Freire could be considered the inheritors of Lucila's quest for worldwide educational equity.

If Lucila had remained a schoolteacher, her educational philosophy would never have left the confines of the Elqui valley in Chile. However, Lucila Godoy Alcayaga became Gabriela Mistral, the much loved and renowned poet—the first Latin American writer to win the Nobel prize for literature. As such, a record of her educational philosophy and maxims survives in her published poems and prose.

Lucila's life as a teacher greatly affected her perspective on educational issues. She considered herself first, foremost, and eternally a teacher. In *La desterrada en su patria,* Roque Esteban Scarpa quotes Mistral as saying, "Teaching has been and is for me an innate quality. All my energies and aptitudes I have given with my whole soul to teaching. Literature for me is only a far secondary entertainment and pastime" (Scarpa, 114). Teaching for Lucila was not a profession; it was her sacred mission and calling. Teaching was an innate part of her being. It was her family's profession, vocation, and avocation. Both her father and her half sister were teachers.

Her father, Juan Jerónimo Godoy Villanueva, was a talented educator and musician. Proficient in Latin and French as well as a skilled guitar and violin player, he wrote songs and poems. Some of the poetic creations for his daughter Lucila were in song. Lucila's father transmitted to her his love for nature, his inquisitive mind, and his wanderlust. His zeal for adventure and travel led him to abandon his family when Lucila was only three years old.

It was her half sister, Emelina Molina de Barraza, a country teacher, who inspired Lucila to follow in her footsteps. Fifteen years older than Lucila, Emelina was the eldest and only daughter from a previous marriage of Lucila's mother. For more than thirty years, Emelina dedicated her life to teaching in the rural Elqui valley and Montegrande in Chile. As her first formal teacher, Emelina introduced Lucila to the wonders of reading, writing, and arithmetic.

Until 1900, under the tutelage of her mother and sister, Lucila's childhood in the Elqui valley and Montegrande was blissful and serene. Her pastoral surroundings inspired her curiosity and reverence for nature, a recurring theme in her literary work as well as in her pedagogical writings. During the last year of primary school, she was sent to a small school in Vicuña to complete her education and to serve as companion to the blind school director, Adelaida Olivares, a friend of her mother's. The move marked a change in Lucila's carefree life.

At her new school, students took advantage of her youth, shyness, and sensitivity. She was teased, called derogatory nicknames, falsely accused, and even physically assaulted by peers. One of Lucila's tasks was to hand out paper for assignments. Lucila was accused of mishandling or stealing paper and was sent back home. This first experience with injustice scarred her deeply. The incident sparked Lucila's passionate fight for and defense of those who were powerless. Her first educational experience away from home was also a precursor of the obstacles that would mark Lucila's pedagogical history. Her academic life was plagued by conflicts with superiors and peers. Controversy, hostility, and envy followed Lucila from one teaching post to the next (Pincheira, 65).

Starting from her very first attempt to become a member of the official teaching corps, Lucila experienced difficulty with the educational status quo (Pincheira, 65). She was not admitted to study for her teaching certificate at the Escuela Normal de la Serena; some say it was due to the leftist-leaning articles she had published in the Coquimbo and Elqui newspapers. Consequently, Lucila opted to enter the profession through the practice of teaching, rather than through formal training (Valenzuela-Fuenzalida, 57–58). After her rejection, however, she took a job as a scribe, not as a teacher, at the Inspectoría del Liceo de Niñas de la Serena. When she registered poor children along with children of wealthier families, she was fired. As in past and future occasions, her activism for social justice had hindered her pedagogical career.

However, these early challenges did not impede the fulfillment of her goal. There are different versions of her early life as an educator.

Lucila's twenty-year journey as a teacher started either in 1904 or 1905, at the age of fourteen or fifteen. At her first actual teaching job, as a teacher's assistant at the primary school in Compañía Baja, Lucila taught poor children during the day. At night, she taught adult workers. Teaching the working poor was a labor of love she would continue throughout her life as an educator. Although there are disagreements about when she left Compañía Baja, researchers agree she held various posts as a primary school teacher at the Escuela de la Cantera and at the Escuela de los Cerrillos in Coquimbo.

Another turning point in Lucila's educational career came in 1910. At the time, she was a teacher at the elementary school in the town of Barrancas, near Santiago. Encouraged by friends, she took and passed her secondary school teaching certification exams to teach high school at the Escuela Normal N° 1 of Santiago. During the exam she was able to demonstrate the knowledge she had taught herself. A number of biographies reveal that Lucila was allowed to write her first subject area exam, botany, in verse, thanks to the director of the institution, Brígida Walker, who understood Lucila's apprehensions and sensibilities. Lucila later dedicated one of the poems in *Desolación* (Desolation) to the educator.

Teaching health for two months in 1911 at the Liceo de Traiguén was the start of her secondary school career. Next, she was transferred to the Liceo Femenino de Antofogasta as a history teacher. In 1912 she taught history, geography, and language arts at the Liceo de Niñas de los Andes, where she remained until 1918. Although Lucila had been publishing her writings prior to her move to los Andes, it was here that she developed as a poet and writer. During this period she began to be known as Gabriela Mistral, a pseudonym she chose to honor the French poet Federico Mistral (Gazarian-Gautier, 42). She gained recognition as a poet, winning the Los Juegos Florales poetry competition. Her fame grew in Chile and surrounding areas as her works were published to a wider audience. But the attention she was earning as a writer started to interfere with her vocation as a teacher (Gazarian-Gautier, 47).

Lucila's journey as a secondary school teacher continued in Punta Arenas, also known as Magallanes, in Patagonia, the southernmost tip of South America, where she became director and language arts teacher at the high school. She reorganized the school and dedicated time to the Sociedad de Instrucción Popular de Magallanes. Nevertheless, Lucila was not satisfied with her achievements, believing she had failed to raise sufficient funds to establish satisfactory educational facilities for the local population (Valenzuela-Fuenzalida, 15). In 1920 she transferred to Temuco as principal of the high school for girls. Thanks to influential friends, she was moved to Santiago, Chile's capital, and was named the first director of the Liceo N° 6 de Niñas de Santiago. This, the last educational position held by Lucila in Chile, was the highest post within the country's educational hierarchy (Gazarian-Gautier, 51).

Intrigues and conflicts followed Lucila from her first teaching position to her last (Pincheira, 65). At the beginning of her pedagogical career, Lucila had difficulty entering the profession. At the end of her career, even though she had reached the pinnacle of administrative power, she still had to battle problems of educational bureaucracy. She resigned her last post in 1921 to protest a new law that excluded anyone without a college degree from becoming a certified teacher (Gazarian-Gautier, 52). At the end of her educational career, as in the beginning, influential people came to her professional rescue. This time it was José Vasconcelos, Mexico's secretary of education, who invited her to become part of his country's educational reform. Her move to Mexico in 1922 marked the beginning of her travels throughout the world.

Her educational work in Mexico signals the end of Lucila Godoy Alcayaga, the educator. Gabriela Mistral, the writer, started to supersede Alcayaga, the devoted country teacher. Transformed but not overtaken, Lucila Godoy Alcayaga had fulfilled her destiny of becoming the symbol of the Latin American teacher. Gabriela Mistral, the poet, and Lucila Godoy Alcayaga, the teacher, fused into her book, written in Mexico, *Lecturas para mujeres* (Readings for women), in which she combined pedagogy and literature in a compilation of essays, short stories, and poems targeted to teach literacy to women.

Even though there is a record of Lucila's teaching career, we will probably never know her impact on her pupils' lives because their voices are mostly absent in Lucila's records and biographies. Nevertheless, especially in her native Chile, she is recognized as a precursor of pedagogical tenets and educational democracy. During interviews conducted by Marcia López, a research assistant at the University of Santiago, to obtain current Chilean teachers' thoughts on Gabriela Mistral's pedagogical assumptions, many interviewees highlighted Lucila's role as an agent of educational change. Ana María Madrid Hellman, a teacher in the Liceo Osmán Frein in the Machalí region, summarized the thinking of Chilean teachers: "For her time, she was a transgressor, defiant; for us, she is current, actual, lucid, and sensitive to the social reality of our poor countries" (interview by Marcia López, 2001).

Throughout Latin America, Lucila Godoy Alcayaga is a respected symbol in the world of public education. Schools are named after her alter ego, Gabriela Mistral. In addition, specific educational reform projects in her native Chile have been forged on the basis of her pedagogical philosophy. Currently, El Proyecto Montegrande, a government initiative to better educational quality as well as educational equity at the middle school level, is an example of Lucila Godoy Alcayaga's legacy. The description of the project demonstrates the influence of her vision: "The name of the project is explicitly in honor of our own Gabriela Mistral, brought up in the small region of Montegrande in the Elqui valley. The goal is to rescue the innovative and visionary spirit that she held on educational matters and that she developed in her pedagogical writings as well as in her job as a teacher. Also to rescue the capacity she had to jump from the local reality to the global world, from Montegrande to Stockholm, forging a universal message" (Ministerio de Educación, 1).

Specifically, Lucila is admired for her unending fight to achieve social justice for marginalized populations through educational opportunity. "Gabriela knew and loved the poor and defenseless and could never abandon them. She visited the prisons and hospitals and helped small children both materially and spiritually, especially those that suffered from malnutrition and rickets. She once said, 'I want to dedicate myself fully to the education of the masses'" (Gazarian-Gautier, 49). Women, poor people, and indigenous populations were the focus of Lucila's educational fervor. She might well be considered the first Latin American educator with a written account of her efforts to bring educational opportunity to all. For Lucila, school was the place in which social justice begins and ends. She declared, "If we do not accomplish equality and culture inside school, where can we demand it?" (Scarpa, *Mistral,* 39). "It is necessary not to consider the school the home of an individual, but everybody's home" (42). "Place in my democratic school the splendor that hovers over your chorus of barefoot children" (35). Her lasting gifts to educators are the incorporation of *democracy* and *equality* as intrinsic components of the world of schools and the concept of schooling as the seed for the creation of a just and participatory society.

Paulo Freire, the contemporary Latin American pedagogical icon, who lived among poor and rural communities just as Lucila had, echoes her view that schools play a major role in the construction of democratic societies: "It is true that education is not the ultimate lever for social transformation, but without it transformation cannot occur" (37).

Even though some of Lucila's educational thinking could be considered old-fashioned, overly sentimental, or inadequate for today's educational climate, many of the recommendations and axioms in her educational writings anticipated ideas now accepted as best practices in the craft of teaching. She had the unique ability to articulate some of the challenges many teachers face daily in their profession. In addition, she was able to voice the aspirations that teachers have for their chosen vocation. Today, teachers can find renewed inspiration in Lucila's pedagogical writings, which include the poems "La oración de la maestra" (The teacher's prayer), "Decálogo de la maestra" (Decalogue of the teacher), and "La maestra rural" (The rural teacher); the essays "Pen-samientos pedagógicos" (Thoughts on pedagogy) and "El oficio lateral" (The lateral profession); and her book *Lecturas para mujeres*. What follows are highlights from these writings that educators will find useful as dialectical tools to explore issues of the teaching profession.

In "La oración de la maestra," which defines the roots of Lucila's educational philosophy, she declares, "That I should build from spirit my school of bricks. / The flame from my enthusiasm should blanket its poor atrium, its naked classroom. / That my heart should be more of a column and my goodwill more gold than the columns and the gold of wealthy schools" (Scarpa, *Mistral*, 36). Lucila saw little connection between effective education and the physical space of the school building. Many administrators and community members still fail to understand that as long as schools are clean, safe, and not overcrowded, the space between four walls does not automatically constitute a place of productive learning. Teachers and students, their work and expectations, play the most crucial role in the learning that occurs in the classroom. Teachers and students, not its material riches, are the spirit and soul of the school.

Lucila recognized that schools can extinguish the joy and enthusiasm students bring to the process of learning, a problem addressed by much research today. In her writings, Lucila underscores the need to infuse education with what she sometimes refers to as beauty or enjoyment: "I believe that there is much weariness in the dry, cold, and dead pedagogy that is ours. The child arrives in our hands with delight, but the lessons without spirit or freshness that she or he almost always receives cloud that enjoyment, tiring the young man or woman [and] logically creating a dislike for study" (*Lecturas*, xvii).

To enhance pedagogical success, Lucila encouraged teachers to connect students' learning to their personal lives, to "brighten teaching with a beautiful word, with the opportune anecdote, and with the relationship of knowledge to real life" (Scarpa, *Mistral*, 39). Today, this concept has been expanded and is labeled personalized or student-generated teaching and learning. It is praxis that proposes teaching based on students' needs, interests, and background knowledge. For example, Lucila's thoughts are present in Freire's well-respected "banking" theory, which suggests that learners' minds are not empty vessels that teachers fill with predetermined material. Instead, education is based on generative themes and words that derive from the real-life experiences and problems of learners.

As with Freire, at the center of Lucila's pedagogical concerns we find students and their crucial role in the educational process: "As it is not possible to retain everything, one has to help the student select and know how to distinguish between the marrow of a reading and the useful, but not indispensable, detail" (Scarpa, *Mistral,* 41). As a teacher, Lucila understood that the student is the one who ultimately makes the decision about what she or he is going to include as an intrinsic part of her or his body of knowledge. In addition, Lucila comprehended the importance of furnishing students with tools of how to learn, not only with the content, what to learn. "It is an intolerable vacuum to offer knowledge before offering methods of how to learn that knowledge" (41). Her thoughts parallel current and emerging fields of educational studies and practices that focus on students' learning skills, learning strategies, and learning styles.

Lucila believed that dignity and respect are at the heart of positive interactions between students and teachers—exactly what educational psychologists urge teachers to practice presently in schools: "Everything can be said, but one must find the right way. The most acrid reprimand can be made without depressing or poisoning the soul" (Scarpa, *Mistral,* 40). "The fingers of the shaper must be at once firm, soft, and loving" (41). "Lighten my hand when punishing and soften it when caressing. Reprimand in pain, so I know that I have corrected lovingly" (36). Classic books on classroom management propose precepts similar to the ones espoused by Lucila. Most experts in the field of education agree that students generally respond well to teachers' guidance and even to reprimands, when the latter are offered in a caring and humane manner.

As far as pedagogical advice for teachers, Lucila left guidelines to create motivational and effective lessons. To her, every lesson can be the basis for inspiring students: "Every lesson is susceptible to beauty" (Scarpa, *Mistral*, 42). Every lesson is a new opportunity to guide students to develop a sense of beauty in their lives and surroundings. When she taught, Lucila's lessons were inspired by her natural surroundings. The Chilean geography, the sea, the mountains, and the flora and fauna were the inspiration of many of her lessons in science and literature.

Furthermore, Lucila reminded teachers that using the textbook exclusively or primarily hinders students' interest and creativity and therefore their learning. Why attend class if teachers merely repeat what is already in the texts? "There is nothing sadder for a student than to find the class equivalent to the text" (Scarpa, *Mistral*, 42). Educational researchers have demonstrated that teachers who enhance lessons with material from outside the classroom text are more effective educators. Lucila anticipated present-day voices urging teachers to explore the world outside the mandated classroom texts.

With regard to lesson delivery, Lucila had specific ideas that will still resonate with teachers and students: "Give me simplicity and depth; free me from being complicated or banal in my daily lesson" (Scarpa, *Mistral*, 35). "Simplify. To know is to simplify without removing the essence or poisoning the soul" (Pincheira, 69). It is commonly stated that the art of teaching is to make clear the very complicated. Talented teachers are able to convert the most complex theories into information accessible for learners.

Lucila expressed a conundrum even the most experienced educators grapple with when planning and executing lessons, the balance between fun and hard work. Each day teachers face the difficult challenge of maintaining students' interest while engaging them in meaningful and complex learning activities. She stated, "Nothing is more difficult than to determine where amenity and joy end and where garrulity and disorder begin in a classroom" (Scarpa, *Mistral*, 41). As a classroom teacher, Lucila understood the many challenges of the profession. Among them is the creation of significant and scholarly lessons, presented in a clear and dynamic manner, keeping students curious and interested in the subject matter.

Because of her personal difficulties entering and remaining in the teaching profession, Lucila explored the topic of preservice and in-service teacher education in her writings, leaving a meaningful legacy for teacher educators and teacher education. She believed that only educators with uncompromising dedication to the teaching profession should earn the privilege of entering and remaining in the world of schools. Going against the tide of one-type-fits-all testing for individuals entering the profession, she reminds us that teaching is an art, not necessarily an entirely teachable skill that can be quantitatively evaluated. If it were not for the unique way she was able to demonstrate her teaching abilities, by writing her competency exams in poetry, she might never have become a teacher. On this subject she said, "The true teacher will always be something of an artist; we cannot accept that kind of boss or overseer into which some want to convert the mover of spirits" (Mistral, *Lecturas,* xvii).

For a teacher to remain adept at the art of teaching, she needs to practice and excel daily at her craft. In the words of Lucila, "The job needs to be earned daily, neither the occasional success or activities are enough." "Make oneself necessary, become indispensable: that is the way to obtain job security" (Scarpa, *Mistral,* 39–40). Moreover, for Lucila, an intrinsic responsibility of teachers is to remain eternal students. She might have been one of the first educators of teachers who stated the importance of teachers becoming lifelong learners, "A teacher that does not read has to be a bad teacher: by not renewing herself spiritually she has lowered her profession to mechanics" (39) "Develop yourself. To give, you need to have a lot" (Pincheira, 69–70).

So, according to Lucila, who are the rare individuals that deserve the title of teacher? Who are the ideal educators? Lucila had very specific ideas on the paramount teacher persona. In her pedagogical writings she painted recurring images of the portrait of the ideal teacher. First and foremost, Lucila's ideal teacher is loving (Valenzuela-Fuenzalida, 78). The adjective *loving* is abstract and hard to define. Nevertheless, educators recognize love of students as key to positive student-teacher interaction and this quality is mentioned often in Lucila's pedagogical writings: "Love. If you cannot love a lot, do not teach children" (Pincheira, 69). "The love for students reveals more paths to those who teach than knowledge of pedagogy" (Scarpa, *Mistral,* 41). And Paulo Freire concurs: "another quality needs to be added: Lovingness, without which [teachers'] work would lose its meaning. And here I mean lovingness not only toward the students but also toward the very process of teaching" (40). Freire's definition of love is an extension of Lucila's definition. It is a quality that does not diminish with time as a teacher faces the mounting challenges of the profession.

The ideal teacher for Lucila is the surrogate mother of students while they are in her or his care. She writes, "Let me be more mother than the actual mothers, to be able to love and defend like them what is not flesh of my flesh" (Scarpa, *Mistral,* 35). Even though this might seem an exaggerated statement, in Latin America it is not unusual for teachers to take the place of parents during the school day. In loco parentis is a concept intrinsic to schools throughout Hispanic cultures. Teachers are expected to educate the whole child, not merely teach subject matter. Their responsibility includes inculcating moral values, protecting, giving *cariño* ("affection," "tenderness"), and disciplining by punishing or rewarding (or both), just as a mother would do. For Lucila, the influence of a teacher on students is as lasting, or more so, as that of a mother. In her poem "La maestra rural," which honors rural teachers, she emphasizes their importance in the lives of children. "Peasant, . . . a hundred times you looked at her, but you never saw her, and in the being of your child, there is more of her than there is of you!" (Mistral, *Desolación,* 93). Very astutely, she speaks of the lack of respect and recognition for the teaching profession, even by mothers, whose work is as important but as undervalued as that of educators.

The consequences of Lucila's image of teacher as mother are dangerous for the future of the profession. Freire understands the ramifications of equating the teaching profession with motherhood: "The more we acquiesce to being made into coddling mothers, the more society will find it strange that we go on strike and will demand that we remain well behaved" (34). Mothers as teachers and teachers as mothers are different concepts with different implications for the role and the status of educators.

For Lucila, a true teacher mostly views her work as a higher calling, not as a job. Teaching is a spiritual mandate. It is a profession inspired vertically, directly from a higher power, by the holy—more specifically, by Christian beliefs and scriptures (Valenzuela-Fuenzalida, 149). Teachers are religious leaders, doing God's work. Here are a few examples from Lucila's "Decálogo de la maestra" equating teaching with a religious vocation: "Lord, You who have taught, forgive that I teach; that I carry the name of teacher, which you carried throughout the world"; "Remember that your profession is not merchandise but a heavenly profession"; "Realize that God has placed you here to create the world of tomorrow" (Pincheira, 69–70).

Not only is teaching a higher calling, it is a calling that implies absolute sacrifice. "Everything is for the school, very little for ourselves" (Scarpa, *Mistral*, 39). The sacrifice includes setting aside all personal rights, wants, and needs. In Lucila's archetypal model of the exemplary teacher there is no room for personal disappointment, desire for personal justice, or feelings of hurt due to lack of recognition: "Teacher, make lasting the fervor and transient the disenchantment. Pull from me this impure desire for justice that still disturbs me, the wretched insinuation of protest that grows in me when they hurt me, that I should neither be hurt by the lack of understanding nor be saddened by the forgetfulness of those I taught" (35). Indeed, according to Lucila, a teacher has no other concerns or problems but those related to teaching. A teacher is always a teacher. She is an example of moral behavior both inside and outside the school context. Teaching to Lucila is not merely a calling that occurs within the school context, it is an all-encompassing way of life: "Teach always: in the patio and on the street as well as in the classroom. Teach with your attitude, your gestures, and your words" (39).

Choosing the teaching profession is a vow of poverty. The higher calling implies that teachers are willing to give up not only their heart and soul but all material wants as well. Lucila gives us this picture of the rural teacher: "The teacher was poor. . . . She dressed in dark skirts and did not jewel her hand" (Mistral, *Desolación,* 93). Like the image of teacher as mother, the representation of teacher as a selfless and sacrificing being might have negative repercussions for the profession. In a world where success and political power is equated with income, teachers will have to carve out a new reality to gain voice in shaping their own and their students' destiny. As Freire admonishes, "It is urgent that we drum up more support . . . for public schools that are popular, effective, democratic, and happy and whose teachers are well paid, well trained, and in constant development. Never again should teachers' salaries be astronomically lower than those of the presidents and directors of government corporations, as they are today" (35).

For Lucila, abnegated and virtuous teachers shoulder the awesome responsibility to create a more equitable world of respect and love for children, even if they themselves do not have many rights or privileges. Teachers are the conscience of an intrinsically unfair society: "All the vices and wretchedness of a people are the vices of its teachers" (Scarpa, *Mistral,* 40). It is important to question if teachers could or should carry the responsibility and guilt for the world's mishaps and missteps. Should they be held to unattainable standards, without any tangible power or recompense? Or can Lucila's thoughts propel teachers to be agents of societal change? Can her views about teaching as an extraordinarily sacred and momentous profession serve as the basis for raising its prestige in the present social order? There are complex issues concerning social and political changes implied in Lucila's portrait of the ideal teacher. In interviews conducted by Marcia López concerning the importance of Gabriela Mistral's thoughts for present-day teachers in Chile, one of the respondents, Francisca Gómez, teacher and director of the María Villalobos school, shed some light on how teachers feel concerning some of these questions:

> the pedagogical thinking of Gabriela Mistral . . . seems a utopia—the teachers are deceived, the work of the teacher is not valued, there is no respect from the authorities, from the people in power; there is no gratitude, and the result is that teachers, in general, have no major commitment; the teacher is hurt; she or he is overworked. . . . the foundation of what Gabriela Mistral proposes, it seems that respect and love for what one does not go out of fashion, teaching is a mission that necessarily encompasses the love for children, for others. . . . I do not believe that what Gabriela thought will come to be, but I believe it should. We should have it as an objective.·

Elizabeth Horan sees Lucila's image of the humble, ever-sacrificing teacher as a way for her to engage in social criticism from a safe confine: "This is a disarming humility: by admitting the very charges that can be used against her she robs them of their potency" (Horan, 57). In her time, as a woman, and especially as a woman of a certain socio-economic background, Lucila could not publicly decry the situation of women, but she could make women and teachers aware of their status. It is very plausible that this was her intention. In later years Lucila, as the well-known and respected Gabriela Mistral, wrote about the profession of teaching in a more unsentimental and realistic manner. In her essay "El oficio lateral," written in 1949, she had become more attuned to the socioeconomic-political situation of teachers throughout the world:

> Our modern world keeps venerating two things: money and power, and the poor teacher lacks, and will always lack, these two important and callous powers. It is common that men and women enter the public

schools as happy youngsters and leave hurt by the profession and by dashed illusions. The meager wage [of teachers], which is beneath the salary of a hand laborer, the family obligations . . . and mostly, the disdain of the upper classes toward vital problems, all this and much more will gnaw at their faculties, and the good wine of youth will turn to vinegar. (Scarpa, *Mistral,* 45–46)

Furthermore, Lucila wisely recognized that the teaching profession is in turmoil throughout the world, not only in Latin America. Even in more prosperous countries, such as in the United States, teachers still struggle for political and social power: "All alone is the unfortunate teacher, almost all over the world, because this sickness, which covers most of Latin American, also appears in the prosperous United States, dominates a good part of Europe, and infests Asia and Africa" (46).

However, these later views neither contradict nor negate the importance of her earlier and more guileless perspective on educators and education. Lucila Godoy Alcayaga, as Gabriela Mistral, left a legacy of profound pedagogical thought, an articulate and poetic collection that reveals the soul of educators, their challenges and aspirations. Her quixotic maxims can serve as inspiration to unite teachers in the quest to make their profession deserving of its own Nobel prize.

Note

Unless otherwise indicated, all translations are mine.

Works Cited

Freire, Paulo. *Teachers as Cultural Workers: Letters to Those Who Dare Teach.* Boulder: Westview, 1998.

Gazarian-Gautier, Marie-Lise. *Gabriela Mistral: La maestra de Elqui.* Buenos Aires: Editorial Crespillo, 1973.

Horan, Elizabeth. *Gabriela Mistral: An Artist and Her People.* Washington, D.C.: OAS, 1994.

Ministerio de Educación, Chile. Proyecto Monteverde, 1988.

Mistral, Gabriela. *Desolación.* 3d ed. Santiago: Editorial Andrés Bello, 1990.

———. *Lecturas para mujeres.* 7th ed. Mexico City: Editorial Porrúa, 1988.

Pincheira, Dolores. *Gabriela Mistral, guardiana de la vida.* Santiago: Grupo Fuego de la Poesía, Universidad Católica de Chile, 1979.

Scarpa, Roque Esteban. *La desterrada en su patria: Gabriela Mistral en Magallanes, 1918–1920.* 2 vols. Santiago: Editorial Nascimento, 1977.

———. *Gabriela Mistral: Magisterio y niño.* Santiago: Editorial Andrés Bello, 1979.

Valenzuela-Fuenzalida, Alvaro. *La vocación vertical: El pensamiento de Gabriela Mistral sobre su oficio pedagógico.* Valparaiso: Ediciones Universitarias de Valparaíso, 1992.

Chapter 4

Gabriela Mistral
Meritorious Member of the Sandinista Army

Patricia Varas

THERE IS A CONSENSUS AMONG scholars of Gabriela Mistral that the study of her poetry has taken precedence over that of her prose. Even though in the last fifteen years a concerted effort has been made to undo this oversight, the Nobel laureate is still better known for her lyrical production. Perhaps her prose has received less attention because much of it belongs to what René Letona calls the "ephemeral condition of journalism" (86).

I would like to address this omission by discussing a series of articles Mistral wrote for *El Mercurio* on the United States' intervention in Nicaragua. These articles, which are little known and yet of great importance today, are "Sandino, contestación a una encuesta" (Sandino, an answer to a survey) (4 March 1928), "La pobre ceiba" (Poor silk-cotton tree) (25 March 1928), and "La cacería de Sandino" (The hunt for Sandino) (7 June 1931). Although Sandinismo and the Sandinistas no longer hold sway in Nicaragua, and the United States—"the superpower that is afraid of small countries" (Chomsky, 34)—no longer needs to fear this small, poor country, the feelings of anger and disempowerment that Mistral captures in her writings are still felt in the region.

Mistral's prose is abundant, since her work as a journalist was not a pastime but a vocation. She wrote brief news articles as the best way to address a vast American audience about her views on an extensive array of subjects as she traveled around the world.[1] Journalism was the best forum for Mistral to make public her opinions on politics, society, education, art, and so on and to respond with urgency to what was happening in her beloved America. Letona goes so far as to suggest that this prose work could serve as a contextual frame for her poetry (86). Mistral, in her constant search to revolutionize expression, even created a personal prose genre: *recados,* messages sent from her self-exile.

In this chapter I consider two of the several characteristics that define Mistral's prose. First, her prose contains a distinct social and political vein that not only allows us to perceive her social and political agenda but also entitles her to enter the public world of politics. Second, the language she uses reflects a dual nature: on the one hand, it has a unique colloquial, informal quality; on the other, it encompasses a lyricism and a passion for the sculpted image and metaphor that reminds the reader of the poet behind the scene. Several critics, such as Letona and Soledad Bianchi, have pointed out Mistral's admiration for José Martí and have seen similarities in their prose.

The three articles in question were written while Mistral was in Europe, and there is a thematic unity and urgency of tone that permits the critic to read and study them as a collection even though three years (1928 31) separate them. The first article, "Sandino, contestación a una encuesta," was written as a direct response to the events taking place in Nicaragua. In it, Sandino is compared to a David fighting and defeating a mighty Goliath. Mistral undoubtedly expresses her dismay at the intervention of the United States and the fact that at the Pan-American Conference in Havana there are no expressions of solidarity for the courageous Sandino. Mistral calls for action, since remaining neutral is not an option. The second article, "La pobre ceiba," does not refer directly to Nicaragua and Sandino but was written only twenty-one days after the first. In it she continues to condemn the interventionist policy of the

United States and its ideology of Manifest Destiny. Mistral also denounces the false unity extolled at the Pan-American Conference because it excluded Nicaragua. Her sadness at the charade, and at the hypocrisy of Latin America, tinges her words. In the last article, "La cacería de Sandino," Mistral's anger coalesces in strong criticism against "Mr. Hoover." She reproaches the media for portraying Sandino as a bandit and hopes that this injustice will bring the countries of Latin America together against the common enemy: the United States.

The topics, organization, and language in these writings are overtly political. Mistral displays a tendentious agenda that is paradoxical, as she herself acknowledges. Mistral, the mother and teacher of Hispanic America, rejected both talking about and actually carrying out politicking—perhaps because it was not in her nature to intervene in this corrupt and patriarchal realm, perhaps because it saddened and angered her to see the injustices perpetrated against her peoples, perhaps because it was too public a space. But in "Contestación" she states, "I hear talk about politics half the year—the time I spend in Paris—but I would not want to know anything of all that" (228). This conditional tone ("would not want to") implies the impossibility of her desire to remain outside the political debate. Her dismissive tone ("all that") hides her anguish and acknowledges that she is a public figure, that she is an Americana, and that she must inevitably become involved in politics.

The inevitability of Mistral's engagement in politics is accepted by the poet, who immediately explains: "nevertheless, I am beginning to convince myself that giddy new times are approaching America in which not only women but children will have to talk about politics, because politics will be (perverse politics) the surrender of the wealth of our peoples" ("Contestación," 228). This apology—and her qualification of politics as perverse—soon and ironically becomes a political commentary that criticizes exploitative *latifundismo*, obsolete education, chauvinistic leadership, and foreign powers exercising undue influence over Latin American governments.

Mistral in this felicitous prologue to her answer to a survey conducted by the Chilean newspaper *El Mercurio* encompasses all the constituencies that were always dear to her—women, children, peasants—and all the institutions and problems that have concerned her—latifundismo, education, prejudice, and foreign intervention. Mistral calls for a growing awareness of and the empowerment of the oppressed by demanding that they "must talk" and thus bring their silence to an end ("Contestación," 228).

Although this forceful beginning sets the tone for the rest of the articles it is nevertheless interesting to note the apologetic caveat with which she cloaks her words. In the last sentence of her prologue Mistral carefully warns us that she is responding to a survey by her friend at *El Mercurio,* that she is writing only "to serve him" (228). With characteristic modesty, Mistral deflects any possible criticism for meddling in an area that does not belong to her by assuring her readers that these words are but a compilation of what she has heard from politicians in Paris: "more than my observations [they are] commentaries heard in Paris from South American leaders" (228). This disclaimer, however, does not hide the fact that Mistral is joining her voice to that of several other "leaders" who support Sandino and condemn U.S. intervention. In effect she is voicing a feeling of Latin American solidarity.

Mistral articulates her solidarity in two vital and progressive manners: a stance against intervention that requires action, and a clear rejection of the United States. Here her *Americanismo,* nourished by Martí and the Darío of the "Ode to Roosevelt," embraces an activism that takes over her pacifist and religious ideas. Letona emphasizes that Mistral's thought was "eminently reformist and conciliatory" (90); and Fernando Alegría also stresses the poet's religiosity and her commitment to nonviolence (87–88). But in this article she certainly advocates the "will of action" ("Contestación," 229). The poet encourages Hispanic Americans to give themselves to the cause, or at least to make a "continental contribution" to show they care (229). Furthermore, Mistral invites young blood to come forward and join Sandino and his army in the struggle. She asks young Argentineans, Chileans, Ecuadorians,

"Where is the very natural, the logical Hispanic American Legion of Nicaragua?" (230). It is as if the greater outcome justifies the means—in other words, that justice and freedom are worth the struggle.

This call for action is framed within a denunciation of the United States—the enemy not only of Nicaragua but of the whole South. Mistral is aware of the imperialism that the Colossus of the North embodies and warns Hispanic America, as Bolívar and Martí had done before her, of the impending danger. In her article "El grito" (The scream), written in 1922, the poet had already alerted the South about the neighbor to the north. She also warned the region about its complacency since she realized early on that the North could penetrate the South only with its willing complicity. "Hatred against the Yankee? No! He is defeating us, he is bulldozing us, and it's our own fault" (14).

The second article, "La pobre ceiba," is devoted to describe the ideology of Manifest Destiny and to criticize the ongoing complicity of Latin American countries with the United States. Manifest Destiny has been the assumption that has explained and rationalized U.S. dominance in the region. In her conversation with a man from the United States she heard the following explanation: "A strong and magnificently organized country has the natural right, about which it needs not consult with anybody, to watch over his neighbors, whose obdurate disorder can harm him" (233). In one sweeping paragraph Mistral ironically describes in dialogue form U.S. policy in Latin America, including the Monroe Doctrine and the "big stick" era, and prefiguring with great vision the Good Neighbor policy to come.

As in the previous article, Mistral's love for her America in "La pobre ceiba" is not mere sentimentalism nor solely aesthetic identification (Alegría, 91) but a much more profound political commitment that envisions revolutionary change to achieve justice. Mistral's political awareness once more throws her in the vortex of doubt: "Why do I write this little article on politics, I, who have no interest in politics?" (235). And again she is quick to respond that it is because she is angry about the discussions taking place in Havana. The mystic and divine

Gabriela is concealed in these words, as Gabriela Mora astutely points out (193). Where she takes a clear stand for the poor, her religiosity becomes closer to Liberation Theology. That is why it is simply inconceivable for her to remain neutral, to fail to do something to achieve justice for the meek and oppressed.

Those who forget that her Christianity was social and not contemplative do so because they do not want to reconcile the humble, reserved schoolteacher with the militant who was deeply concerned with the social problems of her region and was firmly committed to solving them. Cida Chase, for example, sees in Mistral a moral integrity and "Christian humanism" that makes her reject politics because she "hated exhibitionism" (165). But I believe that, quite the contrary, Mistral's prose especially advocates a disposition for political thought, for the display of critical thinking about Chilean and Latin American society. It is in her prose that she criticizes latifundismo and the plight of the peasants and indigenous peoples; that she denounces fascism and supports the republican cause in Spain; that she advocates for education and the rights of children and women; and that she calls for aid for Sandino (Mora, 193). Actually, what can be more "anti-evangelical"—as Jaime Quezada suggests (78)—than the animosity that accompanies her malediction, "Un fortunate may they [Hoover's marines] be!" ("Cacería," 239).

The last article, "La cacería de Sandino," was written only three years before Sandino's assassination. With her usual foresight, Mistral writes about the hunt for Sandino and with uncanny exactitude predicts that the marines will be sent to pick up a trophy (238). The poet condemns U.S. intervention and violation of international law, the arrogance of a country that is beyond the law and international denunciation, at the same time that she warns against complacency and complicity, pointing to the "wretched Nicaraguan politicians" (237) that requested United States aid to fight against Sandino.

As we read the three articles in the order they were written, we notice a crescendo and a desperate cry of hope that can come to fruition only through solidarity, the unification of the countries of Hispanic

America. In "Contestación" Mistral calls for the creation of a *legión hispanoamericana* (Spanish American legion) and firmly believes that a Nicaraguan defeat will only bring the South together. The same idea is expounded in "La pobre ceiba" through the metaphoric use of that American tree that has been hypocritically used to represent a Latin America that is not truly united. In this manner, Mistral feels sorry for this poor silk-cotton tree, which has been wrongly misappropriated to represent a false and weak "Pan-American friendship" (235). Finally, in the loudest and most incensed manner Mistral sanctions the hunt against Sandino. In "La cacería de Sandino" Mistral warns the United States against its presumption, since its predatory acts will turn the region into a united front, a block: "Mr. Hoover will achieve, unknowingly, something that we ourselves had not been able to accomplish: with Sandino's death, feeling like one from head to toe of the continent" (239). The crescendo is clear, the bigger the United States transgression, the stronger the region's response, and the more united it will become. Sandino is not a local hero "but rigorously racial" ("La cacería," 239). In this form, Mistral joins the ranks of the Latin American writers who have used their writing to configure a Latin American conscience. That conscience stems directly from the fear of and the anger against the neighbor of the North.

Mistral chooses to articulate her concerns in a colloquial or dialogic manner. The colloquial aspect of these articles stems not only from their journalistic nature but also from Mistral's urgent desire to talk about issues that worried her with an audience that needed to learn the plight of the Nicaraguans. In all three articles Mistral uses speech either in the form of direct quotes or as if overheard. In this manner, her words seem to be from a larger community—of leaders or intellectuals—or a direct reaction to some reactionary thought. In "Contestación" she quotes a "Nicaraguan youth" who supports U.S. intervention in Nicaragua because that country supports a democratic government. Mistral reacts promptly to this foolish comment: "and [the words] did not burn his mouth, or even his face, when he was repeating them to me" (230).

Mistral uses the verb *burn* in two ways. On the one hand, such ignorant words should cause pain in he who dares pronounce them and "burn his mouth"; on the other hand, they should produce embarrassment and "burn his face." Mistral, ever the teacher, answers the youth because she has experienced "similar ugliness from politicians" (230) and gives him a lesson in "rights" and "justice" and on the traitor within every mestizo who poisons Latin America.

The same colloquial strategy is employed in "La pobre ceiba." This time Mistral reconstructs a conversation with a Yankee, a "sort of Mr. Pershing" (233), about the invasion of Dominican Republic and the ideology of Manifest Destiny. As before, Mistral reacts with anger and calls this man a cynic who, hiding behind the Bible, claims that as Christians North Americans should help and intervene in the "daily killing in those countries. We for the most part help the best ones [countries]" (234). Mistral is quick to retaliate: "Most of the time you help the worst ones—I told him—because it must be the worst ones who ask the foreign police to help them fix their fights" (234). In this response Mistral spreads the blame for what happens in the region. She denounces not only the neighbor to the North and his policies, but those traitors in Latin America who ask for intervention.

Finally, in "La cacería de Sandino," the whole article is a response to "Mr. Hoover." She sets the record straight with this man who is "misinformed, regardless of his twenty-one embassies" (238), and informs him that his hunt for Sandino is only increasing the world's solidarity with Nicaragua. Mistral uses a series of plastic and informal images to describe her dismay: "to turn against anyone's blood" (238); and "perhaps now that uncombed head will fall that is driving the combed heads of the marines mad" (238). And she characteristically uses the possessive pronoun to express ownership and identification: "their Sandino" (238).

The informal, colloquial quality of Mistral's words reflects her desire to share her views with the people and to identify with them ideologically. She enjoys talking with, not down, to her audience. And in this open and democratic dialogue she demonstrates her quick wit, her knavish sense of humor, which does not hesitate to laugh at the expense of the Latin American oligarchy and the United States. In the expression of this wit Mistral employs a lyrical voice that concretizes through metaphor and intertextuality. Thus she produces a text rich in meanings on different literary levels. First, the political message as factual journalistic information is made overtly available to the reader. Nothing gets in the way of decoding this news. Second, a personal tone or style pervades the news article, characterized by a verbal abundance that contrasts with the usual brevity and directness of journalism. The final outcome is the product of an artistic tension that she resolves by embracing the news article as an essay through her deep commitment to social change. Ana Pizarro remarks that this is one of Mistral's main characteristics as a modern writer: "to assume in a natural form what must be the product of permanent tensions, the essay as a genre, and to make of this discourse a professional form of expression" (50). Mistral prefers archaism and that also reflects an ideological position. Jaime Concha writes that she identifies with the peasantry and adopts their speech in her writing (101), and Jean Franco suggests that Mistral seeks refuge from modernization in a "pre-modern peasantry" (32) where folklore and oral tradition are highly valued. Mistral constructs a space where, with her magnificent verbs, she exposes political truths. Mistral's prose is full of preemptive gestures, of strategies that allow her to say what she urgently feels must be said and reach as wide an audience as possible.

All three articles contain metaphors that come from the Bible, Greek myths, or Latin American culture. Mistral's religiosity obviously guides her choice of the Bible as a source of images about the oppressed. In "Contestación" Sandino is identified as David with his sling. While in "Pobre ceiba" she skillfully mixes the classic with the Hispanic and the fairy tale to create the myth of Sandino. Mistral compares Sandino to a hunted animal—sentient imagery that will come to fruition in "Cacería"—a "fabulous beast, like the Onager, like the

Hydra of Lerna, like the dragon that ate towns, in a small ravine of the mythic Nicaragua" (233). The irony is established in the fact that this mythic being—ferocious animal, devourer and destroyer of human-kind—inhabits a small country like Nicaragua. But the dominating metaphor throughout the article is the silk-cotton tree, the ceiba, com-mercially prized as the source of Kapok.

Mistral with ironic wit claims that she decided to write because she was angered at the hypocritical use of nature, of a symbol of Latin America, for political demagogy about unity at the Pan-American Con-ference in Havana. The ceiba was adopted as a symbol of the fraternity among the peoples of the New World, and one was planted during the conference. She writes, "It has irritated one of my strongest passions: the passion for forests, as strong in me as that for the beasts" (235), and wonders, "Why handle them and reduce their vegetable prestige?" (236). Mistral is simply outraged at this misappropriation and remem-bers other illustrious trees in Hispanic America, "the tree of the sad night" and "the rush tree in Oaxaca," which this "pobre ceiba" will join through "the back door" of infamy (235). Thus, through a rhetori-cal art that is by no means hermetic, Mistral, like Saint Francis, em-braces the poor through metaphors of the outside world. She advocates the importance of symbols and reclaims nature. All in Latin America must be harmonious and unified; even the trees must be re-spected and must reflect the pure struggle of the region.

"La cacería de Sandino" is one big hunting metaphor in which the hunted beast is Sandino, and the bloodthirsty hunter is the United States. Since the article is being indirectly addressed to Mr. Hoover, Mistral adopts a series of metaphors to depict Sandino as the perse-cuted hero. Thus she disclaims his bandit status and renames him hero. Borrowing from Greek myth, she identifies Sandino with Hercules and rejects his demonization as the "infernal Pluto" (237) that Hoover has created. He is the "little man Sandino" (238) to the eyes of his enemy, but to his followers, Sandino has the "admiration of his race" (238). And this *guerrillero* embodies each and every one of the precursors who freed Hispanic America. It is in this last article of the series that Mistral's esteem for Sandino comes to the fore. Her obsession about those who never speak up and permitted the Dominican Republic and Haiti to be invaded taints her open praise for Sandino. The object of her writing is not only to lavish praise but to create solidarity.

Mistral's political and social awareness finds a resolution in her writing. As we have seen, even in the most overtly political prose she takes the time to construct a metaphorical world and to develop intertextualities based on the realms of literature and politics. She even defines her own genre, the *recado*, a popular traditional form of oral expression and stylizes it in a written form characterized by the agility of the "the magic world of her conversations" (Gazarian-Gautier, 23).

Although Mistral came to her political commitment slowly, "her *Americanism* grows gradually, at the beginning, as a cultural opposition to the United States" (Concha, 29; emphasis Concha's). This cultural protectionism, together with her humanist religiosity led her to embrace an active militancy and solidarity with those struggling against the United States. Concha argues, accurately, "her [two] impressive articles about Sandino and his struggle in Nicaragua—impressive not only because they are a call alerting the continent, but because they demand an active and concrete solidarity, and above all, because of the deep foresight they reveal—are the product of her ability to feel, of course, as well as a refinement of her sense of history" (30).

One should not forget that Mistral was not admitted to continue her studies as a teacher because a priest deemed her writing anti-Catholic (Concha, 20); that one dictator cut her consular salary and another censured her writing and prohibited its publication in *El Mercurio* (Concha, 22); that Mussolini blocked her appointment as Chile's consul to Italy (Marchant, 100); and that one of the first acts the Chilean junta undertook after the coup was to erase her name from the Edificio Cultural "Gabriela Mistral" (Bianchi, 9). Mistral's political writings are an anguished scream for change and for unity in America. At the same time she contributes to her cultural agenda of originality and Americanismo. Mario Céspedes attributes her search for innovation to the fact that "she was aware that she was a teacher of style thus—with the responsibility of the true creator—[she] invented new forms of expression and brought to life formulae that had been worn out by usage" (5). Claire Pailler remarks that the myth of Sandino has been created mainly through poetry (26); I would add that Mistral prose has also contributed to his myth.

As much as she suffered for embracing the poor and publicly making her ideas known, there were rewards, such as the admiration and acknowledgment of not only the most destitute—Indians, peasants, workers, women—but some of the greatest intellectuals and political leaders of her time. Mistral also received a high honor, a most well deserved recognition from the hero she so admired: Sandino proclaimed her Meritorious Member of the Sandinista Army (Quezada, 75). La Mistral, the teacher, the writer of Christian poetry, the pacifist and poet who did not like politics, did not hesitate to donate her major resource to Sandino's cause: her literature.

Notes

Unless otherwise indicated, all translations are mine.

1. I use the term *America(n)* in the same way José Martí used it, to refer to the whole region where the *Americanos* dwell (North and South), not just to the United States.

Works Cited

Alegría, Fernando. "La prosa de Gabriela Mistral." *Boletín de la Academia Norteamericana de la Lengua Española* 8 (1992): 81–93.

Bianchi, Soledad. "Descubriendo la prosa de Gabriela Mistral." *Araucaria de Chile* 6 (1979): 9–19.

Céspedes, Mario. Prologue to *Gabriela Mistral en el "Repertorio Americano,"* 5–9. San José: Editorial Universitaria de Costa Rica, 1978.

Chase, Cida. "Perfil ético de Gabriela Mistral." *Discurso literario: Revista de temas hispánicos* (1984): 159–67.

Chomsky, Noam, and Heinz Dieterich. *Latin America: From Colonization to Globalization.* Melbourne, Australia: Ocean Press, 1999.

Concha, Jaime. *Gabriela Mistral.* Madrid: Ediciones Júcar, 1987.

Franco, Jean. "'Loca y no loca': La cultura popular en la obra de Gabriela Mistral." In *Re-leer hoy a Gabriela Mistral: Mujer, historia, y sociedad,* ed. Gastón Lillo and Guillermo Renart, 27–42. Santiago: Editorial Universitaria de Santiago, 1997.

Gazarian-Gautier, Marie-Lise. "La prosa de Gabriela Mistral, o una verdadera joya desconocida." *Revista chilena de literatura* 36 (1990): 17–27.

Letona, René. "La prosa de Gabriela Mistral." *Cuadernos hispanoamericanos* 472 (1989): 85–92.

Marchant, Elizabeth. *Critical Acts: Latin American Women and Cultural Criticism.* Gainesville: University Press of Florida, 1999.

Mistral, Gabriela. "La cacería de Sandino." In *Gabriela Mistral, escritos políticos,* ed. Jaime Quezada, 237–39. Mexico City: Fondo de Cultura Económica, 1994.

———. "El grito." In *Gabriela Mistral en el "Repertorio Americano,"* ed. Mario Céspedes, 13–14.

———. "La pobre ceiba." In *Gabriela Mistral, escritos políticos,* 233–36.

———. "Sandino, contestación a una encuesta." In *Gabriela Mistral, escritos políticos,* 228–32.

Mora, Gabriela. "La prosa política de Gabriela Mistral." *Escritura: Revista de teoría y crítica literarias* 16, 31–32 (1991): 192–203.

Pailler, Claire. "Sandino y otros héroes: Historia poetizada y mitos primordiales nicaragüenses." *Hispamérica: Revista de literatura* 17, 49 (1988): 13–26.

Pizarro, Ana. "Mistral, ¿qué modernidad?" In *Re-leer hoy a Gabriela Mistral,* 43–52.

Quezada, Jaime. *Un viaje por Solentiname.* Santiago: Editorial Sinfronteras, 1987.

Chapter 5

The Death of the Beloved in the Poetry of Gabriela Mistral

Eugenia Muñoz

LIFE AND LITERATURE ARE profoundly linked. It is a human being, male or female, who creates literature through his or her representation of subjective or collective experiences, through his or her reactions, attitudes, point of view, ideology, and cultural values as a result of events, realities, dreams, expectations that inspire his or her creativity. Life can be found in literary texts transformed into symbols, images, expressions, figures of rhetoric, meaningful words, and sounds, all of which are organized in a narrative, dramatic, or poetic structure.

The analysis of a literary text, however, should not be based primarily on the biography of its author. In doing that, there is a risk of imposing the life events of the author, which are not necessarily the sole aspect of the text's significance. Authors, in addition to using their own experiences, apply them to their understanding of the human condition, their questions about transcendence, their nonconformity or conformity to social, political, religious, and cultural values. All of that gives universality to the literary text, and thus the author's voice becomes the voice of other human beings.

The treatment of the work of Chilean poet Gabriela Mistral (1889–1957) is an interesting example: many critics have taken her biography as a point of departure for their literary criticism. They emphasize the events in Mistral's life, her longings and frustrations, especially those related to her private, emotional, psychological, educational, and religious life. Even more, some critics demonstrate an interest in the poet's sexual orientation.

The present study is based primarily on the poetic texts and the present moment of their enunciation, which I designate the poetic situation, where the poet develops the poetic text as a response to that situation or event that affects her inner self. Once the poetic situation is identified, the analysis of the text follows and the manner in which that poetic situation is expressed with language: images, symbols, reiterations, oppositions, denotations, and connotations. From that analysis comes the interpretation that points back to life, as Martin G. Taylor says when he quotes poet Louis MacNeice: "A poem, though an individual thing, derives from and has to be referred back to life, which means, in the first instance, the life of the poet. In the same way, the life of the poet, though also an individual thing, derives from and has to be referred back to life outside him" (Taylor, 1).

I shall analyze a group of Mistral's poems that deal with the death of the beloved: "Soneto de la muerte III," "Soneto de la muerte I," "Volverlo a ver" (To see him again), "Soneto de la muerte II," and "El ruego."[1] But here these five poems are not studied in the order in which the poet wrote them. They are organized in a natural sequence of actions, desperate reactions, denials, questions, feelings of depression, and appeals for mercy as a result of the tragic loss of the beloved man, which the female speaker expresses poetically, along with her fantasy of and hope for eternity. Talking about Mistral's poems related to the death of the beloved, Elizabeth Horan comments, "More than any other aspect of the poet's lifelong production, a single section of less than two dozen short lyric poems (out of some 120 items in *Desolación*) has constituted the base for the narrative construction of the poet's life that has continued up to the present day" (129).

IN "SONETO DE LA MUERTE III," the poetic situation is that of a female speaker looking back to a past time when her beloved felt trapped in evil hands that disgraced him and her subsequent opposition and desperation to save him from those hands. In spite of her pleas to the Lord, the evil has such power over her beloved that she feels it is better for him to die, no matter what human judgment she has to face because of that desire.

The first stanza of the poem opens with the words "evil hands" (*malas manos*). For the only time in the poem, the speaker talks directly to her beloved, stating that those hands took (*tomaron*) his life. The word *took* implies, on the one hand, a strong will or desire to act without his consent. On the other hand, he appears unable to resist the action of those hands in his life, a life that in the second stanza is represented as being as beautiful or as fragile as the snow-whiteness of lilies (*nevado de azucenas*). But due to a bad sign of the stars that life has left the place where it was flourishing. Also, the metaphor of the flowers, "en gozo florecía," reinforces the significance of the beloved's short life. This first stanza ends with the repetition of "evil hands," to make clear that this was what made him go the wrong way, taking possession of his inner self in a tragic manner: "Evil hands got tragically into him." By beginning the first and last lines of this stanza with *Malas manos,* Mistral suggests the inevitable continuity of the tragedy.

The second stanza recounts the actions that the female speaker took in order to save her lover from the power of the evil hands. Without hesitation she calls on the opposite power, God: "Lord: through mortal paths they are taking him, beloved shadow whom they do not know how to guide!" The words "mortal" (*mortales*) and "shadow" (*sombra*) contrast with "it was blossoming" (*florecía*) and "joy" (*gozo*) in the first stanza; now the young man is surrounded by darkness; death is aggravated by the blindness in which he must walk. The

79

speaker cries out to the Lord, "Snatch him from those fatal hands"; the word "snatch" (*arranca*) signifies the force necessary to liberate him from the powerful hands. If the Lord does not rescue her beloved, the speaker imagines that he is better off dead than alive.[2]

In the third stanza the speaker's impotence and desperation reach a crescendo because she can neither call her beloved nor follow him. He is already in the realm of death. Here the reader can see the use of the Greek myth of Caronte, the boatman who was in charge of transporting the dead to the underworld and whose boat (*barca*) is pushed away at high speed by a stormy black wind. Thus, she is not able to follow him because she is not in the same domain and his boat is taken so quickly. Once more she strongly requests the Lord, in a motherly rapture, "Return him to my arms!" The significance of this plea is communicated through the figure of the mother, whose arms protect the son from any danger. Even more, going back to the second stanza, when the speaker says that those evil hands do not know how to guide him, it is implied that it is she who knows how. The poet thus portrays the beloved as an innocent, vulnerable child, a victim of the evil manipulation of another or others, since the plural of "hands" is ambiguous. The last line of this third stanza is parallel to the last couplet of the second, in the sense that the speaker is implying that the beloved would better be dead through her will and that of God, than be part of that other kind of death, where he is incorporeal and has become a shadow. "Return him to my arms or cut him off in the flower of his life," exclaims the loving voice. One can argue that the speaker is not necessarily asking for his death, because the line can also signify that if the Lord does not do anything to save him from these adverse circumstances, then He is contributing to cutting the flower of the beloved's life (observe again the use of the flower metaphor to signify beauty and freshness). But the poem's conclusion contradicts the idea that the speaker did not prefer him dead, as we will see.

In the fourth stanza the end of the ordeal is revealed in the first line: "The rose-colored boat of his life stopped . . ." It is possible that this interrupted line refers to the abrupt end of a young life that should have continued for many more years. This interrupted life again is compared to a flower, the rose. Also, "rose" can refer to the color pink, a symbol of freshness and innocence.

The last two lines return to the present tense. Once she finishes her remembrance or recounting of the events of the unfortunate turning point in her beloved's life that concluded with her own request for his death, in a kind of climax the speaker exclaims, "So I do not know about love, so I did not have compassion?" (¿*Que no sé del amor, que no tuve piedad?*). Throughout the poem the speaker has been emphasizing how she desperately suffers for the love of that young man, but here she expresses her ignorance of love and, even more, the hardness of her heart. The explanation for this apparent contradiction in her behavior and feelings is at the level of the implied meaning of the whole poem. She feels subject to the accusation of the others who realized she preferred his death, if he were not going to be under the influence of her love and protection from wrongdoing. For that reason she has prepared her own defense, telling all that she did to save him, appealing to the Supreme power for His salvation, and giving evidence of her own impotence. The binary opposition of the speaker with other human beings is evident, but she resolves it by ignoring their final verdict for her, and she talks with the Lord as a way of showing her direct relationship with Him. She needs no intermediaries or intruders, for they will not understand her experiences of love and what is truly in her heart. As she states in her last words, only she and the Lord really know what it is to feel love. She is therefore confident in His wisdom: "You that will judge me understand it, Lord!"[3]

IN THE SECOND SONNET, "Soneto de la muerte I," the poetic situation presents the female speaker talking to her deceased beloved. She tells him how she will take him with her and put him in better resting place.

The first stanza develops the conflict between the speaker and those who have buried her beloved in a dark, cold place. In the first verse the grave is described as a cold niche (*nicho helado*) from which the loving woman wants to take him into the warm earth. And despite the action of others who seek to separate her from him, she will sleep secretively next to him on the same pillow (*almohada*). The word "sleep" (*dormir*) probably refers to her own death.

The second stanza continues the opposition of the speaker with those who carelessly put her lover in a dark, cold place. However, in contrast to the coldness, the speaker sees herself as a mother who will tenderly lay her sleeping child to rest (*acostaré*) in the shining, warm earth. This idea is reinforced by the identification of the earth with another mother, who will herself become a soft cradle by receiving the suffering child in her womb. The word "suffering" (*dolorido*) creates the impression of an innocent boy who has pain that the mother cannot eliminate, although she tries to mitigate it with her love for him. In addition, observe the opposition of the words "put" (*pusieron*) versus "lovingly lay to rest" (*depositar*), and "niche" (*nicho*) versus "cradle" (*cuna*). In using "put," the speaker conveys the meaning that the men simply took her beloved as a dead body, or a thing, to that cold, impersonal place. She, on the contrary, is mothering and carefully deposits her little sleepy boy in the cradle (which, unlike a niche, is soft), trying not to wake him.[4]

The third stanza presents the sequence of the speaker's actions and the continuity of her struggle with the rest of the world. But here her identity is not the maternal one she adopted in the first and second stanzas. The speaker talks now as a woman in love with a strong will to possess the object of her desire by force, one who, in conjunction with the earth and the moonlight, will take prisoner the insubstantial remains of the beloved.

The fourth stanza concludes the intentions and actions the speaker had been exposing to the beloved and to readers. It also reinforces the position of opposition and rivalry of the woman in love when she takes "revenge" on rival women who have tried to take the man away from her: she will put him in that new and profound place, which only she knows: "I will go away singing my beautiful acts of revenge." Observe the contradiction "beautiful revenge," complemented by the act of singing. The speaker is full of joy for her "victory" over the men and women that took him away from her, but only temporarily, because she in her strong determination and desire for him, hasn't given up fighting for her "possession" even after his death.

THE THIRD POEM, "Volverlo a ver," continues in accordance with the sequence of actions, reactions, and feelings of a woman in response to the death of the man she loves. In this poem the speaker expresses her disbelief at the reality of the eternal absence of a person she was accustomed to seeing through loving eyes. "And never, never anymore? Not on nights filled with the trembling of stars?" asks the speaker in the opening line. At first, the use of "never" (*nunca*) appears to be an acceptance of that reality. However, when the speaker repeats it twice, it acquires the opposite meaning: denial and disbelief that she will never see her lover again. The stanza continues with an enumeration of places where the speaker used to see him. All of them relate to nature: "the pale pathway," "the field," "the tremulous fountain whitened by the moon." The adjectives "pale," "tremulous," and "whitened" can be seen as a romantic projection of the physical state of the speaker in her suffering.

The third stanza continues the enumerations related to nature, but now nature is closed and dark. The woman can't get any answers to her anguished outcries calling her lover. The only reply she receives is the echo of his desperation, and she claims that even in those places she has entered, she cannot listen to him: "Nor in the cavern that returns my echoing outcry?" The reader realizes at this point that the speaker's feelings and actions arise out of desperation when the initial disbelief in his death is contradicted by the silence and his physical absence despite her strong outcries and relentless search for him.

Stanza four starts with a climactic exclamation of the rejection of hard and implacable reality: "Oh, no!" This is followed by the speaker's expression of her ardent but frustrated desire to see her beloved, whether the place be pleasant ("in all springs") or terrifying ("in a livid horror"). What matters to her is to be able to see him again.

In the final stanza, as in the fourth, the speaker has accepted what she cannot express anywhere in the poem: the tragic death of her beloved. But she must see him in order to stay with him, regardless of the circumstances: "And together with him to be all spring times / and winters, in an anguished knot around his blood-stained neck!" These expressions of desperation over the loss of a lover are what Margot Arce de Vázquez defines as "the representation of all human sorrow in its most solitary, inescapable moment" (115).

"SONETO DE LA MUERTE II" ALSO revolves around a woman who has experienced the death of her beloved. She no longer can stand her separation from him and has lost her desire to keep on living. She talks to him about her being buried beside him as a way to remain close through eternity. With regard to the dialogue to an absent beloved, Manuel Alcides Joffre compares some of the poems of Pablo Neruda and César Vallejo to Mistral's poem, where there is no current romantic relationship between the speaker of the poem and the addressee. The communication really is a monologue masked as a dialogue. However, it is pertinent to observe that in the poetic situation the speaker has in mind the other one to whom he or she needs to talk.

The poem opens with the speaker's mention of her lack of enthusiasm for life: "This restlessness will become bigger one day." The word "this" (*este*) emphasizes that the speaker's depression is in the present; she wishes not to continue living: "And the soul will tell to the body it doesn't want to continue / dragging its mass along the rosy path." "Dragging" (*arrastrandro*) signals the difficulty in keeping alive that heavy life after the separation from her beloved man. The latter is reinforced by the use of "mass" (*masa*) to describe the body. Here, the body is like a thing without energy or self-animation. The last line of this stanza shows the speaker's conflict or alienation from the others, who live their lives so differently from hers, even though she walks in the same path people are walking, happy to live.

The second stanza begins a dialogue between the speaker and her beloved, in the future tense. She tells him in advance that others will spiritedly (*briosamente*) bury another sleeper (*otra dormida*) beside him. However, in a secretive tone she tells him that she will wait until they have finished covering her dead body. The speaker, despite opposition from the others, desires to remain close to her beloved and plans to deceive them. First, she is like any other woman who has died: "You will feel another sleepy one arriving in the quiet city." And later, when the others have left the cemetery and can't overhear, she will have a dialogue with him that won't be interrupted by death: "And later we will talk through eternity." The speaker in her grief and frustrated desire, evades her pain, expresses the wishes of her soul and heart, and imagines lying very close to her beloved in his grave. But contradicting the reality of death, they will be "alive" and speaking with each other.

The third stanza continues the poem's second part, which began in the last line of the previous stanza. The speaker now expresses further products of her imagination related to the broken love relationship she had with the man while he was still alive. In this stanza the woman reveals to the man that his body has not yet "ripened" (*madura*) into the deepness of death, that he did not die as an old man. The implication is that his body has to wait for hers so that both of them would be in the same condition and able to reunite.

The fourth stanza is linked to the third by the revelations the woman predicts when she meets him again: "There will be light in the darkened zone of the fates." Here "light" has two meanings: First there is the revelation that the speaker is giving to the man, and second, their reencounter as light will drive out the darkness of their two separate lives. But surprisingly that separation wasn't caused by the man's death. It occurred when the love relationship between them was broken. The speaker doesn't mention who initiated the separation, but she is the one who knows that their relationship was immutably destined by the stars (*signo de astros*).

This is similar to what is stated in Sonnet III, "to a sign of the stars" (*a un signo de astros*). For this reason she is informing him about the will of the stars and the "real cause" of his death: "and, the great commitment having been broken, you had to die . . ." This ending seems to contradict the poem's beginning, when it is clear that the speaker is grief-stricken over her beloved's death and wishes to join him. The explanation, as stated before, is that the speaker needs to escape from her sorrow and find a kind of consolation in imagining a reunion while denying that they were separated before his death. Rafael Gómez Hoyos says that Mistral wanted to express "the conception of immortality and hope of eternity" (40). Gómez is speaking in terms of Catholicism, and he overlooks the fact that the poem reflects hopelessness, grief, and the desire to die. Eternity is a product of the imagination of the poem's speaker.

"EL RUEGO" (THE PLEA) DIFFERS from Mistral's other poetic responses to the death of the beloved in that the speaker has abandoned her attitudes of desperation, anxiety, denial, rejection, grief, and the evasion of the reality of the departure and permanent absence of the beloved. In "El ruego" a woman has accepted the reality of the death and separation of the beloved, but she remains overcome by a grief increased by her certainty that religious doctrine condemns her beloved man to exclusion from the glorious eternal life because he committed suicide. In the group of poems analyzed here, this is the only time the speaker mentions the cause of the beloved's death (even though she alludes to it). Her attitude to the verdict of condemnation is to fight it, in spite of all the evidence against her beloved. But unlike the other four poems, the speaker does not mention the men or the women who are opposed to her wishes and actions, perhaps because she knows they will adhere to the religious verdict. However, as in "Soneto III," here the speaker ignores any human judgment and deals directly with the final judgment of God. Ana María Cuneo says that religious speech can be the only consolation for human anguish. In "El ruego" it is quite easy to understand the reasons for Mistral's use of religious discourse.

Before analyzing this poem, it is relevant to point out the role of the two speakers in the dialogue engaged throughout the poem. The poet-speaker assumes the role of defense lawyer for the lost cause of her beloved, who has already been sentenced to the maximum penalty. The lawyer must now present her appeal (the poem) to the Lord, the only judge with the authority to reverse sentences given by human courts. It is also significant that the lawyer in this case is not only deeply involved intellectually with the defense of "her client" (in writing the document for the appeal, the final creative poetic act) but also emotionally. As in the other poems analyzed here, the speaker is conflicted. Here, God's law has been seriously broken by the speaker-lawyer's defendant and she knows He severely punishes this kind of criminal act. The defender's strategy is to appeal not to God the Father but to God the Son, or Jesus Christ, probably because He also experienced human nature and suffered as a man.[5]

The poetic structure of "El ruego" can be divided into five parts. The first, second, and third stanzas form the first part, in which the speaker states the importance her defendant has for her and tells the kind of person he was. She tells the Lord that He knows how ardently she appeals for strangers, and this time He should know how much more important this case is for her: it is the case of one who was "my glass of freshness," "the honeycomb in my mouth," the "sweet reason for life," the "warble to my ears." Knowing that the Lord's omniscience extends to the speaker, the reader can perceive that she is using her persona to persuade Him. And she requests of Him: "Do not have a fierce look if I am asking you for this one." The speaker's use of "this one" (*éste*) indicates how close the defendant is to her, that he is different from others she does not know but for whom she also frequently prays to God. In the third stanza the speaker delineates the defendant's moral qualities. He is "sincere as daylight" (*franco como la luz del día*), "gentle" (*suave*), and "full of miracles like the spring" (*lleno de milagro como la primavera*). And when she is describing her beloved she repeats, "I am telling you, I am telling you," to emphasize her persistence in gaining the Lord's attention.

The second part of the poem is made up of stanzas four, five, and six. Here the speaker mimics a reply from the Lord. She knows He will address her severely, given the seriousness of her client's offense against divine law: "That one who didn't wait for the Lord's sign to die and destroyed the temple of his head, doesn't deserve a prayer." In this stanza is the only mention of suicide, and it is from the Lord's (imagined) reply. Continuing in her role as defense attorney, the speaker uses her arguments to prove her beloved deserves a defense: Once more she gives her own testimony and reveals her intimate knowledge of her beloved, saying she has "touched the chrysanthemum of his forehead, his sweet and tormented heart" (*he tocado el nardo de su frente, su dulce y atormentado corazón*), and he was like "the silk of an opening bud" (*la seda del capullo naciente*). The positive, delicate images that represent the accused have as their purpose the contradiction of the bad image he already has for his unforgivable deed.

In the sixth stanza, which ends the second part of the poem, we find the last reply of the Lord, who now appears concerned with the suffering the beloved has caused the woman; He makes her conscious of all the offenses the sinner has committed against her. Perhaps the strategy of the Lord is to defeat the offender's defense: "That he was cruel?" (by abandoning her). But instead of accepting the beloved's guilt in this matter, the loving speaker replies: "You forget that I loved him." The word "forget" (*olvidas*) sounds like a criticism of the Lord for not being attentive to her loving feelings, and she reinforces that blame by saying her beloved "knew that her tormented entrails were his" (*el sabía suya la entraña que llagaba*). It also appears like a defiance to say that the beloved knew how profound and tormented her love was for him and yet he ignored it. Even more, she acknowledges that his voluntary death destroyed forever her sources of joy. And in spite of all the beloved's wrong actions and their consequences, she strengthens her challenge, exclaiming, "It does not matter! Understand: I loved him, I loved him!" (*¡No importa! Tú comprendes: yo le amaba, le amaba!*). Here, the defender's speech comes to a climax when she dares to command the Lord, and she repeats twice to Him, raising her voice, that she loved the defendant. The image of her the speaker projects is one of great influence and importance in the Lord's eyes. But now she is growing desperate because the Lord seems indifferent, forgetful, and resentful toward her important client.

Stanzas seven and eight make up the third part of this poem-appeal. But this part actually begins at the last line of stanza six, in which the speaker proclaims her love for the offender and sinner. The theme of love becomes the speaker's greatest argument for winning her case. In a kind of parody, she compares her acts of love to Jesus Christ's acts of love for humankind.[6] But in a contrary fashion, she is here the one willing to forgive and suffer for love while she has to "remind" Jesus Christ about those practices that He doesn't acknowledge in this particular case: "And to love (you know well about that) is a bitter practice" (*y amar [bien sabes de eso] es amargo ejercicio*). She continues her exposition by referring to the generosity in the suffering and the bravery Christ demonstrated on the path to Calvary—to which she maintains hers is equal. Note the images that refer to Christ's suffering. For example, the speaker says: "The iron that perforates" means the lance with which the dying Christ was hurt in Golgotha, but also in the analogy with the speaker's Calvary it is associated with the sharp pain she received from the self-imposed lance-death of the beloved. The defender finishes this allusion of Calvary in her argument when she clearly reminds Jesus of the way the loving heart responds to the weight of the cross: "And the cross (You remember, oh King of the Jews!) is taken softly as though it were a bunch of roses." The contrast of images between the exhausting weight of the cross and a light, delicate bunch of roses is relevant. The epithet King of the Jews could show the speaker's intent to remind Jesus of his nobility, of the inherent greatness of such a title. Mistral might also have the speaker use this allusion to persuade Christ to accede to her requests because the poet considered herself to have descended from the Jews.

In the fourth part (stanzas nine and ten), the defense changes its tack and adopts an attitude of humility and persistence in hopes that the Lord will tire of such an obstinate beggar (who is willing to remain on her knees the rest of her life): "Here I remain, Lord, . . . talking to you the whole night / or all the nights of my life, / if You delay telling me the word I am waiting for." From one perspective, the reader can observe that the "night of her appeal-prayer" resembles the night Jesus spent praying to His Father on the Mount of Olives. From another perspective, the speaker shows fear or unexpected shyness to say directly the word she needs to hear, to win her case which is: "forgiveness" for the defendant. But in the tenth stanza the speaker returns to her attitude of persistence ("I will exhaust your ear with my sobs and supplications") and humility ("timid whippet").

The first line of the eleventh stanza (the beginning of the final part) presents the climax of the whole poem, or the reason for the speaker's appeal and her arguments, strategies, manipulations, anxieties, and ultimate urgency. In this line, the defender finally pronounces the most important word of this case she hopes to win, no matter how: pardon. "Say the pardon, say it at last!" The speaker's anxiety and urgency are evident in the repetition of her command to the Lord, who has been withholding that magic and magnanimous word that could save her beloved from eternal damnation, to which he is supposedly already sentenced. She knows how difficult this case is, but she has tried to reverse the verdict, with her love and her trust in her own merits in the eyes of the Lord. The speaker's last resort is to enlist nature as her support, and describes how it will join her in incredible joy when the Lord finally decides to give his pardon: "The word will scatter the perfume of a hundred fragrant fruits on the wind . . . the desert will flourish . . . wild beasts will be moved to tears / and the mountain made of rock, in its understanding, will cry through its icy eyelids." The images of nature the speaker chooses as her personified allies are precisely those that convey the unimaginable: mountains crying, deserts flourishing, wild beasts softened. If the speaker's beloved can be absolved by the Lord, any kind of miracle can happen in nature. The last line of the poem is an exultation of the Lord's generosity and love: "The whole earth will know that You gave Your pardon!" However, the speaker uses the future tense, which indicates that these actions are still only a desire.

Through the study of these five texts the reader sees how in her poetry Mistral profoundly represents feminine nature and its capacity for lyricism through feelings of sorrow, opposition to cruel reality, desperation, denial, anguish, and the capacity to love and to forgive.[7] She expresses hope and trust in the feminine spiritual relationship with God, and her artistic language becomes a vehicle of imagination and the sublimation of pain and loneliness.[8] Finally, one can see how Mistral responded poetically to her life experiences. She relates her views, reactions, and her method of coping to the realities of masculine loss and abandonment.[9] She shows stoicism and will power in order to overcome the depths of her emotional pain and the impossibility of a fulfilled cherished love relationship.

Notes

1. Quotations of these poems are taken from the 1970 edition of *Poesías completas.* Translations of most Spanish citations and all poems are mine.
2. Nelson Rojas's analysis of this sonnet infers that Mistral was referring to a rival woman who took from her the man she loved, Romelio Ureta, who later killed himself. I do not agree with this interpretation because in the poem Mistral doesn't directly allude to the other woman and the situation with her beloved. Also, the "evil hands" could be a reference to Ureta's friend who, in urgent need of money, induced Ureta to steal money from his workplace in order to satisfy the friend's need. This deed and the dishonor Ureta was going to face in public lead him to commit suicide. What matters in the poem is the idea of an evil influence on the beloved that causes him to end his life.
3. The image of the mother that Mistral includes in her poems has been the subject of diverse studies. Some of them exalt the traditional image of the loving mother. Others, like Susana Mulnich's study, connect this image to the abandonment Mistral repeatedly experienced from men. "The fear of abandonment," according to Mulnich, "gets incredible extremes in

Mistral's poetic world, when the female speaker at times wishes the object of her love to petrify as a rock, or that it was better not to have a son from the man she loved, because this son would leave her as did the father" (132). Maryalice Ryan-Kobler says that critics "have been silent about passages that reveal the conflicted, anguished treatment of the maternal and an unresolved sense of identity" (328).

4. Many critics have studied the theme of children in Mistral's work, with emphasis on its positive aspects. Marie-Lise Gazarian, for example, says that "Mistral lived simultaneously in the magical world of children and in the adult world" (137). However, certain poems about children do not refer to joy and fantasy; they are linked to pain, death, and poverty. See "Un hijo" (A son), "Canción de la muerte" (Song of death), and "Piesecitos" (Little feet).

5. Mistral said she was introduced to the world of the Bible when she was ten years old by her grandmother Isabel Villanueva. As a little girl she understood that the God of Israel, from whom people requested strength, was the same God to whom we are all accountable. She also understood that He was both a terrifying God and the merciful Father.

6. Francisco Sánchez-Castaner mentions the profound identification that Mistral felt with the suffering of Christ, caused by humankind, and His endless capacity to forgive them. In "El ruego" the image of Christ is the opposite: he doesn't want to forgive; it is the woman who espouses love and forgiveness.

7. Mistral said of *Desolación* that "a painful past bleeds throughout these one hundred poems" ("En estos cien poemas queda sangrando un pasado doloroso," quoted in Subercaseaux, 220).

8. Regarding the religiosity expressed in Mistral's poems, Jehenson says that Mistral "explicitly represses her feelings of anger and her sense of abandonment by sublimating them in the context of religion and of a universal love of humankind" (95).

9. Mistral repeatedly suffered the trauma of the loss of or abandonment by men, beginning with her father and continuing with her first love, Romelio Ureta. Later she felt the same with another man she also loved hopelessly and to whom she wrote these words: "It seems to me that you are another dead one that didn't give me a bit of happiness" (in Triviño, 1). The last such tragic loss Mistral suffered was that of her adoptive son, who also died by suicide. In spite of the pain men inflicted on her, Mistral depicts these cruel situations in her poems. And the image she presents of her beloved is positive, innocent of guilt. One can explain this attitude to-

ward men as part of the traditional social and religious values that Mistral had internalized.

Works Cited

Arce de Vázquez, Margot. *Gabriela Mistral: The Poet and the Work.* New York: New York University Press, 1964.

Cuneo, Ana María. "El discurso religioso en Mistral." *Revista chilena de literatura* 45 (November 1994): 19–38.

Gazarian, Marie-Lise. "El anhelo de eternidad: El mundo personal de Miguel de Unamuno y de Gabriela Mistral." *American Hispanist* (1976): 129–45.

Gómez Hoyos, Rafael. "Gabriela Mistral, poetisa cristiana." *Boletín de la Academia Colombiana* 40 (1990): 34–45.

Horan, Elizabeth. "Gabriela Mistral: 'Language Is the Only Homeland.'" In *A Dream of Light and Shadow: Portraits of Latin American Women Writers,* ed. Marjorie Agosín. Albuquerque: University of New Mexico Press, 1995.

Jehenson, Myriam Ivonne. "Four Women in Search of Freedom." *Revista/ Review interamericana* 12 (1982): 87–99.

Joffre, Manuel Alcides. "Indeterminación de los roles maternos y recepción crítica de la obra de Gabriela Mistral." *Literatura y lingüística* 3 (1992): 15–33.

Mistral, Gabriela. *Poesías completas.* Ed. Margaret Bates. Madrid: Aguilar, 1968.

Mulnich, Susana. "El sentimiento de abandono en los textos de Violeta Parra y Gabriela Mistral." *Atenea, revista de ciencia, arte, y literatura* 475 (1997): 125–36.

Rojas, Nelson. "Eje temporal y estrategia discursiva en Los Sonetos de la Muerte." *Revista chilena de literatura* 49 (1996): 27–46.

Ryan-Kobler, Maryalice. "Beyond the Mother Icon: Rereading the Poetry of Gabriela Mistral." *Revista hispánica moderna: Boletín del Instituto de las Españas* 2 (1997): 327–34.

Sánchez-Castaner, Francisco. "Lo religioso en Gabriela Mistral." *Revista de cultura mejicana* 30 (1966): 398–414.

Subercaseaux, Bernardo. "Gabriela Mistral: Espiritualismo y canciones de cuna." *Cuadernos americanos* 205 (1976): 208–25.

Taylor, Martin. *Gabriela Mistral's Religious Sensibility.* Berkeley: University of California Press, 1968.

Triviño, Consuelo. "Con tu verso me he dormido en paz: Gabriela Mistral." *Quimera* 123 (1994): 1–2.

Other Sources

Alegría, Fernando. *Genio y figura de Gabriela Mistral.* Buenos Aires: Editorial Universitaria, 1966.

Hernández de Trelles, Carmen. "Del mito al misticismo: El símbolo religioso judeocristiano en la poesía de Gabriela Mistral." *Revista de la Universidad de Puerto Rico* 18 (April–June 1991): 157–69.

Mandlove, Nancy. "Gabriela Mistral: The Narrative Sonnet." *Revista/Review interamericana* 12 (1982): 110–14.

Marchant, Elizabeth. *Critical Acts: Latin American Women and Cultural Criticism.* Miami: University Press of Florida, 1999.

Mayhew, Jonathan. *The Poetics of Self-Consciousness: Twentieth-Century Spanish Poetry.* Lewisburg, Pa.: Bucknell University Press, 1994.

Mistral, Gabriela. "Mi experiencia con la biblia." *Noah* 1 (1987): 83–90.

Oelker, Dieter. "La actitud mítica, poético, religiosa en las 'Historias de Loca' de Gabriela Mistral." *Nueva Atenea, revista de ciencia, arte, y literatura de la Universidad de Concepción* 45 (1968): 79–123.

Chapter 6

Jewish Issues and Gabriela Mistral

Darrell B. Lockhart

GABRIELA MISTRAL WAS NOT ONLY the first Latin American Nobel laureate (1945) but one of the first women to receive the prestigious accolade. As such, she became an almost instant icon of Latin American literature in general and of Chilean letters in particular. The national pride she inspired only intensified upon her death in 1957. The bibliography of Mistral criticism is extensive, though perhaps not quite as extensive as one might expect the work of a Nobel author to garner. One of the most enduring and overriding impressions of Mistral that remains today—via numerous biographies as well as the folk culture that has developed around her—is that her life was clouded with ambiguities. Fixity, in fact, seems to be almost entirely absent from her life. She lived a protean existence from her beginnings in the Elqui valley of her native Chile to her final years. The multiple ambiguities (sexual, religious, political, philosophical) of her life have left many—if not most—critics scrambling to define Gabriela Mistral, uneasy with the uncertainty, the unanswered questions, the vagueness, the rumors. The apparent need to label, to know, and most of all to lay claim to her legacy has resulted, by and large, not in the revelation of who she was but in the construction of an ideologically charged symbol. Gabriela Mistral the person quickly became Gabriela Mistral the object. Elizabeth Rosa Horan describes this phenomenon, in part, as "the reactionary appropriation of Gabriela Mistral as 'la Divina Gabriela,' 'Santa Mistral,' *la maestra*,' and ultimately 'Madre de América'" ("Alternative Identities," 147). Horan also explains elsewhere, and in candid terms, the rush following Mistral's death to lay claim to her: "As a ghost she could be a permanently virgin mother representing all that the national institutions of church, state, and school would ostensibly honor. Motivating the hot air of official homages following her death was a tremendous sigh of relief among those institutions who had always sought, with varying degrees of success, to appropriate her to their own ends. Now that she had slipped away, her image could be fully co-opted without fear of querulous, unpredictable interruption" ("Gabriela Mistral," 122).

When Marjorie Agosín first approached me about writing an article on Jewish issues in the literature of Gabriela Mistral, I embarked upon the task from the most obvious starting point. That is, I undertook an examination of the many poems, essays, and letters in her vast oeuvre that in some way reflect an interest in or the obvious influence of Jewish tradition or history. It should be fairly apparent to the reader familiar with Mistral's works that evidence of such interest and influence abounds. Moreover, when I began to research the topic I soon discovered an intriguing critical discourse unraveling itself before me, which seemed to unveil an attitude of what I will call, for lack of a better term, Jewish panic. I use this term, borrowing from the designation *homosexual panic* in queer theory, because I hope to demonstrate that both expressions are relevant to the official versions of Gabriela Mistral the object and because much is at stake for those who zealously endeavor to maintain such a cultural construct. In fact, as Licia Fiol-Matta has demonstrated, homophobia has played a significant role in the fabrication of Gabriela Mistral as canonical icon. Homosexual panic has contributed to the creation of a discourse on

Mistral that at best glosses over and at worst erases sexuality from her history. Critics such as Fiol-Matta and Horan are now cogently addressing these issues, thus breaking new ground in Mistral scholarship and at long last affording us some meaningful discussion on her works and her life. Mistral's religiosity, like her sexuality, is a topic that has suffered from a lack of inclusive scholarship.

I hasten to clarify that the intent of this essay is by no means yet another attempt to categorize Gabriela Mistral. There is no interest, or useful purpose, in trying to establish proof of Mistral's obscure—dare one say, closeted—Jewishness. It is irrefutable, I believe, that she was a profoundly spiritual person and a devout Catholic—at least later on in her life—as biographies of her attest. My aim is to examine Mistral's religiosity from the perspective of her relationship to Judaism (particularly the almost constant presence of the Old Testament in her work) and Jewish issues (her strong political stance against Jewish persecution) and how she incorporated it into her work. Both aspects ultimately reveal much about Mistral's character, her position on cultural plurality within the hermetic Catholicism of Chile, her deep understanding and embracing of Christianity's Judaic roots, and her humanitarianism. Her adherence to Jewish tradition, both textual and to a lesser degree cultural, has been the stimulus for a good deal of debate and speculation. Therefore it is interesting to sift through what has been written about Mistral with regard to Jewish *and* Christian tradition since it ultimately discloses a great deal about how such information has been processed through the cultural image-making machine. I do not intend to tear down the pedestal upon which Gabriela Mistral has been placed, but to widen the focus on the image.

Let us return to the question of Mistral's ambiguous identity(ies). Rumors historically have swirled around Mistral fed by the "need" to answer the question, Was she or wasn't she? The question itself implies that one is in the know regarding what it insinuates with a textual wink and a nod. Why is there so much concern when it comes to outing, or for that matter maintaining the closet door permanently sealed against,

Gabriela Mistral? It is, I believe, precisely because the stakes of cultural politics are so high. The competing ideological camps need to retain Gabriela Mistral in their respective corners as battle standard and beacon. Thus far, Mistral—like Sor Juana Inés de la Cruz—has managed to remain elusively out of reach, not wholly one thing or another, just slippery enough to avoid compartmentalization. The ambiguity that surrounds, and indeed defines her, endows Mistral with the appellation of dissident queer, in both sexual and religious terms. One can broaden the Was she or wasn't she? question beyond sexuality to encompass religious identity also. Was she Jewish? And if she was, is it significant to understanding her life, her work, and the way we interpret both?

Queerness as a social marker is something much broader than gay or lesbian identity. It suggests a whole range of nonstraight expression within or as a reaction to mass culture. This range includes specifically gay/lesbian/bisexual expressions, but it also includes all other potential nonstraight positions. Queerness is anything that exists outside the heteronormative paradigm (Doty). While Horan speaks of Mistral's sexual dissidence, she does not pigeonhole her as lesbian. Rather, she states, "For Gabriela Mistral (as for others involved in the bohemian worlds of poetry and theosophy) queerness is constituted by the tension between historical context and her writing. The evidence of that subversion appears in her early, explicit, reiterated rejection of heterosexuality and in her multiple efforts to express an erotic subjectivity beyond the simplistic male/female binary" ("Alternative Identities," 147–48). The issue of Mistral's (sexual) queerness is germane here because it ties into another aspect of her identity as dissident queer: the question of Jewishness. If we understand queerness to be the lived expression of those who exist outside the heteronormative hegemony, then by extension one can postulate that any identity (sexually defined or not) that is ex/centric is also a queer identity. Given the fact that Jewish communities (and individuals) very much live at the edge of the dominant Hispano-Catholic center in Latin American societies, Jewishness can be effectively equated with queerness. This is an instance of being not only an outsider but an unacceptable outsider. Being Jewish is viewed as an ontological act or state of dissidence. It is being queer (quintessentially and irreparably Other) by virtue of birth.

The way in which sexual and religious ambiguities (because they are based on hearsay, popular belief, or just plain gossip) are conjugated into a queer vision of Mistral is made evident in Marjorie Agosín's fictionalized account of the poet's visit to a school in southern Chile: "When Gabriela Mistral arrived the school became solemn and silent. She had green eyes and a displaced gaze; she wore a long skirt and men's shoes. I approached her and gave her the bouquet of freshly cut flowers. And she kissed me on my cheeks drenched in sweat and shame. From that moment on I loved her because everyone also laughed at her and called her a dirty Jew, an ugly lesbian, and friend of the unfortunate Indians" (83).

This is (was) the popular image of Mistral in her native Chile, as expressed through the voice of the young narrator (Agosín's mother). This is also the image that, to a certain degree, has been successfully erased and replaced with one more sterile. To be a truly suitable model of mother and nation, she cannot be Jewish, lesbian, or indigenous. Nevertheless, none of these aspects of her identity can or should be ignored if we are to come to a meaningful understanding of Mistral the person and the poet.

The exploration of the matter of queerness is helpful in attempting to dismantle the constructs built around her—as has been done in (a)sexual terms with the appellations "la Divina Gabriela," "Santa Mistral," "Madre de América"—with regard to her relationship to Jewish issues. I would like to break through the constructs of *poetisa cristiana* and Christian Matriarch of Latin America, not to try and strip Christianity from her life and works—which would be impossible and absurd—but to rediscover, acknowledge, and embrace the Judaic elements as well, as she so obviously did.

The question of Mistral's ethnoreligious identity as a Jew (Was she or wasn't she?) has been commented on by several critics and debated (debunked?) contentiously by others. Most of these deliberations commence by turning to her "abuela judaizante" (Judaizing grandmother) as a point of departure, mostly as part of the popular folklore, at times accepted at face value, and at others ignored as a possibility. Critics Ciro Alegría and Fernando Alegría, both friends of Mistral, include the poet's so-called Jewishness as a nonissue, but a nevertheless interesting aspect that adds to the mystery of her life. Ciro Alegría states straight up, "It so happened that her grandmother was a Judaizer, a determined and cunning Judaizer, and naturally she tried to influence the young girl" (45). He goes on to say that "Gabriela was never religiously Jewish" but that she did show a "great affection for the Jews" (45). Fernando Alegría goes into greater detail regarding Mistral's actual Jewish ancestry, stating at first, "Gabriela never made truly clear the intimate nature of her Judaism" (98). In light of this, he falls back on the statement of Edwards Bello: "Within Lucila there is an unmistakable Jewish substance. Her rebellious creative spirit, her eternal displeasure, her aimless wandering stem from Jewish roots, from ancestors persecuted by the Spanish Inquisition." Here Mistral is referred to by her given name, Lucila Godoy Alcayaga.

He further cites sources that establish Jewish ties on both sides of her family by showing that Villanueva (her father's maternal surname) and Alcayaga (her mother's surname) are Sephardic in origin, although the term *hebreo* is used (99). In spite of attempting to establish Mistral's Jewish heritage, both critics rely heavily on the influence of the Old Testament when speaking of Jewish elements in Mistral's works and life. In her verse and in her relationships with others, Mistral herself adds to the confusion. In the poem "Nocturno de la derrota" (Nocturne of defeat, *Tala*) she writes, "I was born of a flesh cut from the dry kidney of Israel, / a Maccabee who brings forth Maccabees, / wasp's honey that turns to mead" (119). Are we to take her statement literally, as a declaration of Jewish identity, or figuratively, as an empathetic gesture? Most have chosen to interpret it as the latter, but it does add to the ambiguity that Mistral seems to have purposely shrouded herself in. Brazilian writer Cecília Meireles alludes to that same ambiguity, relating that Mistral seemed to hint at her Jewishness while never confirming it. Furthermore, the much-repeated anecdote of Mistral taking to her deathbed a recording of the kol nidre adds more fuel to the fire of equivocalness (Taylor, 65; Ciro Alegría, 45). This is a particularly curious choice of music if we take into consideration that "at times of forced conversion to Christianity, Jews associated the formula of the kol nidre with the annulment of vows taken under duress" (Unterman, 114).

Other critics have been less willing to accept Mistral's Jewishness, even if they accept (tolerate?) Judaic elements in her writing, her apparent symbolic relationship to Jewish tradition, or her penchant for supporting Jewish causes. Germán Arciniegas aggressively disputes the possible Jewish identity of Mistral. He doesn't quite call her a bald-faced liar, but he does sardonically portray her as being prone to hyperbolic storytelling. Even Martin C. Taylor, who wrote the book on religious issues and Gabriela Mistral, clearly maintains, "without more satisfactory proof, it is difficult to accept the supposed Jewish ancestry of Gabriela Mistral" (62). In his chapter dedicated to Hebraic tradition, he goes to some length to prove just the opposite. He states there are three essential categories that must be taken into consideration when assessing Mistral's relationship to Judaism: (1) study of the Bible, which led to an affinity with biblical characters and lit in her a Hebrew spirit; (2) her concern for modern-day Jews, which was part of her overall concern for humanitarian issues; (3) her own personal suffering, which she related metaphorically to the suffering of the Jewish people, whom she identified as being symbolic of persecution and exile (63–64).

The crux of Taylor's argument in relationship to Jewish issues in Mistral's writing is that she was profoundly influenced by her early (and later constant) reading of the Old Testament, to such a point that she identified with the characters on a personal level and used them as sources of inspiration. He convincingly argues that Mistral's poetry is indeed imbued with "Hebrew spirit," but in summary he equates this with a lot of weeping, lamentation, and long-suffering, "In effect, the tears, the protestations, the separation from and final reconciliation with God, in spite of his blind injustice, mark the poetry of Gabriela Mistral with the attributes of the Hebraic tradition" (108). Is this really what Jewish tradition boils down to? Taylor's choice of the expression "Hebrew spirit" cannot be overlooked. This would seem to be a conscious decision to use the archaic term Hebrew in order to keep the association unmistakably linked to the Old Testament, rather than use the modern term Jewish, which would imply association with present-day Jews. In all fairness, Taylor does acknowledge and argue for a true Judeo-Christian heritage in Mistral's poetry, something not all critics are willing to do.

For example, Carlos D. Hamilton, in his study that traces the biblical roots of Mistral's poetry, does so from a decidedly Christian perspective, making a concerted effort to gloss over, explain away, or disavow any real ties with Jewishness or Judaism outside what is the Jewish heritage of Christianity. Even this he seems to accept reluctantly. Hamilton begins his article by contesting the opinion of Hernán Díaz Arrieta (pseud. Alone), Chilean critic and friend of Mistral, who wrote openly about the poet's possible Jewish lineage and enthusiastically about her close adherence to Jewish culture and tradition. Hamilton asserts, "Gabriela's Jewish origin, which no one has proven, seems to me to be as much a myth as her indigenous origin" (201). He goes even further: "Gabriela's Bible is the Christian Bible, in its entirety" (202). The message from Hamilton is quite clear—even if Mistral showed some seemingly Jewish influences, they were purely textual, nothing that could possibly taint her image as Christian (Catholic) matriarch. After all, as Hamilton points out, she did experiment with Theosophy as well, but returned to the true path (and to her senses!) by ultimately confessing her faith in Christ, as Jorge Isaacs did on his deathbed (204). Hamilton not only wants to make sure Mistral remains unscathed by Jewishness, he attempts to clear Isaacs's reputation as well; Isaacs, in fact, reaffirmed his Jewish identity on his deathbed, and well before (Sommer).

The subtext running throughout Hamilton's discourse recalls the Hispanic (inquisitorial) ideal of *pureza de sangre,* or purity of blood. Hamilton also compares Mistral to the Golden Age Spanish mystics, clearly positioning her within that tradition as the modern-day heir to Teresa de Avila (Santa Teresa de Jesús), San Juan de la Cruz, and to a lesser degree Fray Luis de León. This comparison is rather ironic, since his purpose is obviously to situate Mistral within a steadfast tradition of Catholic religious writing. Needless to say, what he fails to recognize is the fact that all three of the exemplary Catholic writers he uses to illustrate his point came from *converso* (i.e., Jewish) families (Swietlicki). Hamilton is correct in pointing out the similarities between these Golden Age mystics and their contemporary counterpart, for in fact they have much in common, namely their suspect Jewish origins and the kabalistic nature of their mysticism.

In her article "Gabriela Mistral: The Christian Matriarch of Latin America," Alicia G. Welden argues against the idea of Mistral as mystic poet, stating outright, "We cannot say that Mistral achieves mysticism" (24). Welden goes about constructing her image of Mistral the "Christian Matriarch" by focusing on Christological imagery, "images of the cross and a suffering Christ as symbols of the passion and of redemption through sacrifice" (24), "adherence to Christian thought" (27), and "symbols of biblical origin" (29), though she never suggests any kind of Jewish, or even Judeo-Christian, influence. Her article reads much more like a hagiography of the poet than a critical appraisal of her work—not uncommon in Mistral criticism.

Even Monsignor Rafael Gómez Hoyos, in his article "Gabriela Mistral, poetisa cristiana," acknowledges that Jesus Christ himself was a Jew, as was his mother, as were the apostles, and the prophets. And although Gómez Hoyos wishes to bestow the title of Christian Poetess upon Mistral, he is surprisingly ecumenical in how he goes about it. Other critics, such as Carmen D. Hernández de Trelles and Ana María Cuneo, likewise have been open to viewing the religiosity of Mistral as being much broader than a strictly Catholic theology. In the introduction to his volume of Mistral's collected prose on religious topics Luis Vargas de Saavedra provides a well-balanced view of Mistral's vision of religion as a fundamental and important aspect of the human experience. Through a selection of quotations he succinctly outlines her broad knowledge of and appreciation for different religious traditions (Buddhism, Theosophy, Judaism, Christianity, etc.).

The foregoing survey of critical attitudes with regard to Jewish/ Judaic aspects in Mistral's personal history as well as in her writing should provide an overall view of how the ambiguity of the matter has led to multiple interpretations of the content, significance, or very existence of such elements. As stated from the beginning, Gabriela Mistral's (non)identity as Jewish really carries very little weight. One can undertake a Jewish, or Jewishly informed, reading of her work without taking into consideration her personal history. Whatever her ethnoreligious identity may have been—whether descendent of crypto-Jews (Ciro Alegría; Fernando Alegría) or Catholic and "Castilian and Basque on all counts" (Hamilton, 201)—and however she may have chosen to self-identify, Mistral is unique among Latin American writers specifically for the Jewish content of her work. As a non-Jewish writer (because really I think she cannot be considered a Latin American Jewish author) she is certainly second only to Jorge Luis Borges for the manner in which she includes Jewish/Judaic elements into her literature. Having said this, I would like to examine but a few examples of how this is achieved.

One of Mistral's most quoted and often anthologized texts is her essay "Mi experiencia con la Biblia" (My experience with the Bible). It was originally a public lecture delivered at the Sociedad Hebraica Argentina in Buenos Aires and subsequently published in the SHA's *Revista* in 1938. I have chosen to cite from the version published in *Noaj,* the journal of the Asociación Internacional de Escritores Judíos en Lengua Hispana y Portuguesa (International Association of Jewish Writers in Spanish and Portuguese), which in turn was taken from a book titled *Chile escribe a Israel* (Chile writes to Israel) compiled by

Sima Nisis de Rezepke, precisely because the *Noaj* version points not only to the Jewish content of the essay but to the significance of it within the Jewish literary environment of Latin America. Mistral maintained strong friendships with many famous figures from the Jewish communities; among them was the Argentine actress and performer Berta Singerman, who in her "Recuerdos de Gabriela Mistral" (Memories of Gabriela Mistral; included in a special issue of *Cuadernos israelíes* dedicated to Mistral) likened Mistral to the prophetess Deborah (6), which Taylor characterizes as exaggeration (69). Mistral likewise gave an elegiac presentation of Singerman in Puerto Rico, extolling her as the embodiment of the ideal Latin American citizen ("Berta Singerman"). While living in Brazil, Mistral became an intimate friend of Stefan Zweig and suffered greatly when he and his wife committed suicide in 1942 (Gazarian-Gautier, 73–74).

Like Sor Juana's famous *Respuesta,* "Mi experiencia con la Biblia" contains a good deal of autobiographical information, as well as details regarding the poet's early influences and formation as a writer. The anecdote Mistral relates about her introduction to Old Testament characters and especially about her grandmother who would read to her the Psalms of David is perhaps one of the most commonly known stories of Mistral's early life. This early formation is cited in virtually all biographies of the author and used as a source of reference when explaining her devotion to the Old Testament and the personages she so admired: Rebecca, Esther, Judith, Jacob, and David (whom she refers to as her hero) to name only a few. Taylor identifies fifteen women and nineteen men from the Old Testament who appear in her poetry, in contrast to sixteen men and women combined from the New Testament (267–69). Aside from merely identifying with Old Testament figures and stories, Mistral reveals a deeper connection made during those formative years: "My contact with Jewish lyricism, which would be the lyricism with which I nourished myself, came when I was ten years old, from my grandmother, doña Isabel Villanueva" (85). This statement is revealing because it speaks not only of the thematic influence of the Old Testament but of the Jewish lyrical style she learned from authors such as the poet David. This statement is further supported by another equally telling observation: "Now I must speak of formal aspects, which are also the essence of the Bible's contagious effect upon me: for in Hebrew, content and form are entwined and work as closely together as muscle and tendon" (88).

Mistral clearly recognizes that she was influenced not only by the symbolic nature of characters and events, but by the richness of the scriptural style contained in the Old Testament and how she endeavored to adapt it to her own writing from an early age (88–89). Her admiration for this Jewish style of writing is summed up in the following words: "The science of expression in the Bible, the Jewish comportment with the word, even when considered separate from religious matters, is a great lesson of integrity given by Israel to other languages and other races" (90).

Numerous poems by Mistral contain Old Testament symbolism and figures, and many more, particularly the poems of *Desolación*, emulate a Jewish lyricism mentioned previously. One of the more promising areas for future study would entail an in-depth analysis of the influence of biblical Hebrew style in Mistral's poetry. This would be similar to the kind of criticism that has been conducted in the area of kabalistic influence in Borges's writing, for example. Critics tend to point to Mistral's predilection for Old Testament themes as examples of the lamentation she felt in her soul, especially when it comes to the long-suffering of characters like Job, or many of the tribulations and trials that biblical women endured. But can we not also see her references to Eve, Judith, Naomi, Rachel, Rebecca, and Sarah as models of feminine strength and empowerment? In her poem "Eva" (Eve; *Poesía y prosa*), for example, she paints Eve as the suffering mother (a common theme) holding the dead body of her son Abel in her lap. All nature is attentive to her pain and mourning, which slowly dissipate with time, and in the end she rises triumphant and empowered against the "boughs of death" (309–10). She accomplishes this without the aid of Adam (in fact, she rejects him) or the succor of God. The predominant imagery in the poem is derived from nature, and nature provides the healing elements. In another nature-based poem, "El Ixtlazihuatl" (*Desolación*), Mistral derives spiritual strength and inspiration from the Jewish heroine Judith, who not only represents courage in the face of adversity but who also was a chaste and pious woman. Judy B. McInnis provides an insightful analysis of the poem and the symbolism of the figure of Judith within it. More important, she illustrates how Mistral identified with Judith. Contrary to what the typical image of Mistral has been (self-sacrificing, celibate, submissive, docile), McInnis affirms, "it is precisely Judith's capacity for violence that most appealed to Gabriela" (162). In addition she states, "The attractiveness of Judith is quite clear, also an isolated and childless woman, she acted autonomously and violently to assure the survival of her tribe" (162). McInnis calls Mistral "la Judith chilena" (the Chilean Judith). This is a welcome and favorable appellation that emphasizes another important facet of Mistral and expands on the rather exclusionary Christian Matriarch image propagated in the vast majority of the bibliography.

Mistral's three sonnets dedicated to Ruth (*Desolación*) constitute one of the best examples of her use of Jewish themes. They have received a significant amount of critical appraisal. Ruth is in many ways the opposite of Judith. As McInnis also observes, Ruth "is the epitome of the obedient wife/daughter. The songs of praise that Mistral dedicates to Ruth, one of the women in direct line of succession to the Messiah, reflect her acceptance of patriarchal norms" (163). Howard M. Fraser perceptively analyzes how Mistral goes about taking the biblical material and reformulating it into a modern adaptation: "The Book of Ruth is ideally suited to the poet's aesthetic goals because the four compact chapters of the Bible story continuously oscillate between desolation and a search for human dignity and love" (8–9). In other words, she is attracted to the Hebrew narrative for its universal appeal while at the same time she finds the story personally appealing. As Fraser also affirms, "In the story of the outcast Moabite woman,

Mistral was able to channel her deep sense of identity with the Jewish people which appears throughout her work" (10). Fraser is able to show, contrary to what Taylor and others seem to conclude, that Mistral is capable of restructuring Judaic narratives that seem to be wrought with suffering, anguish, and sacrifice into refreshing modern-day tales with a positive twist to them. He concludes, "While the traditional theme of life's renewal through the regeneration of family is present, the austerity of the original treatment is gone. Now the poet offers the reader an aesthetic celebration of life" (16). This clearly is in opposition to the fatalistic (Jewish) characteristics that Taylor and Hamilton seemingly associate with the Old Testament, while finding the values such as hope, redemption, joy, and celebration to be New Testament (Christian) values.

Mistral plainly had a deep appreciation for and identified with Jewish history and culture, and not only in a symbolic sense. To presume that she simply utilized Jewish historical imagery because she found it a practical source for poetic tropes in that it spoke to her emotionally, is to reduce not only her intellectual capacity but her profound spirituality and pantheistic religiosity. In her poems "Emigrada judía" (Jewish emigrant; *Lagar*) and "Al pueblo hebreo" (To the Jewish people; *Desolación*), Mistral identifies with the Jewish phenomenon of exile, the Jew as persecuted victim and social pariah. "Emigrada judía" is a highly lyrical evocation of the anguish experienced in the endless wandering of exile, the home left behind, and the uncertain future of the road ahead. While these emotions were ones that she personally felt while traveling the path of her own life, it is simplistic to maintain that the poem does not also eloquently reveal the Jewish experience of *galut* (diasporic exile) and delve into the spiritual and psychological effects of exile upon the individual. In other words, the poem consists of far more than just a metaphor for Mistral's own life. It should be read as an homage to the perseverance and continuity of the Jews.

Mistral first published "Al pueblo hebreo" in 1919 in the Santiago Jewish publication *Renacimiento* (Taylor, 64). It is well known that she was inspired to write it in response to the pogroms against the Polish Jews at the beginning of the twentieth century. One can argue that the poem is similar to many others that she dedicated to diverse persecuted, oppressed, or underprivileged social groups (indigenous peoples, the poor, children, etc.), and this fact has been used to downplay any inkling of a more intimate relationship with Jewishness. However, one cannot ignore the intimacy expressed in the poetic voice of the poem. The sorrow in the poet's lamentation of the pain endured by the Jews is not merely that of a distanced, yet empathetic, observer. It comes across as being truly more personal than that in Mistral's expression of her love for the Jewish people and culture. Moreover, what is most striking in the poem—and we see this in other instances though not quite so clearly—is her embracing of Jewish culture and history as the cornerstone of Christianity. She identifies, in no uncertain terms, both Mary and Christ as ancestors of those modern-day Jews suffering in Poland. By unequivocally associating the two major figures of Catholicism with Judaic tradition, she thus recognizes and praises the Jewish heritage of Christianity. In fact, Mistral's religious-themed poetry consistently imparts a genuinely Judeo-Christian outlook based on the ideal of religiosity more than on the tenets of any one religion. In her essay "El sentido religioso de la vida" (The religious meaning of life) she outlines her belief in a model of religiosity as a code for daily living. Mistral's writings on the predicament of the Jews are not confined to her poetry. Her essay "Recados sobre los judíos" (Notes on the Jews) is her treatment of the phenomenon of anti-Semitism, which she views in general terms as the result of a historical East-West culture clash. She vehemently denounces anti-Semitism, stating that there is no place for it in Latin America and that as a religious issue it is nonsense. She ends the essay by calling for Latin American countries to open their doors to receive at least a portion of the Jews that "Europe spews from its twisted Christian entrails" (*Prosa religiosa,* 50).

This brief overview of Jewish issues in Mistral's works scarcely opens the door to the avenues of inquiry that need be pursued. There is a great deal of work to be done with regard to the topic of Jewish issues and Gabriela Mistral, but the waters are still difficult to navigate it would seem, clouded by the murkiness of ambiguity and channeled by political and ideological forces. Nevertheless, it is necessary to undertake the journey if we are to arrive at a truly comprehensive understanding of Mistral and her works, since Jewishness/Judaism is an integral and consistent element in both. As a concluding point, let us remember that we must avoid the pitfall of labeling. The purpose of exploring Jewish issues in Mistral is not to prove or disprove ethno-religious identity or affiliation. Rather, it is to examine the expression of Jewish cultural, historical, and religious reality in Mistral and understand its origins, significance, and influence in Mistral as an artist. Bringing Jewishness out of the darkness of the closet and into the full light of academic inquiry—along with issues of sexuality and any other elements that heretofore have been deemed too queer for the officially sanctioned image of Gabriela Mistral—can only enrich our knowledge of and enable us to see the authentic Gabriela Mistral. These are not exercises of replacement (out with the old category, in with the new) but of inclusion brought about by the desire to see the whole Mistral. The goal is not to dismiss the obviously Christian/Catholic facets in Mistral, but to enhance them by adding another related component, just as the criticism on sexual(ity) issues only helps to broaden our awareness to the complexities of this seminal figure.

Note

All translations of Mistral's texts and of Spanish-language criticism are mine.

Works Cited

Agosín, Marjorie. *A Cross and a Star: Memoirs of a Jewish Girl in Chile.* Trans. Celeste Kostopulos-Cooperman. Albuquerque: University of New Mexico Press, 1995.

Alegría, Ciro. *Gabriela Mistral íntima.* Bogotá: Editorial Oveja Negra, 1980.

Alegría, Fernando. *Genio y figura de Gabriela Mistral.* Buenos Aires: Editorial Universitaria de Buenos Aires, 1966.

Arciniegas, Germán. "Gabriela, la fantástica chilena." *Cuadernos israelíes* 4 (1960): 22–26.

Cuneo, Ana María. "El discurso religioso en Mistral, Uribe, y Quezada." *Revista chilena de literatura* 45 (1994): 19–38.

Doty, Alexander. *Making Things Perfectly Queer: Interpreting Mass Culture.* Minneapolis: University of Minnesota Press, 1993.

Fiol-Matta, Licia. "The 'Schoolteacher of America': Gender, Sexuality, and Nation in Gabriela Mistral." In *¿Entiendes? Queer Readings, Hispanic Writings,* ed. Emilie Bergmann and Paul Julian Smith, 201–29. Durham: Duke University Press, 1995.

Fraser, Howard M. "Gabriela Mistral's Sonnets to Ruth." *Studies in Twentieth-Century Literature* 3 (1978): 5–21.

Gazarian-Gautier, Marie-Lise. *Gabriela Mistral: The Teacher from the Valley of Elqui.* Chicago: Franciscan Herald Press, 1975.

Gómez Hoyos, Rafael. "Gabriela Mistral, poetisa cristiana." *Boletín de la Academia Colombiana* 40, 168 (1990): 34–45.

Hamilton, Carlos D. "Raíces bíblicas de la poesía de Gabriela Mistral." *Cuadernos americanos* 20, 68 (1961): 201–10.

Hernández de Trelles, Carmen D. "Del mito al misticismo: El símbolo religioso judeocristiano en la poesía de Gabriela Mistral." *La torre* 5, 18 (1991): 157–69.

Horan, Elizabeth Rosa. "Alternative Identities of Gabriel(a) Mistral, 1906–1920." In *Reading and Writing the Ambiente: Queer Sexualities in Latino, Latin American, and Spanish Culture,* ed. Susana Chávez-Silverman and Librada Hernández, 147–77. Madison: University of Wisconsin Press, 2000.

——. "Gabriela Mistral: Language Is the Only Homeland." In *A Dream of Light and Shadows: Portraits of Latin American Women Writers,* ed. Marjorie Agosín, 119–42. Albuquerque: University of New Mexico Press, 1995.

McInnis, Judy B. "Gabriela Mistral—la Judith chilena." In *Modalidades de representación del sujeto auto/bio/gráfico femenino,* ed. Magdalena Maiz and Luis H. Peña, 157–69. San Nicolás de los Garza, Mexico: Facultad de Filosofía y Letras, Universidad Autónoma de Nuevo León, 1997.

Meireles, Cecília. "Um pouco de Gabriela Mistral." *Cuadernos israelíes* 4 (1960): 19–21.

Mistral, Gabriela. "Berta Singerman y la lengua criolla." In *Recados para hoy y mañana,* comp. Luis Vargas de Saavedra, 22–26. Vol. 2. Santiago: Sudamericana, 1999.

———. *Desolación. Ternura. Tala. Lagar.* Introduced by Palma Guillén de Nicolau. Mexico City: Editorial Porrúa, 1986.

———. "Mi experiencia con la Biblia." *Noaj* 1, 1 (1987): 83–90.

———. *Poesía y prosa.* Ed. Jaime Quezada. Caracas: Biblioteca Ayacucho, 1993.

Nisis de Rezepke, Sima, comp. *Chile escribe a Israel.* Santiago: Editorial Andrés Bello, 1982.

Singerman, Berta. "Recuerdos de Gabriela Mistral." *Cuadernos israelíes* 4 (1960): 5–7.

Sommer, Doris. "Jorge Isaacs." In *Jewish Writers of Latin America: A Dictionary,* ed. Darrell B. Lockhart, 268–74. New York: Garland, 1997.

Swietlicki, Catherine. *Spanish Christian Cabala: The Works of Luis de León, Santa Teresa de Jesús, and San Juan de la Cruz.* Columbia: University of Missouri Press, 1986.

Taylor, Martin C. *Sensibilidad religiosa de Gabriela Mistral.* Madrid: Gredos, 1975.

Unterman, Alan. *Dictionary of Jewish Lore and Legend.* London: Thames and Hudson, 1991.

Vargas de Saavedra, Luis. Introduction to *Prosa religiosa de Gabriela Mistral.* Editorial Andrés Bello, 1978.

Welden, Alicia G. "Gabriela Mistral: The Christian Matriarch of Latin America." In *Nahuatl to Rayuela,* ed. Dave Oliphant, 23–33. Austin: Harry Ransom Humanities Research Center, University of Texas, 1992.

Chapter 7

A Hungry Wolf
The Mask and the Spectacle in Gabriela Mistral

Ivonne Gordon Vailakis

> *At this moment, we are witnessing the spectacle of*
> *ourselves.*
> —MANUEL MAPLES ARCE, *Hoja de vanguardia*

(Re)Reading Mistral in the Vanguardia Movement

Gabriela Mistral has typified for some critics a radical conservatism. Although she published in Chile during the height of the *vanguardia* movement from 1920 through 1950, critics do not consider her to be part of that movement because she chose to use traditional thematic and formal conventions. She is the contemporary of another Chilean poet, Huidobro, whose *Altazor* is widely acclaimed as critical of the vanguardia movement, largely because of its innovative aesthetics. Mistral's aesthetics have traditionally been held apart from Huidobro's, despite her employment of activist motifs of lyric subjectivity and her use of poetic images that prevailed in the movement. Although I admit that there are radical differences between these two poets and that they have very different approaches to the vanguardia movement,

I contend that critics who fail to identify Mistral's work as part of this movement ignore the broader polemics about language and identity in Latin America's vanguard.

Gabriela Mistral foregrounds the interplay of language and identity in her work, and this constitutes her fundamental contribution to the vanguardia movement. To this date, no work has been done that includes Mistral's poetry in this significant Latin American literary movement. I suggest that this poet's production should be classified more meaningfully with respect to the other poets of the vanguardia. This notion is reinforced by the critic Vicky Unruh: "The titles of the anthologies underscore the eclectic substance of materials resistant to tidy classification. . . . These problems in classification reinforce the idea of vanguardism as a form of activity rather than assemblage of canonical authors or works. In their very constitution, these collections also suggest that, to arrive at meaningful understandings of the vanguard period in Latin America, one must go beyond specific individual works, writers, or even genres" (Unruh, 9). In order to go beyond specific individual works or writers, we must take a closer look at a writer's production and consider his or her challenge to accepted categories.

While the artistic endeavor of writers like Huidobro is to reach linguistic purity, to arrive at a "ground zero" expression, Mistral's intent is to change the dominant social order by altering its conventional representations through a poetic practice. Women poets have not only been omitted from the canon, they have also been misinterpreted. This is the case with Gabriela Mistral. Some critics have assumed that she is a traditional conservative writer, and therefore all criticism of her work has been interpreted through this looking glass. Jan Montefiore explains the difficult relationship that poets experience with the authoritative tradition, how they negotiate their paradoxical exclusion (*Feminism*, 27). Unruh addresses the exclusion of women poets from the vanguard in Latin America: "This study does not pretend to present an all-encompassing or conclusive assessment of the movement. Other issues touched on here might well provide the focus for future work by the growing community of *vanguardista* investigators, for example, the complex and problematic relationship of women writers and intellectuals to primarily male-dominated vanguardist activities" (Unruh, 28).

Although Unruh makes no attempt to include women writers in this movement, at least she points out the necessity of a study of this nature. There is no question that there is a big gap in the study of the vanguard. Many women writers have been disregarded as participants in such an important art movement in Latin America. My interest lies in situating Gabriela Mistral in the vanguardia movement. I link her production to the movement and the difficult relationship that this poet encountered with the authoritative male tradition. Most important, I consider the literary strategies she utilized to negotiate her exclusion.

Mistral's way of subverting this authoritative tradition is to use the mask as a deliberate representation and transformation of dominant social constructs—first foregrounding social constructs and then transforming them into new ones. Mistral identifies the critical elements of a political poet's project as mirroring and transgression. Her intent on integrating a different perspective infringes on the norm of her male contemporaries. Mistral's entrenchment on patriarchal society is, in short, in her own use of a mask. My use of the term *mask* is based on Mary Ann Doane's argument that the mask represents a curious norm, one that indicates through its very contradictions the difficulty of any concept of femininity in a patriarchal society (45). I expand this notion of the mask as not only a psychoanalytic way of reading but also a way of intersecting both the imaginary and the symbolic. I would further insist on the effectiveness of the mask as resistance. This resistance becomes the poet's way of negotiating an inclusion in the vanguardia movement. Mistral creates texts that question the relationship between art and society. She uses the spectacle of the mask as a way of hiding behind her true self. In this way she crosses the boundary of expectation between writer and reader. This is an opportunity for the writer to expose the reader's complicity in a society of nonresistance. Taking on Kristeva's notion: the writer must embrace an identity that is not her own in order to reveal the effects of patriarchy on the individual psyche (7–8). Instead the effects are concepts that might easily be transformed so as to disempower none. No one feels threatened with the idealized feminine and the benevolent child, therefore this kind of work must be minor and unimportant. With this concept in mind, Gabriela Mistral subverts the status quo by exposing idealized portraits of the decorously feminine or nurturingly maternal as cultural constructions.

Mistral did not write manifestos of the vanguardia, nor did she write an *ars poetica* that would revolutionize the concept of poetry. Instead, she generated a lyrical discourse that challenged the notions of femininity and of patriarchy. She created a way of thinking about culture that had long-term consequences. During the twenties Chile produced important writers who participated in the vanguardia movement. Unruh explains that the "Chilean vanguardism emerged during a tense and haltingly reformist period," and goes on to say, "Underscoring the pitfalls inherent in characterizing Latin American vanguardism solely in national terms, Chile produced two outstanding figures whose forums for innovative activity were often more international and continental than national or local. Vicente Huidobro—poet, novelist, dramatist, and manifesto and film script writer—is widely regarded as both precursor and the founder of Latin American vanguardism" (9). Unruh has written extensively on the Latin American vanguard, but she continues to reinforce the "major" writers of this movement in Chile. Gabriela Mistral's production during this period is considered conventional and traditional, therefore she is never included in any study of the vanguard. Perhaps her intent in cultivating the spoken word, the unofficial language, and the singularity of vernacular writing maintained her in the margins of this important Latin American movement. Or was Mistral, despite her position at the center of this movement, ignored because she did not collaborate in journals and participated in what was considered "experimental" at that time? She was exploring subjects much more daring than linguistic experimentation, yet this poet was totally excluded from the male-dominated activities of the vanguard.

When some critics refer to *Ternura* (Tenderness) as a minor work, it arouses my interest from a critical perspective. As I claimed before, some critics have mislabeled most of Mistral's poetic work, and this book of poetry in particular has received very little critical attention. Chilean critic Jaime Quezada, who has recognized the importance of this book, says, "These are lullabies that rescue what is genuine and traditional in Chilean folklore, a folklore that is part of the lives of the adult and the child of Chile, of all Latin America, and of Spain" (109). In this book, Mistral recovers the simplicity of form and language yet produces a text rich in cultural ambiguities. She seeks to provide a different perspective on the male-authored tradition and defines new parameters in which women and children get reconstructed as rhetorical figures that may be misread and misinterpreted.

This essay will consider Mistral's relationship to the vanguard with respect to her intention to alter conventional perceptions of *women* and her purpose to challenge the dominant social constructs. She accomplishes this by disguising the subject's position. I will look at "The Mother-Child" and "Little Red Riding Hood" in the poetry collection *Ternura*. These poems represent a paradigm for reading this text. They represent a marked difference in cultural critique that is quite different from her male vanguardistas. The collection was published for the first time in Madrid in 1924. It bore the subtitle *Songs for Children* and contained 105 pages and thirty-two wood engravings.

The author's intention with this book is not only to challenge generic divisions but also to explore the use of vernacular language. Quezada adds that the language of this collection has "a conversational tone that comes from her many readings of the Old Testament and from her people from Montegrande, her birth place" (115). This constitutes one of the most striking features of Mistral's *Ternura:* it is a homage to children's language and their perception of the world. This project cultivates both the spoken and unofficial language as direct speech and also celebrates oral stories transmitted by women. In Un-ruh's words, this linguistic exploration "deflects the vanguardist dis-course of origins toward a specific cultural experience . . . to become instead the birth cries of a culturally concrete linguistic identity" (231).[1] Mistral did not interpret this identity in her writings. These verbal be-ginnings of sound and rhythm become apparent with a critical reading of her work. This poet explores language in an unconventional way, examining language from a child's perspective.

On multiple levels her poems address issues of unconventionality and question the assumptions on which hegemonic discourse bases its definition of women. *Ternura* is a daring example of how she di-rectly questions the assumptions of a male-centered discourse. She addresses subjects such as lullabies, fairy tales, and children's tales in the most serious manner. She presents a series of texts that are aimed at children as her "ideal audience" but the "real audience" she has in mind is the adult reader. The poems represent *women* as the makers, the speakers of history. The role of the speaker in every poem is an ac-tive one. In this volume, she sees her role, as well as the role of women, as an active intellectual, as a compiler and transmitter of folk-lore. According to Elizabeth Horan, Mistral legitimates herself as a women's writer by noting that men have been silent about the subjects she chooses and about the audiences she prefers (450). Was Mistral too ahead of her time to be considered a feminist poet? This is a ques-tion that I keep in mind when reading her work from a critical per-spective. In the poems belonging to the book's section "Folktales" she makes no distinction between the speaker of the poem and the text. Rather, the speaking subject is at one with the poem, as are the listeners.

In the poem "The Mother-Child" ("La madre-niña") she creates a text that disintegrates the models of patriarchal discourse. In this text, the poet offers the readers a different point of view by posing opposite meanings through the discourse. The poem, as evidenced by its title, depicts the contradiction of a mother as a child. This opposition represents an illusion, something that is not possible. Mistral's refusal to enter into a patriarchal discourse is exemplified in this poem:

> Those that go by
> the same as yesterday,
> see the courtyard
> with the *maitén*[2]
> they see the muscatel
> vines
> and my child
> they don't see, they don't see! (lines 1–8)

The beginning of the poem illustrates an undefined lyric subject; the speaker wants to distance herself from the text, she wants to act as an observer. *They* are the ones peeking, yet she is the one making the observations of *them*. The speaker has changed the relationship between observer and observed. Those from the outside are looking inside her home, they peer into her patio. The act of seeing signifies an act of trespassing. The outsiders invade her privacy, yet they do not see the most salient aspect of her home, the child. This poetic statement represents the coexistence of opposing forces and the possibility of a different perspective.

After this initial stanza, the speaker reconstructs the lyric text so the reader can become an active participant in the illusion. The poet consciously repeats "to see" (*ver*). This repetition is significant: the ones on the outside look inside, but they do not see what's inside, thus creating an inverted relationship between observed and observer. This relationship between observed and observer creates a different point of view. There is no transformation in the speaker of the poem; the change occurs outside the home. The subject, *they*, goes through a change by altering their perception of the inside. This inversion of "seeing" is not just a reversal of male and female; it indicates a mode for resisting the dominant discourse.

At the end of the poem, the child transforms herself into a woman:

"a child with braids / now a woman" (33–34). After the child becomes a woman, those from the outside finally see her child: "And my child / they finally see!" (37–38). Through the dissociation of mother and child, Mistral questions the immediate associations of the female to the subject of motherhood. The transformation of the subject causes the ones on the outside to finally see. The speaker of the poem has not gone through any changes. The observed ones have changed their perception, and through this change they acquire the ability to see. The rhetorical closure of the poem invites the participation of the readers. They become witnesses to the textual event. The readers know from the beginning of the poem that the child is there. As the poem develops, we witness the transformation of *them*. The reader as well as the community has been included in the meaning of the text. As Susan Willis points out, "There is a direct relationship between history and community, just as the meaning of stories includes the meaning of the group" (821). This is an important concept in understanding Mistral's poetry. The concept of history and community is offered from a different point of view; it is more inclusive than the concepts proposed by her male contemporaries.

The Spectacle of Gender in "Little Red Riding Hood"

Mistral's poem "Little Red Riding Hood" ("Caperucita roja") shows her efforts to construct a new lyric subjectivity. It also serves to question the validity of discrete epistemological categories, such as gender identity. She accomplishes this by disguising the notion of femininity. Two of the most important themes in the poem are femininity and childhood.

Gabriela Mistral illustrates that a fairy tale aimed at an audience of children is in reality a tale of adult restrictions and conventions disguised as a children's story. Indeed, it is doubtful whether such a radical depiction of cultural constructions of femininity and children's sexuality would have been acceptable outside this context. Mistral explained that she wrote these "lullabies" for the women who were singing them, not for the child who could not understand them (Colofón, 183). Given her projected audience, we might conclude that Mistral's definition of femininity in this context expresses the existence of a multiplicity of unnamable identities beyond those of the feminine created by the phallocentric order. This lyrical text illustrates a specific ideology that children do have a sexual nature, even at a time when laws and society argue they should not. This act of subversion is in itself a radical one for Mistral. It is true that, by retelling a well-known fairy tale and questioning the definition of femininity, Mistral runs the risk of becoming restricted by the plots of the existing tales. As Montefiore points out, "Unless the poet makes her traditional material into a new plot altogether, revisionary storytelling is a limited project. I do not mean by this that the storytelling poems are failures, only that their success is necessarily limited" (*Antología,* 16).

I argue that while Mistral is conscious of the limitations of using the material of a fairy tale, she is also aware that the elements of the folktale or fairy tale offer no threat to her audiences. She draws upon her audience's familiarity with the tales to launch her representation of sexual ambivalence, violence, and the contradictions between a woman and her culture. Mistral accomplishes this by collapsing the speaking subject and the listeners into one. The listener has an important role in the fairy tale. Mistral takes the elements of the fairy tale out of their original context and puts them into a new one. She constructs a new lyric subjectivity without disjoining form and content. She is able to accomplish this by transforming the best-known fairy tale of the Grimm Brothers, Little Red Riding Hood, into a new interpretation of a fairy tale. She changes not only the fairy tale but the genre as well. The reader of the poem is no longer a passive reader of the wolf's attack but becomes a witness to the violence inflicted on the innocent child. For Mistral, the the folktale does not divorce us from the real. Her intention is to shock the reader. The wolf's representation is so grotesque in comparison to Red Riding Hood's innocence that the reader feels total disgust by the end of the poem.

The poet's intention in "Little Red Riding Hood" is not to revise fairy tales, but to use the fairy tale as a masquerade. Her use of the fairy tale is a strategy to demonstrate the ambiguity of human nature and the violence so inherent in Latin America. According to Ariel Dorfman, "What is essential . . . is not the verification of the undeniable importance of the issue of violence in our reality . . . but rather the unraveling of the manifold, specific, contradictory, and profoundly human forms posed by that topic; what is essential is to show how violence has created a worldview found nowhere else and how the Latin American has learned to find in violence the essence of his being, and the ambiguous yet close ties that bind him to his fellow human beings" (9). A closer reading of Mistral's "Red Riding Hood" reveals the preoccupation with violence and the social construction of the individual. The original version of "Little Red Riding Hood" is quite violent. George Groddeck has pointed out that he read the original tale as a metaphor of rape. Mistral draws upon this violent motif to show the violence to children and women so prevalent in Latin America. This violence does not derive only from conflicting ideologies, but from a long tradition of *mestizaje,* the mixing of two races. Mistral once said that she was the product of that racial violence (Colofón, 183). The act of violence sets the perpetuator not just morally outside society but to a world beyond our comprehension. Violence becomes the domain of the Other. Mistral's transformation of Red Riding Hood foregrounds this relation between violence and the masquerade, as she shows that the violent aggressor must disguise himself as a wolf.

Here the natural world is humanized. The wolf as an animal acts like he is masquerading. Costumed in people's clothes, he disguises his true identity. This wolf is a hungry beast: "Three days have gone by and the beast has tasted not a morsel" (line 21).

Latin America's history has been built on the principle that the power of the state is legitimated by its violence. Hungry for power, the state will sacrifice anything that stands in its way. As many critics have noted, Mistral was a strong advocate against the violence of the time. In the poem, the wolf drinks Red Riding Hood's blood down to the last drop. Mistral employs this image to allude to the "spectacle of blood being shed" during the struggles of the 1920s. When there is violence inflicted toward others, the "spectators" tend to show indifference toward the suffering of others. This indifference takes place on both individual and collective levels. After a close analysis of "Little Red Riding Hood," we see the logic of Mistral's choice of the poem to launch her political critique; a reading of any fairy tale is also a tale of individual stories that form our collective history.

Mistral's show of the spectacle is most effective in her representations of the restrictions of sex and gender categories upon individual women. She accomplishes her social critique in a series of oppositions: male-female, sexual-prepubescent, naive-cunning, object-subject, black-white. The heroine, Red Riding Hood, lives in a world surrounded by violence, but a societal veil disguises this violence. Red Riding Hood herself is not cunning or witty; she lives in a fog of naiveté:

> Red Riding Hood is candid like the white lilies.
> . . . .
> She gathers some red berries, she cuts some blossoming sprigs,
> and falls in love with speckled butterflies
> that make her forget about the Traitor's journey. (lines 9, 14–16)

Given the violence of the poem, we might first surmise that Red Riding Hood belongs to a world that is obviously different from the one Mistral inhabits. But Mistral shows us that Little Red Riding Hood's naiveté exists in a world already rife with oppositions. She is aware of the Traitor's presence but she chooses to fall in love with the speckled butterflies. Being aware of the wolf's intentions is not enough, the complexity of that other world must show itself as the structure of the poem advances. The dynamic that complicates the oppositions of male-female appears between the little naive girl, Red Riding Hood, and the grandmother, an older maternal figure. Girl and grandmother stand at the polar extremes of sexual maturity and, therefore, of self-differentiation.

Mistral employs these polar extremes not only to show the difference in their sexual maturity but also to demonstrate the dangers of too rigidly defined gender categories: masculine and feminine, male and female. The girl symbolizes futurity not yet realized, the grandmother, the self-realized in the past. This opposition configures the little girl, Caperucita (Little Red Riding Hood), as an articulation point between the masculine (the wolf) and the feminine (the grandmother). The little girl represents the mediator between the poles of sexuality. Red Riding Hood in the Brothers Grimm tale is a sweet little maiden: "This tender young thing is a juicy morsel" (2). In Mistral's poem, she is also pure and innocent. The wolf is the intermediary; he represents not only the other gender but an animalized sexuality. The wolf is all hair and desire: "The hairy deceitful one, hugging the girl" (35). He tells her to lie next to him: "Leave the pastries alone; come and warm up the bed" (31). When the wolf makes sexual advances on the child, the poem is disrupted by this apparently singular voice. The child is being approached as a woman; the innocent one is soon to become a victim. The child loses her innocence at this point in the poem. There is a transformation when the child becomes the prey and the victim of this animalized sexuality. The transvestite animal is about to rape the child-woman. Through this dissociation of child-woman from her role as prey-victim, Mistral leaves us with the ambivalent interpretation of the role of the child in a violent society and, at the same time, the sexuality of children as seen from an adult's perspective.

Without realizing it, the innocent child transforms herself into the prey of the outsider/other. Whether she wants it or not, the girl becomes the object of this animalized perpetrator's desire. The child turns into the victim of his desire. She speaks only to ask innocent questions about the wolf's appearance: "Grandma, tell me: why those big eyes?" (39). The only ones that remain active and have a voice are the wolf and the reader. At this point, the role of the reader in the transformation of the poem is critical. The reader becomes a textual witness of the event, the reader loses his or her ability to act. The child's innocence and fear incite the beast: "The young tender body makes his eyes open wide. / The child's terror makes them wide too" (37–38).

At this point in the poem, the sexual masquerade is growing to a crescendo. All the sexual implications of the poem come to the foreground in these stanzas. This is the point at which Mistral's transformation of the fairy tale becomes a cultural critique (9–12). Most strikingly, the poem takes a different tone when alluding to the wolf: "And the hairy deceitful one, hugging the girl" (35). Here, the use of the word "deceitful" (*engañoso*) is important. In Spanish the verb *engañar* has a double connotation; it means both to deceive and to seduce a virgin. As readers, we are alerted that a violent sexual act is going to take place. The oppositions of innocence and experience denote the sexual transformation. The wolf is old and experienced, in contrast to the little girl: "And the old Wolf laughs, and in his *black mouth* / his *white teeth* have a horrible brightness" (41–42; emphasis mine).

The opposition that occurs between innocence and experience is highlighted by the contrast between black and white. This sharp difference does not happen in the poem until the last two stanzas. Jorge Guzmán, in his excellent study of two of Mistral's poems, comments on the distinction between white and nonwhite in her poetry: "In essence, the child is the one 'with *golden* locks' and she is 'candid like the white lilies.' The contrast of the two colors, black and white, marks the collapse of the color white, which represents the innocence of the girl. Her heart is devoured by this animal whose mouth is black. The purity of her heart disappears in the darkness of his mouth. This presence of white-nonwhite is important. It adds to the poem an element that would not be present in other societies that are not *mestiza* (mixed ethnicities) like our own" (72; emphasis mine). When Red Riding Hood asks the wolf about his big teeth, he replies, "Sweetheart, all the better to devour you . . ."(44). This distinction between white and black corresponds to the act of devouring. This horrific act corresponds to the violence inflicted on the victim and, as Guzmán suggests, "is the practice of the nonwhite side." He adds that "the speaker of the poem remains on the white side, and from that space she could talk about sexuality, using the fairy tale as a hypogram of Little Red Riding Hood. And she judges this to be an abominable act. This abomination is related and heightened with the 'golden locks' of the girl, in contrast to the 'black mouth' of the Wolf" (72).

The dyadic oppositions that existed up to this point in the poem have disappeared: white-black, female-male. These two important cultural differentiators collapse at the end of the poem. The disappearance of these poles of difference is an attempt to subvert cultural suppositions of femininity and masculinity. All desire disintegrates at the end. The beast has crushed the soft body of the girl:

> The beast has trampled, under his rough hair,
> the trembling body, soft as fleece;
> and has ground the flesh, and has ground the bones,
> and has juiced, like a cherry, her heart. (lines 45–48)

The costumed wolf destroys the body of the girl. The poem ends with the implied rape of the girl. That is the end; no one comes to her rescue. Throughout, the reader has been a witness yet can in no way participate in stopping this rape. This is a critical position in the poem's transformational premise: we witness violence of children and women, and yet we remain mute and immobile as we see these acts of violence.

The presence and then disappearance of the oppositions female-male and white-black adds a particular code to the poem that would not be present in all cultures. Jorge Guzmán adds that the opposition between white and nonwhite could not be produced in any culture, that its semantic and semiotic components would be different. Guzmán explains that this disappearance of the "white-nonwhite category" enriches the cultural signs of the text (72). This poem could have not been written outside a society where the presence of white and nonwhite are important to the society's configuration. In fact, the poem was written in Latin America, so the raped body of the female child, like the bodies of the white and nonwhite, signify a continent wracked with violence, not only with sexual implications but with racial connotations as well.

Mistral crafts this poem in such a way that up to the eleventh stanza Little Red Riding Hood is the object of the wolf's gaze and desire. Throughout the poem, she does not look back or talk back, therefore nullifying her subjectivity. We might surmise that the rape and dismemberment of this girl reproduces the Grimms' tale in largely its original form, although the poem's ending is much more violent. However, the obliteration of Red Riding Hood is much more than an affirmation of a cultural order that is abusive to women and children. There is no happy ending, the family is not reunited. The child is dismembered at the end of the poem.

Little Red Riding Hood is the unwitting victim of a devouring adult character, a figure disguised and costumed. As in the original fairy tale, the child does not wear a disguise. Although we may perceive the wolf as a male perpetrator because of his disguise, he is, in reality, also female, a metamorphosed grandmother. The wolf swallows the grandmother, but he dresses in the grandmother's clothes. The character of the grandmother becomes metamorphosed. Not only does the wolf appear in a transvestite position but the language the poet uses is full of linguistic ambiguity. For instance, we're not sure whether it was the wolf or the woman who was laughing while he was eating her: "Laughing, he slowly ate her all up" (*Se la comió riendo toda y pausadamente*) (23). Again, there is a double connotation in the language; in Spanish, "eating" (*comer*) can also be understood as sexual intercourse.

If we pause at this aspect of the poem, the grandmother has the capacity for mutability, and another possibility opens up. This linguistic ambiguity creates different levels of understanding the text. There are also sexual and gender ambiguities at this point in the poem. The different levels occur simultaneously in the text: the masculine presence of the wolf has evolved into a feminized figure. Once he swallows the grandmother, the masculine figure is no longer at the center of the poem. The erasure of the presence of the older feminine figure, the grandmother (fifth stanza), creates a new feminized figure, the transvestite wolf. The masculine wolf has been transformed into a feminine version of the masculine. After Red Riding Hood enters the grandmother's house, she innocently questions the animal appearance of her grandmother while perceiving her altered yet human characteristics.

Mistral draws our attention to the wolf's transgender identity in order to remind us of the masquerade that is one's gendered identity in a culture. Wearing the grandmother's clothes as a disguise, this metamorphosed character reminds the readers of the ambiguous figure of an outsider. Disguising the notions of bisexual fantasy suggests the ambiguity of the outsider. After the wolf disguises himself as a woman, he prepares himself to seduce the little girl. It is important to note that Little Red Riding Hood's virginity becomes euphemistic for a variety of margins in which she is situated, both as a pubescent girl and as a girl without a sexual identity. The poem traces the blurred acquisition of bisexual identity, with some peculiar representations of femininity.

The transformation between the wolf and the grandmother generates a series of sexual innuendos that end in the last stanza. The questions raised up to this point in the poem question and undermine the ideology of the time. They also present a perspective that goes in total opposition to the external points of view. Bisexual fantasy was in direct opposition with the cultural definition of femininity. No writer or intellectual in the 1920s in Latin America dared such a feat. Mistral destroys all oppositions in this poem, black becomes nonwhite, female becomes disguised male. There are no binaries in direct opposition to each other. The poem gives a semblance of gender disappearance. The undoing of a gender binary is also the undoing of a color binary. The ability to change color, to make it disappear, implies the erasure of genders. All synecdoches, "the flesh," "the bones," and the "heart" are not securely attached to a feminine presence, they are erased at the end of the poem:

and he has ground the flesh, and he has ground the bones,
and he has juiced, like a cherry, her heart . . . (lines 47–48)

At the conclusion of the poem, the feminine presence has disappeared. This retelling of a fairy tale has no happy ending. The text at the end opens imaginatively to the possibilities for a disintegration of the traditional binary opposition male-female. Mistral suggests the possibility of breaking with hegemonic masculinity. This masculinity maintains its power by imposing fear, pain, and violence on others. The poem makes the reader realize that she or he cannot stand on the sidelines as only a witness; the reader, like the witness, is also a coparticipant in the violence inflicted on women and children.

Because of the simplicity of their themes and language, the poems in *Ternura* have received little critical interest.. The themes when taken literally reinforce the critical perception of Mistral. Many at the time believed that since she was an unmarried woman and conceived no children of her own, her female instinct would influence her strongly, so the only themes she would write about would be children and her desire to have them. As we have seen, through different perspectives on this Chilean poet, Mistral went beyond the social constructs of femininity and tried to conceive something beyond the opposition of male-female. Her love for humanity made her an advocate for the less privileged people: women and children. The complexities of *Ternura* illustrate the transvestite position Mistral adopts, not only in the poem "Little Red Riding Hood" but in many others. In her poems Mistral not only dramatizes a refusal on the poet's part to be violated by the conventions of what others prescribe as feminine, but she also refuses to define the opposite. She creates a difference by not acknowledging the two sides as opposite and creates a space for other gender possibilities. Through this posture, as a frequent speaker in Latin America in the twenties and thirties, she was able to transgress oppressive circumstances.

Much of her poetry is disguised under the mask of the feminine. Using that mask as a strategy won her a position among both Chilean and international poets. She was the first woman to win a Nobel prize and the only Latin American woman to this day to receive such recognition. Poets like Mistral seek to keep language accessible, primary, alive by writing about fairy tales and lullabies. Critics in Latin America consider the vanguardista discourse to be a link forged through oral tradition, the concept of a living voice engaged in speech or song. Mistral was aware of this, and she asserted this notion in her writing. In the vein of this movement, Gabriela Mistral used the disguise of a mask in order to affirm the marginal discourses into cultural autonomy in art. As a poet and a visionary, Mistral sought to build a dialogue between the public and the personal. She saw the importance of including women and children in the community and in history. As an intellectual, she believed that this dialogue would create a space that would forge a way of reformulating the relations between sexes, classes, and races. Her poetry is both revolutionary and political.

Notes

All translations are mine.

1. The quote is applied to Vicente Huidobro's poetry, but it also applies to Mistral's poetry.
2. Mistral herself uses a footnote to define the word *maitén*—a tree that grows in Chile.

Works Cited

Doane, Mary Ann. "Masquerade Reconsidered: Further Thoughts on the Female Spectator." *Discourse* (Indiana University Press) (fall/winter 1988–89).

Dorfman, Ariel. *Imaginación y violencia en América.* Mexico City: Siglo Veintiuno, 1970.

Grimm, Jakob and Wilhelm. "Little Red Riding Hood." Quote is from version found at: http://mld.ursinus.edu/Maerchen/grimmred.html. Copyright The Fairy Tale Project, 1996.

Guzmán, Jorge. "Dos poemas de Gabriela Mistral." *Acta literaria,* no. 14 (1989).

Horan, Elizabeth. "Matrilineage, Matrilanguage: Gabriela Mistral's Intimate Audience of Women." *Revista canadiense de estudios hispánicos* 14, 3 (spring 1990).

Kristeva, Julia. *Powers of Horror: An Essay on Abjection.* Trans. León S. Roudiez. New York: Columbia University Press, 1982.

Mistral, Gabriela. *Antología general de Gabriela Mistral.* Santiago: Editorial Roble de Chile, 1974.

———. *Desolación. Ternura. Tala. Lagar.* México: Editorial Porrúa, S.A., 1981.

———. *Ternura: Songs for Children.* Madrid: Saturnino Calleja Press, 1924. Rev. ed., Buenos Aires: Espasa-Calpe Press, 1945.

Montefiore, Jan. *Feminism and Poetry: Language, Experience, Identity in Women's Writing.* London: HarperCollins, 1994.

Quezada, Jaime. "Gabriela Mistral: Algunas referencias a *Ternura.*" *Acta literaria,* no. 14 (1989).

Unruh, Vicky. *Latin American Vanguards: The Art of Contentious Encounters.* Berkeley: University of California Press, 1994.

Willis, Susan. "Histories, Communities, Sometimes Utopia." In *Feminisms,* ed. Robyn R. Warhol and Diane Price Herndl, 821–46. Brunswick, N.J.: Rutgers University Press, 1991.

Chapter 8

Walking South
Gabriela Mistral's Chilean Journey

Santiago Daydí-Tolson

LIKE SAINT FRANCIS OF ASSISI, Gabriela Mistral was "always on the road" (Mistral, *Motivos*, 63), as she wrote about the religious figure she most admired and whose rules and spiritual guide she cherished and followed most of her life. She liked the contact of the earth under her feet, and the nearness of nature, with its animals and plants, minerals and landscapes all around her, a world of matter alive with the spirit of creation:

> It makes the trip so joyous!
> I am stunned by what I see
> By what I look and divine
> By what I seek and find (*Poema de Chile,* 7)

Walking was for her a means to learn about this world and to communicate with it; it was also a vital representation of human life as symbolized in the proverbial road of the traditional Christian allegory of *homo viator,* man the traveler. For Mistral, walking is a recurring motif that acquires particular significance in her book about her long walk along her country.

A territory almost three thousand miles long running like a narrow path between the Andes to the east and the Pacific Ocean to the west, from several degrees north of the Tropic of Capricorn to Cape Horn, Chile encompasses the varied landscapes of several geographical regions, uniting two extremes: on one end the luminous heat of the austere Atacama desert, drenched in the torrid subtropical sun; on the other the not less stark lands of Patagonia, swept by storms and dimly lit by the Antarctic sun, which barely rises above the horizon—two opposing worlds, suggestive in their grandiose landscapes of spiritual life and mystical symbolism. Between these two harsh and awe-inspiring geographical extremes extends a country of serene beauty and natural richness. This was Mistral's country of birth, the one she describes and admires, as she walks it from end to end, in *Poema de Chile,* published after her death. She knew this country well and loved it deeply in spite of having lived in it only half of her life.

At the age of thirty-three, invited by the Mexican government to work in the organization of its elementary education in rural areas, Mistral left Chile for what should have been only a short residence abroad. After her stay in Mexico, circumstances led to other opportunities and commitments that required her living the rest of her life far from her home country. For thirty-five years, until her death in the United States, she moved constantly from one residence to another in Europe and the Americas. Most of her mature life, the period of her highest productivity, she spent in foreign countries, far from a land she never ceased to remember with the nostalgic idealization and the critical eye characteristic of most expatriates.

Of the several lyrical personae Mistral created in her poetry—speakers who represented her innermost character—the figure of the expatriate serves her very well to express a view of herself as exiled from the paradisiacal garden of infancy, that idealized reminder on earth of the eternal heavenly garden of the Father. All her traveling, thus, was not done only for work or pleasure, but because of her never ending urge to look for the perfect place in which to live in true spiritual harmony.

Her country of birth, where she lived her childhood years, must have seemed to her the nearest to that ideal, but in her imagination she traveled there constantly, as is suggested by her many notebooks, in which she wrote for at least ten years, until her death, the plans, drafts, and final texts for the unfinished long poem that became known to the public as *Poema de Chile*.

Published by Doris Dana ten years after Mistral's death, *Poema de Chile* is an incomplete work in need of careful editing if its place among Mistral's works is to be understood. The book contains seventy-seven compositions, each one with its own title, forming all together a long poem. More than a series of nostalgic compositions devoted to the natural beauties of Chile, more than a text conceived as a didactic defense of the natural riches of a country in danger of being hurt by uncontrolled progress and misguided national policies, more than a patriotic song of praise, *Poema de Chile* is above all a personal spiritual journey, the intimate experience of a poet who at the end of her days considers her life and her transcendental destiny and imagines a long walk along a path she always wished she had followed while she lived: the length of the country she left behind in her youth.

The basic structure of the book is made clear in Mistral's drafts: after dying in a foreign land, the poet returns in spirit, her "second body," to her country of origin:

> and I arrive like the arrow
> this, my second body
> to the point where they begin,
> the Homeland and Mother that were given to me (7)

There she finds a child and a *huemul,* or Chilean deer, wandering in the desert:

> I was crisscrossing
> thickets, wastelands,
> meeting up with the cactus's eyes

and battalions of anteaters
when suddenly,
from a frond of ferns,
your neck and little body sprang
into the light, like a new pine tree. (8)

She decides to show the country to them and the three together begin
their walk south: "You well deserve that I take you with me / along the
land I had, my kingdom"(5). At the end they have covered all the Chilean territory, from the Atacama Desert in the north to Patagonia at the
southern end of the continent,

Where tired Chile,
at the end of roads and space
wants to die like everyone,
gazelle, coyote, or goose (241)

"Hallazgo" (Finding) and "Despedida" (Farewell), the opening and
closing poems of the collection, respectively, set the narrative frame
within which the rest of the compositions find their place and meaning.
The first establishes the basic components of the book's story, among
them the identity of the first-person narrator, the ghost of Gabriela Mistral. As the unhappy soul of a dead person would do in the popular
Christian conception of the world of the spirits, the poet descends to
earth from above, "through space and air," attracted to her land by her
desire to be in her motherland one last time. In an apparent contradiction characteristic of Mistral, presented by the juxtaposition of opposing terms—"without a call and being called"—she suggests the very
personal need for her return and the lack of interest on the part of others
to call her back to them:

I descended through space and air
and more descending air,
without a call and being called
by the force of desire,

and the more I walked
the steeper was the descent
and the livelier my joy
and the more certain my prophesy. (7)

From the northernmost region of the Chilean desert, a place that geographically represents a beginning and might be symbolically related to transcendental spiritual experiences, the ghost of the poet travels south all the length of the country to reach at the end the snowy lands of the Antarctic region, which in the context of the poem must be understood as representation of a geographic limit and the end of a journey of atonement and purification. Atonement for having been away from the fatherland for most of her life, atonement perhaps for the death of her adopted son; purification of the Christian soul in search of its final rest in the presence of the Divinity. In this journey, which takes an indefinite length of time, being a mostly spiritual trek, Mistral completes what she left unfinished in life.

In her last composition the poet hears the call of the Lord, her "Dueño." Leaving the earth and her companions behind, she returns to Him. With this text Mistral fulfills her desire for a final transcendental destiny in the everlasting realm of the Father, the promised mystical union desired by every Christian soul. This is the call that cannot be ignored, the call she had been waiting for all her life. All travels are now completed and there is no more exile for the soul:

I go now because I am being summoned
by a whistling from my Lord;
he calls with the ineffable
sting of a ray of lightning. (243)

This simple narrative plan is based on the traditional motif of the journey. In the commonly accepted geographical reading of maps from north to south, the journey begins in the north, where the geography of Chile begins, and ends in the south, where the land ends. Following a spatial succession of steps along a geography naturally defined by its roadlike narrowness, the poem cannot but proceed in a linear direction, uncomplicated by any other plot than the simple anecdotal succession of mostly unrelated scenes.

These compositions constitute the bulk of the collection and touch several issues of special interest to Mistral's evaluation of her own life and work. They provide a good document of her worldview, a sort of intellectual testament, and a literary summary of her work. They are, obviously, the writing of someone who has reached the end of her career and looks back to consider where she has been, and at the same time wonders about what is yet to come. This is a book of the twilight hours, when the spirit faces approaching death and assumes its inevitability. That same univocal direction sustains the strongly emotional character of the book, its urgency, and objectives.

The subtle, mostly implied, allusion to a spiritual journey, vaguely evocative of Dante's trip in search of ultimate knowledge, must be taken into consideration when reading the poem, as it points to the essence of its meaning. For Mistral, *Poema de Chile* is not so much a collection of evocative compositions about Chilean geography, as might appear at first glance, but a spiritual exercise, a lyrical narrative of the poet's most intimate spiritual experience during her last ten or so years of life. Those years were sadly marked by the tragic death of Yin Yin, Mistral's adoptive child, who committed suicide as a teenager in 1943 while living with her in Petrópolis, where they had moved from Europe because of the war. If Mistral was a spiritual and religious person before her child's death, his inexplicable suicide led her into an even more introverted and religious life. *Poema de Chile* grows from this new attitude and because of this can be interpreted as a purgative journey, as if Mistral admitted to a sin that needed, in Catholic theological terms, the cleansing of purgatory. Behind the sentimental praise of the land, with its nostalgic references to a last return, the poet might very well be hiding a feeling of culpability, a sense of failure with respect to her relationship with her land and her people.

Leaving aside the Catholic dogma of purgatory, Mistral chooses, well within her preference for the popular lore, the more superstitious image of the "alma en pena," or "haunted soul" (ghost). She represents herself as such a ghost, suggesting a plan to leave the book behind for posthumous publication. By imagining herself as a ghost, she assumes her own death and even anticipates the purging process by which she expects to free herself of all culpability and remorse and to reach the state of perfection she has sought all her life.

The nostalgic and purgative journey of Mistral's spirit is basically a first-person narrative, a sort of after-death autobiography. The choice of the traditional form of the romance for all the compositions of the book is indicative of its essentially narrative character and points to the figure of the narrator, the poet herself, or more precisely, her ghost. Many are the references in the book to the fact that the main character and narrator is the ghost of Mistral herself. This explicit autobiographical component is essential to the very personal meaning of *Poema de Chile.* The complete identification between lyrical voice and author is a necessary interpretation if the poem is to be understood in its full meaning—a poetic exercise in making things happen through the power of verbal imagination. The ghost is not a literary device per se, but the true spirit of Mistral talking from the world of the dead. By the time *Poema de Chile* became known to the public, the poet was in fact dead.

To make sure the narrator is identified as a ghost, Mistral uses in the poem more times than any other representation applied to the speaker the term *fantasma,* or ghost. In several instances the ghost herself explains to the child that she is dead, that she is nothing but a wandering soul who does not have any human needs, as in these verses from "Huerta" (Orchard): "—Little child, I am a ghost / and you've already forgotten that the dead / do not need anything" (52). In "Flores" (Flowers) she explains to the child her different condition, her having a make-believe body that exists and at the same time does not exist—it appears and disappears, as if in a dream:

With my make-believe body,
I sit where the others sit.
It does not hurt me that they do not see
in the flesh, she who is a dream
that is formed and unformed
and is and is not all at once. (100)

In addition to establishing the nature of the first-person narrator
through the repeated use of a word, Mistral includes other forms of
identification of this apparently purely fictitious literary character in
terms that refer directly to her as an individual well recognized by her
public. The autobiographical fiction of her afterlife journey is thus presented as literary truth and as personal desire. Among the other forms
of self-reference found in different compositions of the book, the most
evident are several instances in which the ghost refers to herself by Mistral's names. She uses both the pseudonym by which she is publicly
known as the poet and writer, and her original first name, Lucila, the
dreaming girl who lived in the idyllic Valle de Elqui and was later to become the poet Gabriela Mistral, as told in childlike imagery in "Todas
íbamos a ser reinas" (We were all going to be queens), from her book
Tala. There is no doubt that she is the ghost, not only because she
identifies herself as such, but also because the child calls her by her
name: "You mentioned the sea, Gabriela" ("El mar," 63). Another
time the boy asks the ghost for her name. In answering him the poet
makes a reference to both her names, insisting on the same identity and
alluding to a personal decision for choosing a different name: "Yes, the
one I was given / and the one I cleverly gave myself" (43).

As if using her own name were not enough to assure the correct
identification of the narrator, Mistral combines in her ghost, in an obvious recognition of the image she presented to the public, those literary and real profiles that characterized her as Gabriela Mistral, the
writer. Her ghost is then characterized in *Poema de Chile* as mother,
teacher, poet, and madwoman, all poetic personae used by Mistral in

her poetry as representations of different aspects of her identity as an individual and as an author.

Of the several identifying masks used by Mistral throughout her poetry, perhaps the best known and the most easily recognizable is the persona of the mother: "your poor mother ghost" (92), she calls herself when talking to the child who accompanies her. Together with *fantasma,* the other word most used in the poem to refer to the ghost is *mamá,* uttered repeatedly by the child. For the readers of Mistral this term and the relationship it implies bring to mind the many poems in which Mistral sings with the voice of a mother. In only a few cases does the boy use in *Poema de Chile* the term *mamá,* suggesting the purely vicarious character of Mistral's motherhood, both in her poetry and her life.

The teacher in Mistral is not clearly distinguished from the maternal figure: both represent the caring attitude of the woman who finds her most cherished function in the raising of children. Both mother and teacher partake of the love for the child and of the passion for showing the world to him, so that he can grow to be a wise man. The teacher is found in *Poema de Chile* in the many lessons and in the advice the ghost gives the child as they walk through the different regions of the country. In these lessons, of course, are contained the most cherished views Mistral had about things. In "Emigración de pájaros" (Migration of birds), for instance, she warns him about the ignorance of the people: "People, little one, know / little or nothing about birds" (28). The teaching in "Flores" relates more specifically to agriculture, a form of productivity essential to the Chilean economy:

> You already saw, you already learned,
> how to sow and plant,
> how to water the peach tree
> and how the drought is defeated
> and the pestilence is scared off,
> until the pestilence is over. (92)

For the spirit of the poet, the various places, animals, and plants seen in her walk south are mostly evocative of a world that was lost to her when she lived in exile, but they also have a pedagogical value, as she uses them to show the country to the boy who accompanies her as a pupil, the inheritor of her poetic wisdom. A teacher above all, Mistral walks her country for the last time for her own spiritual need and to show it and explain it to her people, toward whom she feels a moral obligation. It is difficult to separate in her at this point the poet from the teacher. The pedagogical value of her writing, be it lyrical poetry or journalistic essays, is particularly evident in this extremely personal book.

Showing the world, or teaching, is also the function of the poet. The fact that the speaker in the poem is a poet insists also on the exact correspondence between the author and the lyrical voice. The biographical allusion to her birth as a poet in her Valle de Elqui is well understood as Mistral's most important life experience: "there, where I lived / where I created river and mountain / my words and my silence"(10). In "Viento norte" (North wind), Mistral insists again on the natural character of her poetic voice, learned from the voice of the wind: "Because you must know," she tells her companion, "we / his poets, learned / the wide-open scream, the weeping" (32). Poetry is a distinctly different form of expression that comes from a different perception of the world. The poet is not a normal person and, like Mistral herself, is often considered to be mentally perturbed or possessed by inexplicable spiritual forces. Poet and madwoman are one with the mother and the teacher, and both the child and the ghost herself admit that she is not a normal person, that she talks and acts like someone who is not totally sane.

Madness is related to the poet's talents, which from very early in her life made her different from others:

> That is what they said to me,
> I did not do what was appropriate for my age:
> I did not sew, I did not mend,
> my eyes were lazy,

I asked for stories, romances,
and I did not wash the dishes . . .
Oh! Above all, it was due to
the way I talked, in rhymes. (39)

Even the child himself notices the difference of her inspired words and her uncommon actions. He points to the exceptional nature of the poet:

Mother, sometimes, I must say,
you scare me to death.
How come your walk
is different from ours,
and suddenly, you don't even hear me
and you talk like the insane,
looking without answering
or answering to others?
Who are you talking to, tell me, when
I pretend to be asleep . . . and I hear you?
Maybe it's with the animals,
the grass, or the crazy wind. (22)

The repetition of the word *loco* (insane, crazy) in this text is not so much a stylistic weakness on the part of the writer, but the obvious result of the fact that this composition is only a draft. It points, though, to the importance of madness in Mistral's appropriation of her poetic talents. The child feels a "mad fear," as most people do when listening to the inspired voice of the poet, who, in popular and traditional lore, speaks like a possessed individual, someone gone mad, who talks to animals, grass, and the "crazy wind." People, then, say that Gabriela Mistral is a mad woman: "Now people say / that you are a forgotten thing" (139), the boy tells her; he also tells her that people say she is a pagan woman who writes crazy poems (201).

Madness, a form of self-definition that appears several times in the book, as well as in the rest of Mistral's works, alludes only in part to the

traditional image of the poet as a mad person; it has a more direct relation with Mistral's spiritual outlook on life, so emotionally intense, that
not only appears as very different from the most common forms of spirituality found among people but seems too extreme and obsessive. Her
madness is akin to the madness of mystics, the total abandonment of
the spirit and reason to the overpowering passion for the absolute, the
extreme love that consumes the self in the unity of the Divinity. And
this elation is obtained in *Poema de Chile* when the soul reaches the
final southernmost region at the end of the journey. Having completed
by then her last duty, the soul is swept away by the call of the Father.

These several human profiles found in her work, representing various lyrical voices, have always been attributed to Mistral as an individual, establishing tightly knit relationships between the literary works and
the real life of the author. Based on their presence in her poetic works it
is easy to see how these different lyric personae were very distinct literary creations through which Mistral was able to convey her views and
feelings about herself and about issues affecting the standing of women
in society. She made of these profiles defining characterizations of herself as poet and intellectual, and as such they were interpreted as actual
portraits of her as a real person. Recognizing this appropriation, by
which Gabriela Mistral is concrete, real, individual, and partly a com-
posite of literary voices, she represents herself in *Poema de Chile* as the
wanderer ghost of the poet, teacher, mother, and madwoman.

All these well-recognized literary identities are distinctly feminine. A
combination of all those traits developed in the figure of a woman
molded by Mistral's ideals. Although her views on women probably do
not satisfy the standards of contemporary feminism, they correspond to
a period and culture that Mistral knew and understood very well. For
her, woman has a fundamental role in society, that of forging the new
generations as mother and teacher. This is because woman is an absurd
being who loves selflessly, with no pretensions of fame or recognition.
"I, little one," says she to the boy who wonders about her actions, "am
a woman: an absurdity that loves and loves" (130). It is because she is a

woman that the ghost, the "ghostly woman," in *Poema de Chile* does not roam the land alone, in a solitary and heroic deed of the spirit; she does it in the company of the child she meets in the desert, the Indian boy whom she adopts and takes with her on her journey, as a mother would do. And as a caring mother, she teaches him about the world, out of love for the humanity he represents.

Mistral fulfills in *Poema de Chile* her most cherished function as a woman: providing love and direction to a forsaken child. Actually, she came back to earth because of him—to save her boy from Atacama: "I came down to save / my Atacamanian child" (243). In this Indian boy are reunited all the children of the many lullabies and songs for which Mistral was famous, but also in this child, lost in the desert, Mistral was representing her own Yin Yin, lost to her in real life, and through him, all suffering men in need of the caring support of a woman possessed by her love for all that exists. Her love and teachings, then, are directed to all future generations, as the poem becomes in its many readings a timeless reenactment of her own journey of purification. The *huemul,* or Chilean deer, who in most instances appears as accompanying the Indian boy, and in a few cases seems to confuse him with a fairytale character of a child-deer, represents in its animal and childlike purity the new generations, more in tune with nature and a world in peace.

In *Poema de Chile,* Gabriela Mistral returns to her most cherished themes and her tenets about life. She worked on its composition for several years, adding to it without a plan for its completion, probably because she knew it would be completed only by her death. It is the writing of her last days, the final confrontation with mortality and, more so, with the Christian belief in an everlasting life of the spirit, joyful or miserable, depending on how life was lived.

We can imagine Mistral in those final years, in failing health, beset by the memories of her son, and increasingly more nostalgic of her homeland, probably dreaming of a return that was by then impossible. As a poet she turned to language and imagination and did what she could not do in the world of immediate reality. Instead of going back to the purely wishful land of perfection of which everyone dreams, the paradisiacal land of childhood, which for her coincides with the religious belief in eternal bliss in the presence of God; she actually returned to her country by means of a poetic act of will and desire. Working all those years on *Poema de Chile* was a profoundly spiritual act of faith and a form of anticipation. She was practically writing it from beyond, as if she were already the ghost of herself. Her voice in the poem comes to us from another world.

To interpret *Poema de Chile* as simply a book written to depict the country from the admired perspective of a nostalgic exile is to miss the core and the meaning of the work. In essence it is more than a literary work insofar as it is not finished, and more so, because it grew mostly as an exercise of personal imagination, as a form of meditation and prefiguration of what the poet expected would be her destiny after death. The woman who had imagined motherhood and made it her own through poetic language imagined also in poetic terms her last spiritual experience. By the sheer power of her poetic word she made real, in an ultimate act of selfless love, the purgative journey that freed her from all worldly concerns, allowing for her admission into paradise. There her ghost found her definite identification in the mystical union represented not by a rose, as in Dante, but by the stark beauty of Patagonia, the region where the land ends and the spirit soars free into eternity.

Note

Unless otherwise noted, all translations are mine.

Works Cited

Mistral, Gabriela. *Motivos de San Francisco.* Santiago: Editorial del Pacifico, 1965.
———. *Poema de Chile.* Santiago: Pomaire, 1967.

Chapter 9

The Inconvenient Heroine
Gabriela Mistral in Mexico

Diana Anhalt

TWO DAYS AFTER Gabriela Mistral died in 1957, Mexican poet Carlos Pellicer wrote:

> Everything my memory remembers
> and forgets about you holds vases of flowers. (1)

Everything I remember about Gabriela Mistral holds suitcases. I think of her as the perpetual immigrant crossing and recrossing frontiers, loaded down with suitcases full of books and papers and dreams for the future. She wrote:

> . . . I stop, question, walk on.
> As I walk I do not sleep.
> They've sliced up the earth,
> leaving me only the sea. (in Rodríguez, 83)

Thus, confining her to Mexico, as I have been asked to do for the purpose of this paper, has been a challenge. Gabriela just wouldn't co-operate. She wandered through my head as she'd wandered through life, settling down wherever she felt at home. "When I like a place I don't limit my stay. Time doesn't count and I persevere, getting to know its people, figuring out how far it's come" (in Schneider, 35). (At present, she's still living in my head, perhaps because she likes it there, though, knowing Gabriela, I don't imagine she'll stay for long.)

Nevertheless, no matter where she resides, she was, throughout life, unique, bold, highly principled, honest, stubborn, outspoken, and, on the surface at least, unafraid. In short, she could be an inconvenient heroine. Once she was dead she was perfect. Only then was she incapable of speaking up. People could turn her into whomever they liked and in Mexico they frequently did: "She was a very strange, enigmatic creature, not easy to love," a well-known historian told me, and the librarian at the Biblioteca México seemed to recall her having led a tragic life: "Her husband beat her, you know." In a used bookstore on Donceles Street the young salesman assured me she was one of the greatest living Mexican poets, and an acquaintance asked me if she was the woman who had painted her body and danced naked in Montparnasse. Everyone I asked seemed to have heard of her; practically no one had read her.

However, her first trip to Mexico was not primarily as a poet, nor as the journalist, essayist, and Nobel prize winner she would later become, but simply as an educator whose role there would be more spiritual than pragmatic, closer to that of a muse than of a pedagogical innovator (Arrigoitia, 12).

At the time, Mexico was just struggling back to its feet following the bloody revolution of 1910 to 1920. Wealth was concentrated in the hands of a few; the rural population lived in extreme poverty, ignored by the central government, and was ruled by unscrupulous caudillos. Having taught in night schools for peasants and workers in northern Chile, Mistral was well aware of these problems (Valenzuela, 64).

For a Mexico immersed in a generalized crisis, her humanitarian notions about man's dignity and worth struck a common chord (Díaz, 124). Few, if any, had verbalized as eloquently as she a concern for the well-being of the forgotten masses—the Indian, the woman, the child—nor such fervent devotion to a united Americas, *nuestroamericanismo,* she called it.

Mistral believed the curriculum should address not only the intellectual issues but practical ones as well—agriculture and industry, for example—and emphasize the uniqueness of Hispanic American culture, relying less on European models. It should be current, relevant, and meaningful. "Youth, that living water," she wrote, "cannot love one who bears the dead word upon his living tongue" (Mistral, *Lecturas,* xvii).

She was not alone in her convictions. In Mexico, José Vasconcelos, one of Latin America's more intriguing and enigmatic personalities, became the head of the country's newly conceived Secretariat of Public Education.[1] Under his guidance the widespread printing of classics, practical manuals, and textbooks was promoted; libraries were established and teams of teachers sent out into every corner of the country. In order to develop what would become one of the most significant educational campaigns that Latin America had ever known, he required the assistance of dedicated, energetic, and highly respected young educators with original ideas, people like Gabriela.

In 1922, the year she first visited Mexico, Mistral was just thirty-three years old but she was no longer completely unknown to Mexico: her poetry had appeared in its periodicals; her pedagogical writing, such as *La oración de la maestra* (The teacher's prayer) and *La maestra rural* (The rural teacher), was reaching the rural outposts; she was on excellent terms with the Mexican ambassador in Chile, had corresponded with a number of Mexican intellectuals and writers, and was known to Vasconcelos through *El Maestro,* the University of Mexico's educational periodical (Arrigoitia, 11).

As luck would have it—despite the tragedies that haunted her life, Gabriela would have her share of luck, as well—Vasconcelos's timing was providential. Badly paid and misunderstood, Mistral had considered emigration to Argentina two years earlier. By 1922 she was director of the newly inaugurated Liceo N° 6 de Niñas de Santiago, an incredible feat for a teacher without a formal degree. However, according to her 1951 account in a letter to Radomiro Tomic, the school was boycotted and abandoned because she had a falling-out with the undersecretary of public instruction, a former friend (Mistral, *Tan de usted,* 16).

What she didn't mention is that once she had accepted the invitation, conveyed by Mexico's minister of culture in Chile, Enrique González Martínez, she was overwhelmed by a general outpouring of affection and given a grand send-off. Prior to her departure she made it clear that she had no intention of forgetting either her country or her people. She would carry them with her, if not in her suitcase then in her heart, and as a cultural ambassador she hoped to familiarize Mexicans with the work of young Chilean poets (*Excelsior,* 24 July 1922). Furthermore, her own government had charged her with the task of studying the organization of secondary female education in Mexico and she had agreed to do so. At a farewell banquet Mistral assured her audience that "going to Mexico for me is as if I remained in Chile, because I consider America my own great country" (Valenzuela, 66).

On 20 July 1922 Gabriela Mistral stepped off the deck of the *Leerdam* with the two women who had accompanied her from Chile: sculptor Laura Rodig and teacher Amantina Ruiz. She arrived in Veracruz during the rainy season, when the heat is stifling, the vegetation lush, and the air clammy. According to one spectator, Gabriela was smiling in the photographs, "but with that air of seriousness that made her appear a bit gruff" (Rodríguez, 77).

Vasconcelos did not meet her ship because he was in Brazil on official business (Valenzuela, 68). In his stead he sent Palma Guillén, a college teacher and one of his enthusiastic young supporters. She would become Gabriela's official companion during her time in Mexico. Years afterward Palma wrote, "As far as I was concerned she was stuck-up, badly dressed and girdled, with her skirts too long and her shoes too low . . . her hair swept back into a knot at her neck . . . [and] the eyes of a frightened bird" (Guillén, vi).

Getting along with Gabriela was not easy. They shared nothing in common. Palma claimed Gabriela knew nothing of the provinces or of poetry and that she was standoffish, cultivated, vigilant, and courteous, and she left Gabriela to herself (Guillén, v–viii). As a result, she didn't get to know the real Mistral, the lover of coffee and Coca-Cola whom writer Humberto Díaz Casanueva would describe as "a great conversationalist, or rather monologist, who could speak until daybreak, rocking us with her voice and the magic of her imagination and smoking cigarette after cigarette . . . as the peasant women do, until all that remained between her fingers was something resembling a thimble of ash" (12).

Guillén believes she felt alienated from Gabriela because she was a great poet: "Great poets move in an atmosphere that sometimes asphyxiates mere mortals. In Gabriela there was much depth, many dark zones and mysteries . . . dark things that I didn't understand then or that I never understood" (v–viii).

Eventually, Guillén would become a close friend of the woman she described as "Gabriela the clown, an extraordinary impersonator, who could crack joke after joke, making you howl with laughter." She claimed, years later, that she believes Gabriela would have felt more at ease upon her arrival if a troupe of dancing children waving flags had met her at the pier. "But," Guillén adds, "that wasn't the custom in those days" (viii).

Instead, a small, formal delegation, consisting of Guillén, Jaime Torres Bodet, who would assume Vasconcelos's position during the forties, and writers Julio Jiménez Rueda and Bernardo Ortiz de Montellanos, greeted Gabriela in Veracruz. At her next stop, Jalapa, she was met at the train station by a few journalists, the state band, and a local poet who insisted on reciting a poem in her honor (Schneider, 5). Later that morning, 24 July, her train arrived in Mexico City, where she was warmly received. This time there were crowds of children to greet her.

Her first few days were packed with activities. Three thousand children—some accounts put the number at five thousand—were convened in Chapultepec Park. They sang her poems:

Give me your hand and we will dance.
Give me your hand and you will love me.
We will become one flower.
Like a flower and nothing more. (Godoy, xiv)

Then, within days of her arrival she inaugurated La Escuela Hogar para Señoritas Gabriela Mistral (The Gabriela Mistral school and shelter for young ladies), for which she would subsequently prepare a textbook. She was greeted with a standing ovation and showered with flowers.

A woman's noblest, most significant contribution to her school and society is as a wife and mother, she told the crowd of eight hundred students. She added, "I want to tell you how excited I was when I learned that in the plateau of Mexico, in a land I had only dreamed of, there is a girls' school named for me." "She was close to tears," the *Heraldo de México* reporter wrote (30 July 1922). "God gave me a gift of many souls, an immense garland of souls . . . but the gift of a soul is divine by excellence and terrible in its significance. The gift of so many souls is like a Christmas for my heart" (*El Universal,* 30 July 1922).

Nevertheless, one incident, described by sculptor Laura Rodig, was among the most moving. During a ceremony held in Mexico's main square, adjacent to the spot where the Aztec empire's ceremonial center had once stood, a barefoot Indian knelt before Mistral, bowed his head, and kissed her hand. This symbolic gesture acknowledged their common heritage and her effort on behalf of his people (Valenzuela, 69).

No wonder her first letters from Mexico were so effusive: "[The Mexicans demonstrate an] absolute simplicity, an affectionate simplicity, which is the hardest virtue to find in my Chilean race. . . . They have won my heart" (in Valenzuela, 66).

When she was hired her duties had not been well defined, and it was assumed she would spend her first days in the capital making contacts and settling down. But, according to Vasconcelos, early in the morning following her arrival in Mexico, Mistral presented herself at the Ministry of Education and asked how she could be of service (Iglesias and Garrido, 43).

No doubt, she would have had Vasconcelos's support no matter what her decision, but because she believed Mexico City's culture "was sufficiently elevated so as not to require a foreigner's assistance," she decided instead to work outside the capital. Apparently she had considered offering her services to the Escuela Gabriela Mistral but was discouraged when she learned their ideological tendencies clashed with her own. (They favored the use of birth control [Valenzuela, 73].) Guillén, on the other hand, claims Mistral preferred working in the countryside because "she was terrorized by Mexico City—by the urban ambiance and the commotion—and she had trouble operating in it" (Guillén, vi).

In any case, Mistral joined Vasconcelos's Rural Mission Project and became involved with the traveling library program as well as with the *maestros misioneros,* a hearty band of idealistic young teachers who traveled through the mountains on muleback carrying books and supplies to remote villages and who were charged with educating future teachers through "example, virtue, and intelligence." This meshed completely with Mistral's own vision of what education should be: "Teachers must have saintly virtues and teach brotherhood, love of creation, humanity, peace, and union with God" ("Desolación," xxviii). Guillén wrote: "Like peasants in their fields with sacks of seeds, that's how Vasconcelos sent us out—everywhere—each to do what they knew or to rehearse what they dreamed of doing or to learn, because, in the end, everything was needed by a country famished for bread and culture" (v).

Under ordinary circumstances Gabriela and Palma traveled together, but sometimes Eloisa Jasso, Gabriela's Mexican secretary, accompanied her instead. They took trains or school buses, making their way down unpaved roads, battling dust, drought, and, during the rainy season, floods, to hamlets, towns, and cities throughout the republic: El Chico, Cañón de Tomellín, Acapulco, Guadalajara, Querétaro, Veracruz, Oaxaca, Pátzcuaro, Taxco, Cuernavaca, Atlixco, Puebla. . . . They visited schools in old houses, parishes, and courtyards and slept in hotels, orphanages, or old age homes. Occasionally, they would sleep on the bus or the school inspector or rural schoolteacher would find them a bed, and during their journeys, Gabriela met some of the people who would become lifelong friends: Anita and Dora Busta-mante and Lolita Arriaga among them.[2]

Upon her arrival in a small town, Gabriela would sit down on a bench in the main plaza and read the newspaper out loud to the people who clustered around her. This provoked conversation and helped es-tablish ties between the teachers and townspeople. During her visits she gave talks on the meaning of teaching, on the preparation of teachers, on the goals of the new schools, on libraries, on the teaching of history and geography, and about Chile. She entered classrooms, watched teach-ers at work, chatted with them, and made it a point to speak to every-one who would listen.

Her hectic two years of travel throughout the country were inter-spersed with brief periods in Mexico City, where she had rented a small, sparsely furnished house in the Mixcoac neighborhood. She gave conferences, inaugurated schools and libraries—a few in her own name—elaborated pedagogical projects, received visitors, and wrote (Schneider, 7).

Many of the poems and articles she produced during this period were published in Mexico and elsewhere, but a number were written expressly for inclusion in what was to become her major writing project during these two years, *Lecturas para mujeres,* a textbook for the Es-cuela Gabriela Mistral. Originally conceived by Vasconcelos as a book for girls, Gabriela proposed, instead, an anthology of collected writings that would become a guide for women of the future.

According to some, Vasconcelos had an ulterior motive: in his ca-pacity as minister of education he had encouraged a significant num-ber of women, many from the conservative upper classes, to attend universities, enter the teaching profession, and collaborate with him in his program. As a result, he had been severely criticized. By encouraging the publication of a book devoted to "female readings" and instilling "feminine values" he may have been hoping to counteract some of that criticism. (Ironically, if this was the case, his plan may have backfired: Gabriela was an unmarried, independent, and outspoken woman, regarded by some as a threat. Her detractors claimed this damaged her credibility.)

What made *Lecturas para mujeres* unique was not only its focus on women and its affirmation of maternity, filial love, and the home, but its attempt to reach women from humble backgrounds, who might otherwise have had no other contact with the humanities. As a result, she chose writers not only for their subject matter and stylistic simplicity but for their ability to write well: Rabindranath Tagore, Charles Baudelaire, John Ruskin, Rubén Darío, José Martí, Paul de Saint-Victor, Amado Nervo, José Vasconcelos, Paul Fort, Santiago Rusiñol, and, of course, Gabriela Mistral. Approximately ten percent of the material she wrote herself, and much of it focused on Latin America and Mexico: she recorded her impressions of the Indian, his culture and way of thinking, and wrote about Mexican heroes, the Indian women with their "skirts shaped like roses" (Mistral, *Lecturas,* 61), and the caves of Cacahuamilpa, "as blind as Milton" (Mistral, *Lecturas,* 88). (Now in its eighth edition, the book continues to be read throughout the country.)

One would suppose she would become, during her time in Mexico, an ever greater object of veneration, but such was not the case. According to Vasconcelos, "An old evil of ours is xenophobia. As always happens in these cases her presence provoked resentment. Envious little teachers attacked her because she was a foreigner" (Iglesias and Garrido, 44). Rumors sprung up: Gabriela didn't do anything in Mexico except travel and make a lot of money. In truth, although her expenses were covered, she lived modestly, her salary barely equivalent to what she'd earned in Chile. In fact, her rank was lower: In Chile she had been a school director; in Mexico she was only a school inspector.[3]

Her critics asked, Why should a foreigner be brought to Mexico when local teachers were so much better informed about local problems? Surely there was no shortage of first-rate talent to complete the task, they insisted. What could she possibly know that they didn't? After it became known that Vasconcelos had named a school after her and commissioned a statue by sculptor Ignacio Asúnsolo, the attacks worsened. "I did what I could to keep Gabriela from finding out about such meanness," Palma Guillén wrote (xiii).

Despite this, Gabriela became aware of the resentment directed against her even before *Lecturas para mujeres* was finished. Her disappointment and pain come through in the introduction, which begins with the phrase "Words by the foreigner" and continues "I received, some months ago, from the secretary of public education of Mexico, the task of compiling a book of scholastic readings. I understood that a text should be produced by the nation's teachers and not by a foreigner, and I have compiled this work only for the Mexican school that bears my name. I feel this is within my right and, furthermore, that I have the obligation to leave a tangible keepsake of my lessons" (xiii).

The introduction is dignified, with none of the effusion and warmth that characterized so much of her writing. It is a self-effacing answer—almost an apology—to her critics. Placed in context—this was the woman who dreamed of a united Hispanic America free of borders in which work and thought could circulate freely—one can't help but sense Mistral's hurt. She referred to herself as "the little Chilean teacher" and instead of signing her name, ended the introduction with the words *la Recopiladora*, the Compiler.

According to Palma Guillén, Gabriela was "so mistreated, so unjustly attacked and always so alone," despite having edited a brilliant work (x). As to the quality of her work, Gabriela disagreed: "I think only a third of my book is any good. I don't think I'll write any more verses for children. . . . I go from being simple to being simpleminded" (in Iglesias and Garrido, 17, 21).

Rather than wait until the end of the year—her contract expired in

November 1924—she rapidly terminated *Lecturas*. By then the situation had changed drastically: Vasconcelos had resigned from his position and Plutarco Elías Calles, who replaced Alvaro Obregón as president of Mexico, was less sympathetic to educational reform and subsequently many programs were dropped.[4]

In a personal inventory, probably written shortly before leaving the country, Mistral took stock of her losses and gains during her time in Mexico. The woman who composed this document was certainly disillusioned and somewhat bitter, yet still capable of astonishing objectivity: "I have . . . been hurt and filled with grief. My stubbornly personal character irritates. I don't want to change it. Now, less than ever, am I willing to compromise." She also recognized that "the manifestations toward me were exaggerated but, even lessening their spontaneity and their justice, I still retain a large amount of confidence in my strength. I know I haven't spoken to people in vain. . . . I was seduced at the beginning by [their] sweetness but this has faded slowly. I've seen that many times the gallantry is banal, and I sometimes miss the Chilean sincerity, frankness."

On the other hand, she claims that in Chile: "When I speak of my verses, they speak of my birth and throw my rural school in my face," whereas Mexico was more democratic. But both were disappointing in their narrowly nationalistic outlooks: "in Chilean flowers I'll only see flowers and in Chilean flesh I'll only see flesh," she promises, thus reiterating her commitment to a universal worldview.

Yet her conclusions are by no means entirely negative, and she tallies up the good things along with the bad. She feels she has been able to study the landscape as never before ("as if they had lifted my eyelids") and claims to have acquired a growing respect for Mexico's cultural values. She speaks, as well, of profound gratitude for the affectionate and generous hospitality of its people, their natural refinement and sensibility, and the recognition she has received: "One day I found myself with a name that is more or less respected in the continent. It comforts me after fighting for so long." She adds, "This is my only happiness, that I could eat on any American soil, and that misery is a little farther from my door. This gives me tranquility, something I've never had in my life" (in Iglesias and Garrido, 17, 21).

There were other things as well: While in Mexico she wrote at least thirty-four texts and some poetry; she formed lifelong friendships with Mexican writers and intellectuals like Alfonso Reyes, Antonio Castro Leal, and Enrique González Martínez; through her contact with Vasconcelos and Guillén she was exposed to the Greek and Latin classics; and through the influence of the latter, she regained her Catholic faith.

By the end of the summer of 1924 Gabriela would leave behind not only Mexico but her teaching career as well, devoting herself primarily to journalism and diplomacy. Her lifelong pilgrimage had begun. She did return to Mexico on several occasions, most notably between 1948 and 1950, when she lived, almost exclusively, in Veracruz. She had received the Nobel prize by then, the only Latin American woman to do so. Upon her arrival, Mexico rolled out the red carpet: bands played, children pelted her with flowers, and local scribes recited poems they had written in her honor (Schneider, 5).

Poor Gabriela. Whether in Mexico or abroad she would always labor under one handicap or another: aside from being submitted to the worst sort of doggerel, she was falsely portrayed by the press and, in turn, by the public. She became a legend, a simplified version of herself, based not on truth, but on standards imposed by others: She was stereotyped as the young female poet, sensitive and vulnerable, disillusioned in love, fraught by tragedy, and alone with her memories, when, in fact, she was competent and pragmatic, a true humanist, driven by a mission.

Of her time in Mexico she would write: "I lived according to my own standards and truths; teaching, I was always master of myself; I expressed my agreement with my circumstances and surroundings but also my disagreement. My way of working was not imposed upon, and I was fortunate to be able to choose. They took care not to overwork me. . . . Mexico was my country too" (in Arrigoitia, 13).

Occasionally an interviewer would capture her essence, as did the journalist who wrote, "Those who fail to distinguish believe poets live with their heads in the clouds but, in truth, Gabriela Mistral is a thinker; she walks with both feet on the ground" (*El Universal,* 30 July 1922). (What he forgot to mention was that she almost always carried a suitcase.)

Notes

All translations are mine.

1. In 1929 Vasconcelos ran for the presidency on the National Party ticket in a popular pro-democracy movement. When the official candidate was sworn in, Vasconcelos called for an armed uprising, was briefly jailed, and, upon his release, went into exile. On returning to Mexico in 1940, he became a spokesman for the fascists and director of their magazine *El Timón* (Musacchio, 2131).
2. Guillén mentions that when Gabriela died thirty-five years later, she received condolence notes from people who had known her during this period (vii).
3. On the other hand Hernán Díaz Arrieta (pseud. Alone), with whom she corresponded, claimed she earned three times as much.
4. At the time, Vasconcelos believed Gabriela had approached Elías Calles in an attempt to remain in Mexico; Gabriela claimed Vasconcelos was incapable of dialogue without conflict. In any case they had a serious falling out. Not until 1953 would they exchange a "reconciliatory embrace."

Works Cited

Arrigoitia, Luis de. *Pensamiento y forma en la prosa de Gabriela Mistral.* Río Piedras: Universidad de Puerto Rico, 1989.
Díaz Casanueva, Humberto, ed. *Gabriela Mistral.* Jalapa: Universidad Veracruzana, 1980.

Godoy, Lucila Alcagaya (Gabriela Mistral). *Gabriela Mistral en Mexico: Premio Nobel de la Literatura*. Mexico D.F.: Enciclopedica Popular. Secretaría de Educación, 1945.

Guillén de Nicolau, Palma. Introduction to *Lecturas para mujeres* by Gabriela Mistral, v–xxviii. Mexico City: Editorial Porrúa, 1997.

Iglesias, Augusto, and Luis Garrido. *Vasconcelos, Gabriela Mistral, y Santos Chocano: Un filósofo y dos poetas en la encrucijada*. Mexico City: Clásica Selecta Editora Librera, 1967.

Mistral, Gabriela. *Desolación. Ternura. Tala. Lagar*. Mexico City: Editorial Porrúa, 1998.

———. *Lecturas para mujeres*. Mexico City: Editorial Porrúa, 1997.

———. *Tan de usted: Epistolario de Gabriela Mistral con Alfonso Reyes*. Comp. Luis Vargas de Saavedra. Santiago: Hachette/Ediciones Universidad Católica de Chile, 1990.

Musacchio, Humberto. *Diccionario enciclopédico de México: Ilustrado*. Mexico City: Andrés Léon, 1989.

Pellicer, Carlos. *Siete sonetos por Gabriela Mistral: Homenaje*. Mexico City: Universidad Nacional Autónoma de México, 1957.

Rodríguez Valdez, Gladys. *Invitación a Gabriela Mistral: Presentación y selección*. Mexico City: Tierra Firme, Fondo de Cultura Económica, 1990.

Schneider, Luis Mario. *Gabriela Mistral: Itinerario veracruzano*. Veracruz: Biblioteca Universidad Veracruzana, 1991.

Valenzuela Fuenzalida, Alvaro M. "México y Chile: Gabriela y Vasconcelos." *Revista de educación* (October 1990): 64–69.

Chapter 10

Gabriela Mistral and Brazil
A Journey of Fortitude

Ana Pizarro
Translated by Nancy Abraham Hall

THERE ARE FEW STUDIES of Gabriela Mistral's years in Brazil. Curiously, her time in Mexico has long been viewed as her greatest period of intellectual growth, especially with regard to her connection to Latin America as a whole. And yet, Mistral stayed in Mexico only briefly—first for three months and later for two years—but she made several trips to Brazil and lived there for five years. Evidently, the importance critics attach to the poet's Mexican years rests on two factors. First, Mexico was experiencing domestic changes of international consequence during the creative phase of its revolution. Mistral went to Mexico to participate in José Vasconcelos's educational project, and enthusiastic crowds greeted her at the airport even though she was only thirty-three years old and had yet to publish her first book. By the time she moved to Brazil, on the other hand, she was a mature thinker with much of her important work behind her. As she assumed her post at the Chilean consulate in Brazil, she was welcomed as a respected intellectual. Well connected to other writers and to contemporary literature, she lived there during the second Vargas administration, a key period in Brazilian political and cultural history.

Another reason why Mistral's biographers and literary critics tend to emphasize Mexico over Brazil is Hispanic America's general lack of knowledge about the Portuguese-speaking nation. One need only peruse bibliographies to notice a veritable black hole from 1940 to 1945, precisely the years that Mistral spent in Brazil. And yet, during that very period, she experienced life crises and achieved important milestones, including the death of her son and the announcement of her Nobel prize.

On 10 December 1945, Mistral received the Nobel prize in Sweden. The date marked the end of her association with the Brazilian consulate, as the prize meant new opportunities for travel to various places around the world where she would be honored. Before leaving Brazil for the award ceremony in Stockholm, she told a Reuters reporter: "The New World has been honored through me. Therefore, this victory belongs not to me, but to America" (Samatán, 393).[1]

This statement, which could be taken as just another pro–Hispanic American affirmation, implied something different. It contained an idea that few intellectuals held at the time, an idea that Mistral concretized during her stay in the Portuguese-speaking sector of the continent: the notion that Latin America, in the south, consisted of two cultural blocks, the Hispanic and the Brazilian.

What did the years in Brazil mean to Mistral? How did they influence the direction in which she grew? How did she fit into or remain apart from that cultural universe? What consideration does this period deserve? These are the questions I will address below.

The Chilean writer lived in Brazil during a period fraught with political, cultural, and social difficulties for that nation: the second administration of the populist and dictatorial Getúlio Vargas. In power from his 1937 coup d'état until 1945, Vargas established a new, more authoritarian constitution, the Estado Novo, backed by a huge, fascist-style propaganda machine that constantly raised fears of an imminent invasion by a foreign power (Henriques). The government worked hard to project an image of a homogenous society, what Marilena Chauí has termed "a body organically articulated" (cited by Lenharo), immersed in a fictional universe that ran counter to the rest of the world and to reality. Based on cynicism, lies, denunciation, and torture, the system exercised propaganda and censorship, and the fiction of good government was maintained through a wide variety of civic demonstrations and cultural expositions. An incipient culture industry reached the public by means of phonograph recordings, carnival parades, and song lyrics. The government also developed ways of mobilizing labor, as outlined in handbooks distributed to workers. Schools assumed strategic importance in regard to social control. Behind it all, Getúlio Vargas pulled the strings, as he affixed his name to countless institutions and encouraged his life story to be widely published. The whole society seemed to look into what one analyst has called Getúlio's "luminous, opaque eyes [*vivos ou entre-fechados*]" (Vasconcelos).

An admirer of Hitler and Mussolini, with whom he shared domestic policies, Vargas saw the need for a neighborly relationship with the United States. To this end he allowed for the possibility of U.S. military installations in the northeast of Brazil, and in 1942 he joined the Allies in declaring war against the Axis, despite his admiration for the latter.

Under the difficult historical and political circumstances of a strongly nationalistic discourse, Brazil's incorporation into the war, and an authoritarian environment, Mistral fulfilled her duties at the consulate. Formally, the Chilean government maintained a position of neutrality. Following trips to the state of Minas Gerais and visits to its capital, Belo Horizonte, the poet reported to her government, "Chile occupied my attention during my ten days in that capital, despite the disadvantages anywhere in Brazil that stem from our international stance at present."[2]

Nevertheless, the Chilean intellectual positioned herself clearly within the political landscape and the most profound cultural life of the country. In this way she connected herself to the Portuguese American world, and perceived it as a community linked to Hispanic America. This was an essential element that enriched her discourse during her years in Brazil.

Full of hope for future communication and exchanges between the two Americas, the Hispanic and the Portuguese, she wrote: "One day our nations will celebrate the date of our idiomatic exchange. It is indeed a remarkable turning point, like the beginning of all great highways, moving forward, propelled by the winds of honor" (Mistral, 28).

The driving need to represent America became a trademark of Gabriela Mistral's writing. She consistently focused on representation. It is necessary to see this gesture as a permanent source of authority in her discourse: she represented the poor peasants of the Elqui valley, the indigenous race, the Republic of Chile, womanhood (*el mujerío*), and now America. She lived at a time and in a setting in which intellectual women faced difficult obstacles, especially when they did not conform to canonical images. As they emerged, they needed legitimacy. This "daughter of a new nation," Mistral claimed for herself the role of representative—and the emphasis was important—of one culture with two languages. She explained, "Due to fortunate circumstances beyond my comprehension, I am at this moment the direct voice of the poets of my race, and the indirect voice of two noble languages: Castilian and Portuguese" (in Samatán, 398).

As a writer, she did not call herself the bearer or defender of Hispanic culture alone, as did most of her contemporaries. This is an interesting point since as it makes it clear how ahead of her time she was. During Mistral's life the separation of the two worlds, the Hispanic and the Brazilian, was very clear, a matter of two halves of a totality that knew almost nothing about one other. It is necessary to understand that Mistral's statement could have been made only in the context of her experience in and knowledge about Brazil.

During 1937, Mistral traveled to several different cultural missions throughout the Americas. In 1939 she became affiliated with the Chilean consulate in Niterói, Brazil, and without planning to, remained there for five months. Brazil struck her as an appropriate place to reestablish contact with nature and the land, a tranquil place that could offer a quality of life unavailable in war-torn Europe. Living on the Continent, she felt, would require a certain amount of courage and youthful energy that she no longer possessed. Brazil could become her haven if she bought a piece of land located somewhere as restful as her childhood home in the Elqui valley of Chile. With Europe out of the question for now and her relationship with Chile clouded, Mistral began to see Brazil as a possible refuge, a place where she could take up farming. One biographer wrote, "She saw in Brazil a way to return to the peasantry, encouraged by the example of other intellectuals like Bernanos who, in a similar manner, had fled urban centers" (Samatán, 359).

Soon Mistral moved from Niterói to Petrópolis, the city of imperial history, where don Pedro I had resided. The strong cultural legacy of Petrópolis, and in particular its religious imagery associated with the empire, appealed to Mistral. An unusual place of great esthetic dignity, the city is seductively close to Rio de Janeiro. But for Mistral, the most important aspect of her new home was its location within a narrow valley, surrounded by mountains—like Elqui, only smaller—as well as its temperate climate, so much more pleasant for someone from Chile than the humid air of Rio.

Personal reasons eventually lead Mistral to consider buying land and a farmhouse on the outskirts of São Paulo or in Rio Grande do Sul. While she was in Brazil, Mistral lived with her Puerto Rican friend Consuelo (Connie) Saleva, who held a teaching degree, served as her personal secretary, and took care of the day-to-day matters with which Mistral was unable to cope. A third member of the household was Juan Miguel Godoy (Yin Yin) whom Mistral called her adopted son. Of course, today Godoy's true identity is known, as confirmed by Doris Dana, Mistral's final secretary and friend. Mistral was unable to publicly acknowledge Juan Miguel as her biological child, knowing that neither the public in Chile nor Latin America as a whole would accept the truth. As she would throughout her life, Mistral used subterfuge on this issue in order to lead the life she envisioned for herself, and to be able to claim what she needed. She used the "strategies of the weak," and avoided a situation that otherwise would have limited her life.

As she arrived in Brazil in 1939 from Nice at the outset of war, Mistral began to effectively frame the notion of an "Americanist" spirit, a concept that has always inspired her. When she had arrived in Brazil two years earlier, she used the language she learned while living in Portugal to declare, "Following a long absence, which never caused a diminution in my Americanism, I have returned as a daughter restored to the light, to American soil. Finding myself among you is not that different from living in Chile. I summon the one America, which is greater than we ourselves can possibly say or believe."[3]

This internal Iberian American connection became Mistral's main political and intellectual focus in Brazil. She assumed that there was a wide informational gap between the two Americas: "We know each other very little although we love one another well. . . . Let us do anything other than live the indolent love that Creole countries have for one another or the blind love of complete ignorance."[4] She channeled her consular work, then, in two directions: first, she communicated information about Chile, its literature and art as well as general information of a historical and cultural nature; second, she was in contact with the Chilean Foreign Affairs Office, sending it information that appeared in various newspapers and journals, such as *La Tribuna de Petrópolis, O Jornal de Petrópolis* (which she described as "literary and popular"), *A pequenha illustraçao, O Jornal de Rio de Janeiro,* the important *A Manha* (also based in Rio), and *Diretrizes* magazine, among others.

As a public speaker, Mistral was interested in reaching a popular audience, the social base. For this reason, and along with her deep and lifelong concern for children, she worked on behalf of schools and public libraries in Brazil. Through her consular connections, she requested donations of books from the Chilean Ministry of Foreign Affairs. She ordered basic books, such as those used in high school courses—books with simple language that could be read by students and workers and that could even be of use to writers. The beneficiaries of her efforts included the Biblioteca Municipal de Petrópolis and the Escuela de Perfeccionamiento de Minas Gerais, where she lay the groundwork for the Hispanic American Library. This last endeavor received support from Cecilia Meireles and from prominent poet and intellectual Manuel Bandeira, with whom Mistral discussed this and other matters, as she supported his chair at the Universidad de Rio de Janeiro, a post he occupied until his death.

Mistral's relationship with the Ministry was often pedagogical in nature. She filed reports with the Ministry about behavior and attitudes conducive to modern cultural policies. She recommended, for example, that they distribute Benjamín Subercaseaux's book *Chile, o, una loca geografía* because of its critical point of view: "Any book of propaganda, no matter its country of origin, that offers self-praise rather than critique, is poorly written overall, and is primarily self-interested, will draw fire, but will not be read. The foreign reader will trust neither the information nor the statistics it contains."[5]

When she moved to Brazil, Mistral had some personal goals in mind (among them, to reconnect to the land as a way of reconnecting to reality), as well as political and intellectual ones. The former became clear through her consular work, and in her report on the visit of U.S. writer Waldo Frank, in which she wrote: "In my modest judgment, Iberian America owes a debt of gratitude to Waldo Frank," the only Yankee writer whose books and articles offered her a unique, broad, and fine self-portrait. She owed a debt of gratitude to Waldo Frank for a continued defense of our culture, which the United States challenges. She should thank him as well, because he had given all this without official subsidies of any kind. Frank was an entirely free man, and had not made money by writing for minorities.[6]

This tendency to affirm American connections, especially those concretized in the connection between the Portuguese and Spanish languages and cultures, inspired Mistral to compose a beautiful speech, which later became an article on Hernando de Magallanes, or Ferdinand Magellan. Invited to christen a new airplane named for the Portuguese navigator, she sketched the profile of the explorer and his transcendence: "The supreme Argonaut became part of the planet in such a way as to make praise seem useless and actually constraining. The name Magellan is a pure storm that follows one long track around the earth itself. Our Iberian nations control at least three of the four elements known to the Greeks: air, land, and sea. One needs eulogies to such a man, connected to the planet as an integral element in his own right."[7]

Just as the Chilean writer managed to feel at home amid great expectations in Brazil, so that nation generously embraced her. As the Divine One, she seemed to need no introduction. An article by E. Feder praised the decision of the Chilean government to honor Brazil with her presence: "How much honor the state bestows upon itself when it sees in the artist's creative activity alone a public function worthy of being included as such in the prosaic lists of its budget. What a lovely idea the governors of Santiago have had, to see the very presence of the poet in a friendly nation as a valued function worthy of as much esteem as consuls in the fields of business, emigration, and the protection of national interests."[8]

The impressive reception accorded Mistral by newspapers, radio, educational institutions, and writers during her stay in Minas Gerais was documented by a considerable number of articles in the local papers of the day. She arrived on 16 September 1942, and stayed until the twenty-sixth. The papers noted that the famous Chilean writer spoke with intelligence about poetry, underscoring its beauty and utility for humanity. In her public appearances she drew parallels between Chile and Minas as mountainous places. On 3 December 1940, in a letter to Drummond de Andrade, whom she greets with "admiring and affectionate friendship," she wrote, "I have been thinking that I will be able to communicate well with the miners: I too am a creature of the mountains, perhaps the most arid highlands of our Andes."[9]

This disregard for the established barriers between classes was not viewed negatively by Mistral's hosts but rather served to increase the respect most had for her. Mistral made no concessions to other conventions, either. For example, as a modern professional, she deplored literary circles based solely on ties of friendship and mediocrity. On this and other matters, such as her political views regarding World War II, she was unequivocal, despite any long-remembered personal pain her stands occasioned.

Mistral's time in Brazil was also eventful in personal terms. Two situations developed in the wake of 1942, a year full of intense professional activity. In addition, the Brazilian years are remembered for the unraveling of one of Mistral's oldest and dearest projects. Her almost daily connection to the intellectual world was maintained through her correspondence and a modest social life.

During Mistral's time in Brazil, the universe of comfortable middle-class women seemed to lie somewhere between the French-influenced model of the *femme savante* and the more restrictive ideal of the woman who embraced the positivist spirit of the republic and Varguism. The motto of Varguism—Home, school, and nation—turned some institutions and figures into strategic means of social control. An important propaganda push led to ideological messages appearing on posters, stamps, and coins. Within this framework, the images of women and the norms of sexuality put forth by the machine were intensely repressive, a prolongation of the climate of domination that emanated from the state and conditioned Mistral's world. Regional loyalty, monogamous marriage, patriarchal morality, and sexual repression achieved cult status within Brazilian society (Henriques). As one researcher notes, within this ideology "the body is devalued; the senses are the most degraded part of human beings. The spiritualization of the body and of love go hand and hand with a hatred of sexuality, while misogyny based in patriarchal values is added to the mix" (Vasconcelos). It is apparent, then, that within this climate Mistral's sense of herself as a mother as well as her attitudes toward her own body and sexuality were conditioned in ways similar to those she had experienced as a young person in Chile.

Mistral did not lead the social life of a diplomat. She accepted invitations only from institutions that met with her approval and agreed to perform ceremonial tasks she considered worthwhile, such as the christening of the airliner mentioned above. She visited public and agricultural schools, such as Viçosa in Minas, took an interest in industrial development, and was particularly attentive to information that could be useful in Chile's growth in that direction.

Gabriela Mistral's personal life developed along three fronts while she lived in Brazil. First, there was her relationship with Connie Saleva, with whom she lived and who took care of the details of everyday life, something Mistral seemed unable to do. Second, she had her son, Juan Miguel, a student at the agricultural school in Minas Gerais, with her. Finally, there were regular meetings and conversations with certain writers to whom I will refer later.

Mistral had left prewar Europe and returned to South America because she felt it to be a more suitable environment in which to raise a child. Despite her tireless efforts in Europe, including extensive travel, she and others were unable to impede the inexorable spread of political evil there, and so she chose to leave. But when Brazil entered the war, she once again faced the conflict's proximity. On 22 September 1940, in a letter to Henriqueta Lisboa, she wrote, "This horrible hour for the world depresses me a lot and has me living the tragedy day to day. Therefore I need the help of letters from souls stronger and better than myself to get on with life."[10]

Mistral's interest in Brazil had been persistent. In 1936 she wrote from Lisbon to writer, diplomat, prolific narrator, and poet Ribeiro Couto, with whom she shared an interest in common folk, the anonymous lives of people in villages and suburbs, and who also published in French. She requested of Couto specific information about real estate (prices, locations) for some Chilean friends. Like her friends, she confided, she too thought "of being able to live one day to the Brazilian countryside, a grand dream of mine." Earlier, on 4 January 1936, she had written to Couto: "I have left the Castilians to themselves, in the desert, with their castilianization of the language, etc. As proof of my affection, I will tell you that I put in for a transfer to either São Paulo or Lisbon. This time they have pleased me with Portugal, but another time they will do the same with Brazil."[11]

Mistral's plans to permanently settle in Brazil began to crumble for two reasons. Although she could well afford to buy land, she lacked the skills needed to create and run a business that would allow her to maintain such a property. Moreover, her hopes did not take Juan Miguel's true interests into account. The teenager was simply not interested in country life. Having grown up in France, he did not understand Brazilian ways and therefore did not adjust well to the new location. Mistral's dream went unfulfilled.

Events soon take her in a different direction, however. Her health suffered a permanent setback. She did feel better in Petrópolis than in Niterói, with its hot, humid climate. In Petrópolis she was able to breathe mountain air once again, and acknowledged its appropriateness for her constitution. Emotionally, however, she was caught completely off guard by the double suicide of her friend Stephen Zweig and his wife, who could not bear the onset of war in Europe and the suffering in store for the Jewish people. The Zweigs were close friends of the poet, and she often visited their house, only three blocks from her own in Petrópolis. Not long after the death of the Zweigs, Mistral's relationship with Juan Miguel also began to deteriorate. A troubled teenager, the young man behaved in ways that indicate he was not at all comfortable with how his life was going. Tragically, he too committed suicide, and the writer suffered a second devastating loss within a short period.

Thus, Mistral's time in Brazil came to a close in 1945, under much different circumstances than those she imagined when she arrived. Cecília Meireles wrote:

Gabriela's heart was made increasingly bitter by the suffering and many misfortunes that occurred while she was in Brazil, including the frightening war. Whenever we visited her, in Rio or in Petrópolis, we were sure to find her smoking, seated with a cup of tea, surrounded by people from all corners of the world who had fled persecution and chaos. They all found a comforting welcome at Gabriela's, where they

were able to sip tea, listen to their hostess's long, seductive mono-
logues, and forget the atrocities that were devouring the earth. (12)

When the Nobel prize came her way at the end of 1945, Mistral was
unable to express the joy with which she might have received such
news five years earlier, when she had just arrived in Brazil. "At the end
of her Brazilian stay, Mistral needed to be surrounded by people who
understood her, and who were able to find the essence of who she really
was amid the innumerable accidents that darkened and disfigured her"
(Meireles, 13).

Mistral's social consciousness found its reflection in Brazilian literature around 1937. With prominent authors of the day she shared an
interest in vindicating the dispossessed, the have-nots, the poor of
Latin America—something she tirelessly promoted in her discourse.
Within this same period, a new line of inquiry emerged among thinkers and essayists, related to the analysis of the social sciences, which
attempted to explore the meaning, history, and spirit of Brazilian society. Essays such as "Raízes do Brasil" (1936) by Sergio Buarque de
Holanda, "Casa Grande e Senzala" (1933) by Gilberto Freyre, and
work by Caio Prado Jr. on the political evolution of Brazil demonstrated this tendency, reflecting on the country and its character by
researching its history and behavior.

We do not know to what extent Mistral might have been familiar
with these writings, today considered classics, about Brazilian culture
and society. But clearly, the concerns they raised were in the literary
and cultural air, and they dovetailed with Mistral's own questions
about research into the nature of identity. She too felt a need to name
in order to some way profile the traits, characters, landscapes, flora,
and fauna of one's own land. This is easy to see in her *Recados,* among
other writings, and especially in her *Poema de Chile.*

In 1930 a new phase of Brazilian modernism was initiated by a group
of poets for whom the early, heroic phase of the movement had already
established a language of renovation and an eye toward nationalism.

This was the group to which Mistral became directly linked when she first arrived in Brazil in 1937, and again when she returned to live there from 1939 until 1945. Among this group of poets Mistral found writers who shared her aesthetic code, including the rejection of solemn language, an interest in everyday life, and the revolutionary simplicity achieved after an initial period of experimentation. In contrast to some early *modernistas* who were fascinated by machines and urban life, Mistral was a rural being, and her gestures, sensibility and evolution developed in that register. That was precisely why she left Niterói and Rio de Janeiro to live in the agrarian and mountainous Petrópolis, the beautiful city that conserved the Imperial Palace where don Pedro had taken refuge from Rio's heat, amid banana trees and tropical plants.

This group of poets included Cecília Meireles, one of the writers closest to Mistral and one of the first friends she made upon arriving in Brazil. Their friendship was a permanent one based above all on a sense of shared work. Like Mistral, Meireles had been educated to be an elementary school teacher. She attended the Instituto de Educação do Rio de Janeiro, and lived in that city permanently, traveling abroad often, including once to the University of Texas, where she taught in 1940. Meireles published at a young age and was attracted to the modernist movement as early as 1922. Her poetry was of an intimate nature that, according to Alfredo Bosi, "orients the imaginative processes toward shadows, the indefinite, if not toward a sense of absence or nothingness" (Bosi, 489). The musicality of her verses, as well as the assured posture of her poetic elaboration stand out in a unique book published in 1953, *Romancero da inconfidencia,* a lyrical epic in which she evokes episodes from the history of Brazil since its discovery. This book was a sort of "Canto General" of Brazil in which Meireles captured history through multiple voices that speak of love, pain, heroism; that confess and doubt; voices of ghosts that narrate, in rhymed and unrhymed lines of poetry, short and long measures, an unfolding story in verse that places the reader between presence and legend.

Mistral was interested in Brazil even before she got there. She had requested consular appointments to both Brazil and Portugal and while assigned to the latter, had learned the language that later would allow her to give speeches and participate in public meetings in Brazil with fluency. She held the Portuguese language and its literature in high regard and not only became interested in the classics of Brazilian literature but also worked to reshape its canon to include the nation's women writers by incorporating and evaluating the work of new authors.

In general, women writers were able to achieve canonical status in Brazil—as opposed to other Hispanic American countries, and particularly Chile—relatively early in the century. The initiators of the modernista whirlwind included two women artists: Anita Malfatti and Tarsila do Amaral. Brazilian women had a space that was unavailable to their counterparts in either Mistral's country of origin or in Mexico. The relative celerity with which creative women were acknowledged in Brazil, as well as that nation's cultural variety, of which the rest of Latin America still has little knowledge, must have had a favorable impact on the newly arrived Chilean writer.

A second important friendship for Mistral was that of poet Henriqueta Lisboa from Minas Gerais. A professor of literature, poet, and translator, she was the first person elected to the Academia Mineira de Letras in 1968. Having spent her life in Minas Gerais, Lisboa was Mistral's steadfast interlocutor. She organized the trip that the Chilean writer made to Belo Horizonte, a visit widely covered by the press. There, Mistral delivered lectures that were broadcast on local radio stations, granted interviews, and visited a variety of educational institutions.

Minas Gerais was a universe in which Mistral felt at home. Upon her return to the city, she wrote "Pequeño elogio de Belo Horizonte" (Small praise to Belo Horizonte), in which she stated, "I just spent ten days in an aptly named city, whose beautiful and broad horizon delights the eye and the soul. Its dry, sharp air reminds me of the slices of wind we breathe in the Andes. That said, it is also home to the most perfect American roses these old gardening hands have ever had the pleasure to hold."[12]

In that high place, as she would later confide to Carlos Drummond de Andrade, Mistral reconnected with the natural environment, so much like that of her native Elqui, with its mountain air and sweet-smelling flowers. Minas Gerais was a rather special place in the physical and cultural geography of Brazil. On the one hand, its capital, Belo Horizonte, was brand new. On the other, Ouro Prêto and its other towns and villages were full of history. That history encompassed colonial times, including the era of gold, remarkable architecture, artistic development, and the drama of slavery. A symbol of anticolonial rebellion, a place full of contradictions, Minas was home to the Inconfidencia Mineira, the plot discovered by a group of intellectuals and members of the Portuguese army, such as Joaquim José da Silva Xavier, the leader nicknamed Tiradentes. Cecília Meireles wrote about this episode in Brazilian history.

For her farewell speech in Belo Horizonte, Mistral chose to speak about Henriqueta Lisboa's work, including an analysis of her book *O menino poeta*. She called it a miracle of harmony, observing how well the plasticity of the Portuguese language lends itself to children's literature. After reading Lisboa's work for the first time, on 22 September 1940, Gabriela Mistral wrote the following to her future friend: "Your poetry has interested me in your soul, and I never consider a visit a matter of courtesy but rather a slow and sweet approximation to those who interest me most profoundly."[13]

In effect, to read Henriqueta's poetry is to perceive the particular sensibility the two friends had in common, mainly an interest in the world of children on a continent where children's literature did not exist. "In terms of genre, we two have neither grandparents nor parents," Mistral reminds her. There is in Lisboa's work a transcendent humanism—her gaze is religious, like that of her Chilean friend—and an intimacy, two important aspects of Mistral's poetic and intellectual register. Mistral told Lisboa how she felt, not only with regard to what was happening on the world stage, but in her private life as well, and the two women are able to support one another. The death of Mario Andrade deeply affected the poet from Minas, as she was very close to him. With the voice of experience and maturity, Mistral was able to offer her sympathy, as she too had experienced similar tragedy: "I don't think anyone expected 'the liveliest of us all here in Brazil' to die. And yet that is what happened. Because these days what is absurd happens more frequently than before."

It's as if Mistral was reaching across life and pain to access superior spiritual states that even she herself could not imagine. With regard to her son's death, she had previously written to Lisboa, "There will be enough sorrow for years to come. My health only sets itself right for a few days at a time. This death of Yin Yin's has broken the axis of the wheel. I don't know if it is possible to reinvent oneself at fifty-four, my friend."

How could she not feel close to the poet who, after her first book, *Fogo fatuo*, in 1925, published *Enternecimento* in 1929? Lisboa's subsequent books—*Velário* (1936), *Prisioneira da noite* (1941), *O menino poeta* (1943), and *A face lívida* (1945)—are from the time in which she knew Mistral. She sent copies to her friend and received her comments in return. And when she sent Mistral a copy of *A face lívida*, written between 1941 and 1945, Henriqueta included the following note: "I took the liberty of dedicating to you a page whose subject touches us closely: '*As crianças*' [The kids]." Both had in common a great interest in childhood.

The friendship with Henriqueta Lisboa, as with Cecília Meireles, lasted beyond Mistral's stay in Brazil. The friends maintained a permanent communication based not only on affection, but also on a discussion of their work, recent publications, information, and other intellectual concerns. Lisboa translated Mistral's poems and Meireles her articles, sharing and commenting on the difficulties presented by the Chilean's particular use of language. Mistral's positive assessment stood in contrast with the lack of attention Lisboa's work received at home. As her friend Mario de Andrade indicated to Lisboa, "Brazilian critics have demonstrated, at all times, very little perception in regard to poetry."

The dialogue between Mistral and Lisboa is interesting if we keep in mind that it took place during the first half of the century. In it we observe the capacity to establish a clear affective connection in addition to the intellectual one. Formality did not inhibit the expression of feelings, and as a result the letters between the two women writers differed in tone from Mistral's exchanges with Alfonso Reyes, another dear friend. On 18 January 1941, Lisboa wrote to Mistral, "Since I received your letter of the thirty-first [December], I have felt less alone, or more accompanied, in this communion of spirit that is complete consolation for which two spirits live."[14] And later Lisboa confessed, "the punishment of my dissatisfaction, of my great need to be closer to you, and to your spirit."

Mistral's relationship with Drummond de Andrade was more distant. He was a younger poet and she took an interest in his work—an interest that revealed her awareness of the Brazilian avant-garde movement, whose experimentation Mistral understood and defended in a letter to Povina Cavalcanti.[15] Mistral's interest in literature written by Brazilian women was apparent in an interview published in Chilean newspaper *El Mercurio*.

Brazil's great cultural vitality, then, provided Mistral with a very rich intellectual life, and in that country's social orientation she found much to match her own interests. She joined in the literary life of the nation and, through her contributions to national newspapers, informed the rest of the world about Brazil's writers. In turn, she kept Brazilians abreast of developments within Chilean literature. While her personal life was not happy during these years, she achieved success in terms of the political and intellectual goals she had set for herself.

Notes

1. Mistral uses the term *America* to refer to Latin America.
2. Mistral, *Oficio Consular*, 30 September 1942, Archivo de Oficios Consulares, Ministerio de Relaciones Exteriores (Santiago).

3. Mistral, "Gabriela Mistral saúda o Brasil," *A Noite* (Rio de Janeiro), 29 August 1937.
4. Mistral, "Notas culturales del Brasil," *El Universal* (Caracas), 29 July 1941.
5. Mistral, *Oficio Consular*, 31 January 1942. Archivo de Oficios Consulares, Ministerio de Relaciones Exteriores (Santiago).
6. Mistral, "Sobre el viaje de Waldo Frank," *Oficio Consular*, 30 May 1942. Archivo de Oficios Consulares, Ministerio de Relaciones Exteriores (Santiago).
7. Mistral, "O nome de Magalhaes é a interperie pura e una longa trilha que envolve a propria terra" and "Gabriela Mistral e sua notavel peca oratoria," *O Jornal* (Rio de Janeiro), 12 November 1942.
8. E. Feder, *O Jornal* (Rio de Janeiro), 25 November 1942.
9. G. Mistral to D. de Andrade, 3 December 1940, Arquivo-Museo de Literatura Brasileira de Fundação Casa de Rui Barbosa (Rio de Janeiro).
10. G. Mistral to H. Lisboa, 22 September 1940, Arquivo Henriqueta Lisboa, Universidade Federal de Minas Gerais (Belo Horizonte).
11. G. Mistral to R. Couto, Lisboa, 4 January 1936, Arquivo-Museo de Literatura Brasileira de Fundação Casa de Rui Barbosa (Rio de Janeiro).
12. G. Mistral. "Pequeño elogio de Belo Horizonte," *O Jornal* (Rio de Janeiro), 28 November 1942.
13. G. Mistral to H. Lisboa, 22 September 1940, Arquivo Henriqueta Lisboa, Universidade Federal de Minas Gerais (Belo Horizonte).
14. H. Lisboa to G. Mistral, 18 January 1941, Arquivo Henriqueta Lisboa, Universidade Federal de Mina Gerais (Belo Horizonte).
15. G. Mistral to P. Cavalcanti, 30 November 1943, Arquivo-Museo de Literatura Brasileira de Fundação Casa de Rui Barbosa (Rio de Janeiro).

Works Cited

Bosi, Alfredo. *Historia concisa de la literatura brasileña*. Mexico City: Fondo de Cultura Económica, 1982.
Henriques, Affonso. *Ascensão e queda de Getúlio Vargas*. Rio de Janeiro: Distribuidora Record, 1966.
Lenharo, Alcir. *Sacralização da política*. Campinas: Papirus, Editora da Unicamp, 1986.

Meireles, Cecília. "Un poco de Gabriela Mistral." In *Cadernos Brasileiros N°12: Gabriela Mistral y el Brasil.* Santiago: Brazilian Embassy in Chile, 1963.

Mistral, Gabriela. "Dos culturas: Brasil y América." In *Cadernos Brasileiros N°12: Gabriela Mistral y el Brasil.* Santiago: Brazilian Embassy in Chile, 1963.

Pizarro, Ana. "Mistral, ¿qué modernidad?" In *Re-leer hoy a Gabriela Mistral: Mujer, historia, y sociedad en América Latina,* ed. Gastón Lillo and Juan Guillermo Renart. Ottawa: University of Ottawa/Editorial Universidad de Santiago, 1997.

vinte Samatán, Marta Elena. *Los días y los años de Gabriela Mistral.* Puebla, Mexico: Editorial J. M. Cajica Jr., 1973.

Subercaseaux, Benjamín. *Chile, o una loca geografía.* Santiago: Editorial Universitaria, 1973.

Vasconcelos, Gilberto. *A ideologia curupira: Análise do discurso integralista.* São Paulo: Editora Brasiliense, 1979.

Chapter 11

Translating the Hidden Machine
Gabriela Mistral in English

Randall Couch

ALL TRANSLATIONS FAIL. Good translations fail deliberately. That is, they are the record of a conscious series of significant and signifying choices. Poetry, of all literary forms, is most bound up in the materiality of language—thus the truism that no poem can be brought whole from one tongue into another. If a translator begins with the goal of preserving a poem's central and characteristic qualities while sacrificing only the more peripheral, he or she must adopt some process, whether intuitive or systematic, to decide which are which.[1] Such a process involves an act of interpretive reading that tests the translator's command of the capacities—and limitations—of both source and target languages, as well as testing his or her ability to enter fully into the meanings and effects of the poem as written. Since the factors involved differ for each poem and each poet, a review of specific translations can offer insights into the practice of the poet as well as of the translator.

The poems of Gabriela Mistral have not been frequently translated into English. The first significant selection (74 poems) was published in 1957 by Langston Hughes. A bilingual volume of fifty-six different poems appeared in 1971, the work of the poet's friend and literary executor Doris Dana. For more than twenty years these served as the standard English versions, until the 1993 publication of *A Gabriela Mistral Reader,* edited by Marjorie Agosín with translations by Maria Giachetti. The Dana and Giachetti versions do not cover exactly the same material, and both remain useful to English readers. An illustrated version of the cycle "Poemas de las madres," translated by Christiane Jacox Kyle, was issued under the title *Poemas de las madres/The Mothers' Poems* in 1995. Translations of individual poems and small groups have been published in articles, musical settings, and critical monographs, but it remains true that, unlike her countryman and former pupil Pablo Neruda, Gabriela Mistral is not familiar to most English-speaking readers of poetry.

Why should this be? In the Spanish-speaking world, Mistral is a canonical writer, known to most literate people. No doubt many factors affect her reception in English, but we may suspect three in particular. First is the perception that Mistral is the poet of women and children, the schoolteacher-poet. For the last seventy-five years in the United States, elementary education has not played the same nation-building role that it has in Mexico and many other Latin American countries, so this aspect of Mistral's subject matter has lacked the prestige and political sponsorship it enjoyed in parts of the Hispanic world. To the extent that she has been seen as a voice of sentimental or frustrated maternity, tastemakers may not have approached her work seriously. Her influence was, as Max Daireaux put it, not so much a literary one as "a moral influence that works mysteriously on the heart and the mind" (in Bates, xxii).

When Mistral has not been treated as a spokesperson, she has been the poet of personal anguish. Her early reputation in Chile was won by the searing "Sonetos de la muerte" (Sonnets of death) of 1914, a cycle of poems in which the speaker enacts the dissolution brought on by the shock of bereavement. North American poetry about this time was coming under the sway of the cooler sensibility of high modernism, and by midcentury New Critical notions of formalist analysis ruled the academy. While Mistral's work employs certain devices in common with the European surrealists, she did not identify with that school, nor indeed take much interest in it. Not until near the end of her life would the intensely subjective emotion of *Desolación* or parts of *Lagar* become fashionable again in American poetry, and not until the confessional movement of the 1960s would it find equivalent strength.

Finally there is Mistral's style, which Enrique Lihn calls "without precedent . . . and without heirs" (Agosín; in Giachetti, 20). Mistral is capable of a stark simplicity and a hermetic compression of idea; her syntax can be direct or so strained as to be almost impossible to parse. In a single poem her diction may range from the biblically sonorous to the intimate, from the archaic to the earthily demotic. Perhaps most striking, she recombines elements of classical Spanish prosody in a uniquely expressive practice that complicates the tradition without seeking to abandon it. The mixture is as distinctive to the ear in Spanish as Dickinson or Hopkins in English, and like them she was long seen as a magnificent oddity.

All these factors and more influenced the nature and timing of English translations of Mistral's work. Langston Hughes made his book a dozen years after Mistral had been awarded the Nobel prize; it appeared the year of her death. In his introduction he protests diffidence, "hoping that a woman would have" undertaken the task (10). In keeping with his own poetic voice, Hughes was drawn to the folk elements in Mistral's music and the claims of human affection in her matter. He included poems from all the books Mistral published during her lifetime, but over half the pages are devoted to selections from her first volume, *Desolación*.

It is noteworthy that Hughes describes Mistral's poetry as "simple and direct in language, never high-flown or flowery, and much easier, I think, to translate than most poets writing in Spanish" (10). While he included poems of great sadness, he omitted many difficult and complex poems, among them the "Locas mujeres" (Madwomen) cycle. He also left out the "Sonetos de la muerte" because of scruples about the importance of their "word music" and the impossibility of rendering it in English.

Of Mistral's English translators, Hughes is the only one who regularly attempted formal prosodic effects. In general he did not shrink from employing rhyme in his versions. Particularly in the "Canciones de cuna" (Cradle songs), this decision is quite defensible, despite the poverty of English in rhyme words, because the sound of the poems is so vital to their effect. His success is mixed. The lullabies, for example, are among the most metrically regular of Mistral's poems, as befits the genre. In preserving end rhyme and in seeking the most direct locution, however, Hughes sometimes allows both syllable count and the number of stresses to vary greatly from line to line. The result is a syncopated effect that can be lively and charming but that sounds unsonglike in English—and very different from Mistral's rhythm.

For example, from "Corderito" (Little lamb):

Corderito mío,	Little lamb of mine
suavidad callada:	with such softness blessed
mi pecho es tu gruta	your grotto of velvet moss
de musgo afelpada.	is my breast.
Carnecita blanca,	Flesh as white
tajada de luna:	as a moonray is white,
lo he olvidado todo	all else I forget
por hacerme cuna.	to be your cradle tonight.
	(Hughes, 29)

Allowing for differences in performance, Hughes's "numbers" are much less regular than Mistral's. Where Mistral's *hexasílabos* are nearly perfect, with a consistent trochaic pulse, Hughes ranges from three to seven syllables in each of these two stanzas, and though his opening pair initiates a trochaic rhythm, any metrical regularity collapses with the introduction of at least one foot of triple meter in most of the remaining lines. Likewise in the famous "Poema del hijo" (Poem of the son). Mistral's smooth *alejandrinos,* in *cuartetos* employing *rimas conso-nantes llanas y cruzadas* (alternating consonantal rhymes—ABAB), are rendered by Hughes in lines of variable measure, hovering mostly between ten and eleven syllables but ranging from nine to fourteen. His quatrains preserve part of the rhyme scheme, exhibiting accented end rhymes on the even-numbered lines of each stanza.

In contrast to Hughes, Margaret Bates observes in her introduction to Doris Dana's translations that in Mistral, as in "the great Spanish Symbolist poet Antonio Machado, the effect of utter simplicity is backed up by a subtle, complex, hidden machine that extracts from each word, from each sound and accent, its maximum emotional charge. This type of poetry, because of the complexity beneath the surface, is the least translatable" (xv).

Dana herself is clearly aware of this complexity. Her *Selected Poems of Gabriela Mistral* intends to show us a serious poet. Her selection is balanced more evenly than Hughes's across the four volumes Mistral published in her lifetime. She omits poems that have appeared previously in English translation, and she deliberately strives to show Mistral's stylistic development and a representative range of subject matter (xxvii). Given Hughes's choices, the result is inevitably a darker, more philosophical book. In her translator's note, Dana says, "I have tried for fidelity to the original, above all in tone and content; but I have not bound myself to any precise metrical scheme derived from the Spanish or limited myself by striving for a forced rhyme that cannot be carried over into another language" (xxvii).

We might add to these principles that Dana observes a relatively strict preference for direct subject-verb-object word order in English, emphasizing the plain-style aspect of Mistral's practice. She untangles the poet's dependent clauses and varied syntax, at times more thoroughly than absolutely necessary for clarity. This choice, along with a preference for short Anglo-Saxon words, contributes to a relatively flat, declarative tone, at times intensifying to the hieratic. In leaning toward the plain style, Dana appropriately honors Mistral's avowed humility and aversion to *vanitas,* but it's likely she is also influenced by contemporaneous (late 1960s) North American ideas of what makes a good poem. Though not insensitive to Mistral's rhythms, Dana gives priority to a blunt conciseness. This commitment occasionally leads her to resort to highly colored diction and other devices to gain intensity. I'll look more closely at some of her choices when I compare versions of the poem "La otra" a little later.

The most significant development since the publication of Dana's translations in 1971 has been the contribution of feminist scholarship in recovering the rhetorical sophistication of Mistral's poetic compositions. Writers such as Patricia Rubio, Elizabeth Horan, and Licia Fiol-Matta have used Mistral's letters and prose writings to demonstrate the poet's acute consciousness of the small number of authoritative positions from which she—as a woman in a male-controlled literary and political culture and as a product of the rural middle class—might speak. They show Mistral cultivating not just one but several distinct audiences—adjusting her self-presentation, her literary persona, and the rhetoric of her poems to reach and persuade each one. This work provides an important corrective to the popular picture of "Saint Gabriela" as a kind of naïve, divinely inspired "natural." It is no derogation of her achievement, no contradiction of her ethics, to recall that her very literary self—the name Gabriela Mistral—was both an indirection and a fabrication.

The implication of this more complete picture for Mistral's translators is clear. In the "subtle, complex, hidden machine" behind her words, subtext and context take on greater importance. What is presented as innocent may accommodate irony, what seems subjective may speak through a persona, what appears incidental may in fact be crucial. This larger awareness informs every decision about what can be retained and what must be sacrificed. It steers connotations and therefore affects selection among synonyms. It influences how often pronouns are supplied, how gendered words are rendered, how syntactical variations are interpreted.

And yet it would be as great an error to read Mistral's poems as crude allegories as it is to see them as naïvely sentimental. Apart from the fact that Mistral throughout her life displayed ambivalence toward feminist and other political organizations, she would not be honored as one of the language's great poets if her expressions could be so easily reduced. Rhetorical complexity does not equate to coded speech, in which the surface may be ignored in favor of the buried message. Good poetry always means many things at once. The poet's subjective joy and suffering may be sung without further justification; at the same time they may make her more alert to the experiences of others whom she represents through personae. Neither precludes an active and even calculating artistic concern with shaping her material, with making it beautiful according to her ideas of beauty, and with using language that allows readers to make each poem in some sense their own. The translator, like the poet, must work in all these dimensions.

In a panel on translation at the 2000 Dodge Poetry Festival, poet and translator Edward Hirsch hypothesized that very sophisticated writers, or writers with ironic sensibilities, who choose to work in traditional or folk-derived forms are among the most difficult to translate successfully. I take this to be because every expression must be analyzed to determine such an author's attitude toward the received form. In these conditions, form and content may exhibit even more than usual a complex and dynamic rhetorical relationship over the course of the work, each commenting on the other. While it would be wrong to characterize Gabriela Mistral as having an ironic sensibility, I think recent scholarship shows the conditions Hirsch describes to be present in her content, as Tomás Navarro Tomás earlier showed them to be present in her prosody. The element of poetic craft most affected is tone.

Maria Giachetti's 1993 translations in *A Gabriela Mistral Reader* reveal a dawning awareness of these issues. They have in general a lighter feel than Dana's. They retain an interest in plain speech but are apt to adopt a more conversational tone. With a few exceptions, they don't push so hard for the earnest, exalted poetic moment. Giachetti shows an interest in local detail and sometimes adds words or lines to expand a *chilenismo* or smooth out a highly compressed figure. She seems to trust Mistral's strength to come through intact. She, like Dana, occasionally yields to the temptation to choose more specific or highly colored English words where Mistral's diction is general or elemental.

Giachetti's less striving tone comes at the cost of a loss of tautness in the line. Even less careful of Mistral's rhythms than Dana, her paraphrase on occasion becomes prosy. This quality arguably gives some poems a more contemporary sound. At their best, Giachetti's versions sound fresh and free of exaggerated piousness. Her less effective moments risk flatness. I will consider her work further in the second part of this essay.

I WOULD NOW LIKE TO EXPLORE some specific issues that emerge during the process of translating a single poem, noting how other translators have chosen to approach them. My intent is less to critique particular versions than to isolate questions that bear on Mistral's work and show how they intersect at the translator's moment of choice. I'll take as my text "La otra," from the "Locas mujeres" series. This was a milestone work for Mistral herself (she prefixed it as a prologue to *Lagar,* and placed it at the head of the "Locas mujeres" cycle in *Poesías completas*); as such it has been translated and discussed by several writers, and it raises many of the questions—both of compression and complexity—alluded to earlier. Here's the complete poem as it appears in the 1954 edition of *Lagar:*

La otra

Una en mí maté:
yo no la amaba.

Era la flor llameando
del cactus de montaña;

era aridez y fuego;
nunca se refrescaba.

Piedra y cielo tenía
a pies y a espaldas
y no bajaba nunca
a buscar "ojos de agua."

Donde hacía su siesta,
las hierbas se enroscaban
de aliento de su boca
y brasa de su cara.

En rápidas resinas
se endurecía su habla,
por no caer en linda
presa soltada.

Doblarse no sabía
la planta de montaña,
y al costado de ella,
yo me doblaba . . .

La dejé que muriese,
robándole mi entraña.
Se acabó como el águila
que no es alimentada.

Sosegó el aletazo,
se dobló, lacia,
y me cayó a la mano
su pavesa acabada . . .

Por ella todavía
me gimen sus hermanas,
y las gredas de fuego
al pasar me desgarran.

Cruzando yo les digo:

—Buscad por las quebradas
y haced con las arcillas
otra águila abrasada.

Si no podéis, entonces,
¡ay!, olvidadla.
Yo la maté. ¡Vosotras
también matadla!

Gendered Language

Because its nouns and pronouns are gendered, the translator of any
poetry in Spanish must evaluate how important the gender of a particular substantive expression is to its meaning. The poet in Spanish has a
scale of emphasis available: she may employ a feminine noun or pronoun alone, or reinforce the use of one by a second reference using the
other. Where masculine collective pronouns are conventionally used
to indicate an unspecified group (e.g., *vosotros*), the use of the feminine
counterpart insists on specifically female referents. The translator
must judge whether an expression's gender is mere convention, in
which case an ungendered English word may be used alone, or
whether it represents an act of specifying or emphasis that calls for the
addition of clarifying English terms.

"La otra" comes from the series "Locas mujeres"—a title that establishes a specifically female context for its speakers—but the series title
may or may not appear when the poem is published separately. "La
otra" can be rendered in English as "The Other" and assumed to be female because the author is a female and the poem speaks in first person; Dana and Giachetti both make this choice (as do Horan and other
scholars). The alternatives are bad. "The Other Woman" carries connotations of love triangles that are unacceptable in the poem's context,
while constructions with pronouns sound strained and artificial. Nevertheless, while "The Other" preserves the elemental quality of the

Spanish, it opens the translation with a loss, a kind of gender deficit. As a term of theory or philosophy for pure alterity, "Other" in Spanish would be rendered by the masculine *el otro*. Thus Mistral's explicit signal that the "other" of the poem is feminine is missed in English.

The gender deficit deepens in the first line. A literal rendering would be "One [feminine] in me I killed." The "one" killed will soon be understood to be identical with the "other" of the title. To say simply "one" or "someone" leaves open at this point the possibility that the referent is masculine: a psychoanalytic animus perhaps, a father image, or some other construct. The ambiguity can be settled in the next line, but there is a cost to suspending certainty and allowing the reader's expectations to develop speculatively. Dana (124) and Giachetti (117) render the first stanza as follows:

Dana	Giachetti
I killed one of me,	I killed someone
one I did not love.	inside of me.
	I didn't love her.

There are other ways to handle the gendered pronouns, but before considering an alternative strategy I want to examine another issue raised by the poem's opening—one that complicates this choice.

Rhythm and Idiom

Pablo Neruda is reported to have reassured a guest about some Lithuanian translations of his work: "Don't worry. The rhythm is all right. . . . For a poet, that's what counts" (in Felstiner, 30). The sentiment may be especially apt for Neruda's cadences, but sensitivity to any poet's rhythms is essential if a translation is to develop an analogous "feel" to that of the original.

Mistral's metrical practice, in particular, is worthy of attention here in its implications for the translator. In his 1973 essay, "Métrica y ritmo de Gabriela Mistral," Navarro Tomás noted that in her early books Mistral did not limit herself to using meters and stanzas in their commonly established forms. She sought instead to discover the "implicit modalities" in these forms, from which she "constructed a metrical framework of broad and rich variety." Her later poems were, in general, less tightly interwoven, with less consonance and fewer double rhymes, but her fluency in the expressive deployment of lines of varying measure within a stanza or poem continued to increase. As Navarro Tomás put it, "Under the appearance of improvisation and carelessness, she cultivated a subtly elaborated metric" (325).

Traditional Spanish meters are based on lines of fixed syllable count. Within each meter, stresses may be required on specified syllables of the line (which may lead to a polyrhythmic line) or, in other modes, according to regular trochaic or dactylic patterns. Each of the meters carries its own historical and emotional associations. Without venturing into the intricacies of the system, we can characterize the innovation of Mistral's later work by an analogy.

Any good writer of English blank verse will create liveliness by occasionally replacing an iambic foot with one of another type. Mistral practiced this substitution at the level of the line, interpolating a line or group of lines having one measure (syllable count) into a stanza based on a different measure. In itself this is not uncommon in Spanish prosody, but tradition expects such lines to occur in specific combinations of measures and in specific circumstances—just as we routinely look for trochaic substitutions in the first position of an iambic pentameter line. By contrast, Mistral freely employed unexpected combinations of measures, and similarly reconfigured traditional stanza forms, in order to control pacing, modulate tone, emphasize drama, or create closure.

It is a critical commonplace that English speakers do not hear syllabics. That is, in a poem without a regular accentual meter, the ear will not perceive the regularity in a series of lines of unvarying syllable count. And yet, as Rodney Williamson says, "the task of the translator of Gab-

riela Mistral begins with a decision about the metrical and sonic structure of the text" (162). So what's a translator to do? The target language
uses a primarily stress-based metrical system, and the odds of finding
rhyme words to approximate the running *rima asonante* on the even
lines of "La otra" without doing violence to the sense are vanishingly
small. Even a sophisticated Spanish-speaking reader could be forgiven
for thinking, in a poem like "La otra," that Mistral had simply eschewed
meter rather than constructing a collage or quilt of metrical fragments.

I like to invoke the concept of pattern density to guide these decisions. In the original poem, various types of patterns are established
and several significant variations on those patterns are introduced.
Both patterns and variations carry and create expressive effects. It is
important for the translator to identify as many of the patterns as possible, to understand the number and function of the variations, and
then, as a first-order approximation, to answer the general question,
How orderly is the original, sonically? The translator can then strive,
using the resources of the target language, to create a similar degree of
order or disorder—put another way, to create a version with a similar
ratio of pattern to variation. That ratio is the poem's pattern density.

To create a version with such a ratio, one might begin by looking for
resources that the target language shares with the original that can be
manipulated in similar ways. In "La otra," for example, speech stresses
exist in the Spanish, in tension with those ordained by the metrical
mode. The translator can count the stresses in each line, noting where
in the argument and emotional development of the poem the numbers
vary, with an eye to attempting analogous effects. Although using
stress in this way may slightly exaggerate its importance in Spanish,
when successful it's a way to obtain a feeling of familiarity in the English that's rooted in the original.

On the other hand, Murat Nemet-Nejat speaks for many translators
today when he advocates expanding the capabilities of the target language by incorporating a characteristic resource from the original that
is perceptibly "foreign" to the English version (99). A strict application

of this idea might strive to preserve Mistral's syllable counts precisely. But a start would be simply to be alert to Mistral's line lengths and the points at which they change, and to apply a similar purposefulness to the English version, rather than allowing line lengths to vary arbitrarily to accommodate other needs.

In "La otra," Mistral opens with a two-line stanza composed of a divided decasyllable: five and five. The ten quatrains that follow are based on various combinations of octosyllables and heptasyllables, with their intimations of divided alejandrinos. In the fourth and fifth quatrains, however, Mistral creates expressive closure by substituting the shorter five-syllable line in the final position. In stanza seven it appears again to mark a dramatic turn—the collapse of the dying eagle. Then she returns to the pattern of sevens and eights for two stanzas, until in the final stanza, the intensity of the closure is reinforced by the use of fives in the second and fourth (last) lines: in effect, an interlaced mirroring of the opening couplet.

Clearly this pattern is not arbitrary. Even though English lines tend to be more compact than their Spanish equivalents, the translator can seek to shorten the English line at corresponding points and to avoid departing widely from a stable pattern elsewhere in the version.

Before weighing the contending claims of syllable count, stress pattern, gendered language, and imagery in the poem's opening, however, I must return to the question of stress. Mistral's rhythm in this poem is organized around a three-stress line; depending on performance, some lines can be read as having only two stresses, but the three-stress norm hovers as a ghostly presence. In the opening line, the Spanish has three clear stresses, with decisive emphasis falling on the first and the last syllables of the line. There is at least one unstressed syllable between each stress, preventing any spondaic hesitation.

This rhythm reinforces the sense. The verb "kill" is placed in the stanza's most dramatic possible position: at the end of a short first line, bearing the line's third and terminal stress. The colon's hard end-stop rhythmically reinforces the syntactic emphasis. Such inverted syntax is common in Spanish (as an inflected language), but to reproduce it in English here would give the translation a misleading unconventionality. Dana and Giachetti both revert to subject-verb-object order. In the struggle to capture the proper relationships (of containment, of alterity or identity, of number) between the speaker and the "other," the two choose different strategies. Dana employs the highly idiomatic English construction "one of *x*"—the surprising completion "me" makes the phrase fresh. While this strategy preserves Mistral's exact syllable count in the couplet (though Dana ignores it for the rest of the poem), it results in a very different rhythm from Mistral's. The line may be read with three stresses, but they occur in the first three syllables of the line, which trails off at the end.

One might also question whether "one of me," which seems to imply that the speaker is one of a set of equally complete alternate selves, conveys the same psychological relationship as "one *in* me," which suggests that the "other" is a part or aspect of the speaker. Giachetti chooses to highlight the latter reading by rendering *en* as "inside." This choice entails an even greater departure from Mistral's rhythm than Dana's. Giachetti's sentence now has at least four stresses—more than any line in Mistral's Spanish—so she elects to break this sentence into two two-stress lines, giving her stanza three lines to Mistral's two. Giachetti has clearly given interpretation of the psychic relationship priority over rhythm. Her pattern density is much lower than the original's.

Mistral's poem is a psychomachia, and it opens with self-murder. However partial the killing, it seems to me such an act warrants the short, sharp shock of Mistral's stresses. Bearing in mind the gender deficit observed earlier, one can imagine a third rendering—not perfect, but one which recovers the feminine "other," maintains three spaced stresses per line, and allows the first line to end on a strong rather than a weak beat. Such a provisional first stanza might read:

> I killed a woman in me:
> one I did not love.

This version sacrifices the paired five-syllable measure in favor of stress effects. The relationship of rhythm to sense is not of uniform importance throughout this or any poem, but an opening gesture as dramatic as Mistral's brings the question of rhythmic emphasis immediately to the fore.

Diction and Allusion

Margot Arce de Vázquez pointed out in 1964 that in *Lagar* Mistral makes use of more Latinate words and more biblical phrases and *cultismos* (liturgical, devotional, or other religious expressions) than in her previous books (87–88). An alertness to such formulae helps the translator capture an aspect of Mistral's style, since analogues are often available in English. An example of this occurs in the fourth stanza of "La otra" in the lines *de aliento de su boca / y brasa de su cara.* The first of these lines instantly conjures both the Hebrew scriptures and their function in Anglo-Catholic liturgy.[2] Coupled with the following line, the formula not only contributes its cadences to the poem's tone but also adds the stern shadow of the law and the prophets to its picture of the inflexible "other."[3] Yet both Dana and Giachetti decline the formulaic expression in favor of a more concise and "contemporary" sound:

Dana	Giachetti
scorched with her breath and the blazing coal of her face.	burned by her mouth and face of incandescent coals.

A simpler and yet more resonant rendering, and one closer to both the syllabic and stress counts of the Spanish, might be:

> from the breath of her mouth,
> the live coals of her face.

Image

Mistral shares with the surrealists a fondness for images that shade one into another as if in a dream. In "La otra," for example, the "other" is first characterized as a flaming cactus flower, albeit one that can walk. In stanza seven the extended image pivots on a simile and the "other" metamorphoses into a starving eagle—also fiery—for the rest of the poem. Recognizing the technique, a translator should be prepared to follow such shifts and to be circumspect about insisting on continuity with earlier figures when a passage is ambiguous. In short, the translator must have the courage to give Mistral her strangeness.

For instance, in the fifth stanza two similes occur in an unusual form—and one not common in Mistral's other books. To introduce the similes, she uses the preposition *en* (we might understand the sense of this as "in the form of"). Arce de Vázquez instances four examples of the type in *Lagar,* of which two occur in this stanza (92). Since there has been water imagery earlier, it is tempting to construe Mistral's use of *rápidas* and *presa* in liquid terms, with *rápidas* signifying "rapids" and *presa* signifying "dike" or "dam." Both Dana and Giachetti take this approach:

Dana	Giachetti
Her words hardened in rapids of resin, never freed in the spill of an open dike.	With rapid resins, her speech hardened never to be set free in a glorious cascade.

The more common meaning of *presa,* however, is "captive" or "prey." If we recognize *en* as introducing a simile, we can render the stanza more directly:

> Like quick-setting resins
> her words would harden,
> never to fall lovely
> as a captive freed.

Resinas is a recurring word in *Lagar,* one associated throughout Mistral's poetic career with a personal symbolic vocabulary of trees. In this rendering of the stanza, the resins arise naturally from the "mountain plant"—the comparison of rigidifying speech with hardening gum follows logically. It introduces no third term to the image. The tree speaks: the words *are* the resins, not something caught "in" or "with" them. The image can be clearly visualized without resorting to a vague "insects in amber" idea; and it does not require us to strain for a verb form that makes grammatical sense with "dike" in this context. Mistral's style often makes use of linguistic pairings, and this reading presumes and preserves deliberately paired similes.

Syntax

While "La otra" is less syntactically complex than many poems in *Lagar,* it offers examples of Mistral's penchant for compression, grouping, and repetition. For instance, in stanza three she collapses two parallel thoughts (*piedra tenía a pies* and *cielo tenía a espaldas*) into one clause by relating the pair of landscape elements to the pair of body parts via a single verb. This odd structure does not result from the inflected nature of Spanish; it is only marginally less idiosyncratic in the original than in English. Apart from adding pattern density by creating a pair of adjacent pairs, the construction allows the poet to pack three *ie* diphthongs in quick succession to striking musical effect.

In this situation, both Dana and Giachetti have chosen to distribute the terms of Mistral's little equation into separate phrases or clauses, simplifying syntax to reinforce clarity of sense. The cost of this strategy is the loss of all musical doublings:

Dana	**Giachetti**
With rock at her feet and sky at her shoulder,	She traveled a rocky way, and pressed her shoulders against the sky,

she never stooped	she never descended
in search of cooling springs.	to search for *the eyes of water*
	[italics Giachetti's]

A different strategy might retain as much of Mistral's device as can be parsed without strain. Some indirection is permissible—the slight sorting required by the construction is part of the aesthetic pleasure of the original. This strategy may serve as a mild example of the kind of "foreignizing" described by Nemet-Nejat and Lawrence Venuti. Adopting it allows us to create analogous pairs and to substitute alliteration for Mistral's assonance in the first two terms:

> She had stone and sky
> at her feet, at her shoulders,
> and she never came down
> to seek the water's eye.

A collateral advantage of this approach is that it preserves the original's eerie sense that sky and earth are somehow *attached* to the body of the "other." That effect, together with the poet's choice of the idiom *ojos de agua* for "springs" instead of a noun such as *fuente* or *manantial,* shows Mistral both creating an anthropomorphic landscape and emphasizing, as she does elsewhere, the elemental, almost animistic quality of the "other": she is a force of nature.

Implications of Tenses

The perfect tense contributes decisiveness and concreteness to tone. The imperfect tense makes available an awareness of the repetition, incompleteness, or duration of past events. Mistral employs the imperfect in several places in "La otra." In their versions, both Dana and Giachetti maintain the simple past tense for the entire length of the poem, except where a participle can be substituted. While rendering the Spanish imperfect using the simple past can often be appropriate, as in the stanza just considered, the translator has the opportunity to evaluate where the poet chooses to depart from the perfect tense and what functions that shift might serve. So, for instance, in stanza six, Dana and Giachetti render the imperfect *doblaba* simply as "bent":

Dana	Giachetti
This mountain plant	This mountain flower
did not know how to bend.	did not know how to bend—
I bent	but by her side,
at her side.	I bent.

Both these stanzas end abruptly, Giachetti's decisively so. Both omit the ellipses with which Mistral concludes the Spanish line. Perhaps they were seeking a vigorous effect, but both make the last two lines shorter than any others in their versions, creating a variation in pattern not present in the original.

Another approach might be to assume that the ellipses following an imperfect-tense verb together signify some aesthetic intention. Ellipses suggest incompleteness and trailing off, so we might render the stanza like this:

> This plant of the mountain
> didn't know how to bend,
> and alongside her
> I was bending . . .

Such a reading presents the bending as a *condition* of the speaker, perhaps something repeated or progressive, that contrasts with the "other's" rigidity. Without needing to steer the interpretation, we can suggest the kind of divergence that plausibly precedes the speaker's decision to kill the "other," to starve the eagle.

IN "LA OTRA," AS IN ANY POEM, the translator faces a multitude of decisions, but the foregoing examples illustrate representative issues that arise in translating Mistral's later work. Some involve the increasingly complex rhetorical context that new scholarship is providing for the poems. Others are matters of poetic craft, or of simply being alert to the characteristic gestures of the poet. This discussion represents a preliminary venture into the kind of interpretive reading essential to any serious translation.

It is often said that translations date quickly and that every generation needs its own translators. For a poet like Mistral, whose mix of biblical, archaic, folk, and conversational idioms served her effort to write in a timeless style, it may be that attempts to bring her up to date are in fact least likely to be durable. As scholarly appreciation of the poet increases, however, it seems probable that her voice will be heard in several thoughtful new English translations. That can only be a boon to those who study Mistral and to those who value her poetry.

I'll close with a provisional rendering of the complete poem:

The Other

I killed a woman in me:
one I did not love.

She was the blazing flower
of the mountain cactus;
she was drought and fire,
never cooling her body.

She had stone and sky
at her feet, at her shoulders,
and she never came down
to seek the water's eye.

Where she took her rest
the grass used to twist
from the breath of her mouth,
the live coals of her face.

Like quick-setting resins
her words would harden,
never to fall lovely
as a captive freed.

This plant of the mountain
didn't know how to bend
and alongside her
I was bending . . .

I left her to die,
robbing her of my heart's blood.
She ended weak as an eagle
that is not fed.

The flapping wing grew still;
she bent, spent,
and fell into my hand
her embers dying out . . .

Still her sisters keen,
they cry to me for her,
and the fiery desert chalks
rake me as I pass.

Moving on, I tell them:
"Search in the ravines
and fashion with the clay
another burning eagle.

"If you can't do it, then,
Too bad! Forget her.
I killed her. You women
must kill her too!"

Notes

I would like to thank Reginald Gibbons, Brooks Haxton, Elizabeth Horan, and Clare Kinney for their valuable comments on this essay. Unless otherwise noted, all translations are my own.

1. Certainly not the only strategy. A translator may prefer to concentrate on differences—employing "foreignizing" strategies to emphasize the gulf between source and target cultures. This practice may represent a dissident critique of dominant domestic values (see Venuti, especially chapter 4, "Dissidence"). Use of foreignizing techniques may also serve to nuance a translation with less radical aims, by attempting to enlarge the capacity of the target language to convey some aspect of the original's flavor, rather than striving to assimilate that otherness completely into fluent and familiar discourse (see Nemet-Nejat).

2. See, for example, Ps. 19:14 ("Let the words of my mouth, and the meditation of my heart, be acceptable in thy sight, O Lord . . .") and 33:6 ("By the word of the Lord were the heavens made; and all the host of them by the breath of his mouth.) in the Authorized Version.

3. See, for example, Isa. 6:6–7 in the Authorized Version, in which Isaiah's prophetic vocation is sealed: "Then flew one of the seraphims unto me, having a live coal in his hand, *which* he had taken with the tongs from off the altar. / And he laid *it* upon my mouth, and said, Lo, this hath touched thy lips; and thine iniquity is taken away, and thy sin is purged" (emphasis in original).

Works Cited

Arce de Vázquez, Margot. *Gabriela Mistral: The Poet and Her Work.* Trans. Helene Masslo Anderson. New York: New York University Press, 1964.

Bates, Margaret. Introduction to Doris Dana, trans., *Selected Poems of Gabriela Mistral.* Baltimore: Johns Hopkins University Press, 1971.

Dana, Doris, ed. and trans. *Selected Poems of Gabriela Mistral.* Baltimore: Johns Hopkins University Press, 1971.

Felstiner, John. *Translating Neruda.* Stanford: Stanford University Press, 1980.

Giachetti, Maria, trans. *A Gabriela Mistral Reader*. Ed. Marjorie Agosín. Fredonia, N.Y.: White Pine Press, 1993.

Horan, Elizabeth. *Gabriela Mistral: An Artist and Her People*. Washington, D.C.: Organization of American States (INTERAMER), 1994.

Hughes, Langston, trans. *Selected Poems of Gabriela Mistral*. Bloomington: Indiana University Press, 1957.

Kyle, Christiane Jacox, trans. *Poemas de las madres/The Mothers' Poems*, by Gabriela Mistral. Cheney: Eastern Washington University Press, 1995.

Mistral, Gabriela. *Lagar*. Vol. 6 of *Obras selectas*. Santiago: Editorial del Pacifico, 1954.

———. *Poesías completas*. 2d ed. Ed. Margaret Bates and Gabriela Mistral. Madrid: Aguilar, 1962.

Navarro Tomás, Tomás. *Los poetas en sus versos: Desde Jorge Manrique a García Lorca*. Barcelona: Ediciones Ariel, 1973.

Nemet-Nejat, Murat. "Translation and Style." *Talisman* 6 (spring 1991): 98–100.

Venuti, Lawrence. *The Translator's Invisibility: A History of Translation*. London: Routledge, 1995.

Williamson, Rodney. "Arte de disparidades y de confluencias: Reflexiones sobre la traducción de la poesía de Gabriela Mistral al inglés." In *Re-leer hoy a Gabriela Mistral: Mujer, historia, y sociedad en América Latina*, ed. Gastón Lillo and J. Guillermo Renart. Ottawa: University of Ottawa, 1997.

Chapter 12

Constructions of the Self
The Personal Letters of Gabriela Mistral

Patricia Rubio

GABRIELA MISTRAL WROTE THOUSANDS of personal letters: the first ones were crafted during the earlier part of the century, and the last ones shortly before her death in 1957. She wrote from villages in northern Chile and from cities in the south where she first taught and later served in public school administration. She wrote from various points in the Americas where she taught and lectured in a number of colleges and universities; from several European cities where she represented Chile in the consular corps. She wrote to friends—mostly male, two of whom became presidents of Chile. In her youth, she wrote to two platonic lovers and throughout her life to fellow writers, intellectuals, friends, and to her family in the Elqui valley. Hundreds of these letters have been published in scholarly editions, but with the exception of *This America of Ours: The Letters of Gabriela Mistral and Victoria Ocampo* (ed. and trans. Horan and Meyer), they have not been translated from the Spanish.

Given the interest elicited by Mistral's life, demonstrated both by an abundance of biographical studies, and a preponderance of biographical criticism of her poetry—especially of *Desolación*—it is surprising that her letters have thus far not received detailed attention. As a form of life writing, letters are a particular kind of autobiographical discourse that constructs an egocentric universe in which self-evaluation and judgments of the experiences and the world surrounding the writer are the main focus. As one considers Mistral's collected letters, recurrent themes and preoccupations rise to the fore: concerns regarding financial security, her mistrust and contempt for the Chilean urban elite, her paranoia, her health.

Although the published correspondences include introductions and critical annotations that contextualize the exchanges and illuminate thematic and stylistic characteristics in their intellectual and biographical contexts, what is missing are the "narratives" of the self these epistolaries develop when considered as parts of a whole—the body of her collected letters—rather than as discrete entities—a set of exchanges with one particular person. The study of her published letters, beginning with those she wrote to Alfredo Pineda between 1905 and 1906, to the last, toward the end of her life in 1956, allows us to observe—in Mistral's own voice—her development through time.

Retracing such development, however, faces a number of difficulties. As Barthes proposed, "the I that says I is not the I that writes I." Much is pruned or added, silenced or excluded. Furthermore, her letters have not been published in toto, and an undetermined number of them were lost due to postal mismanagement and interceptions, especially during World War II. Also, the dialogic nature of the epistolary mode is often interrupted by her frequent relocations, which were not conducive to accurate record keeping. A meaningful portion of the letters she received is missing. Her correspondence with Carmen Lyra, the Costa Rican writer, for example, has been lost, and there are few letters available from what must have been an assiduous exchange with Palma Guillén, her longtime friend and living companion from Mexico.

The gaps in the collection of letters underscore the fragmentary nature of epistolary exchange, resulting from its spatial and temporal discontinuity. Mistral's correspondents were usually abroad, which delayed, and often interrupted for long periods, the dialogic exchange. In terms of time, spatial separation causes the present of the writer to never coincide with the present of the intended reader. Thus, although Mistral frequently refers to her letter writing as conversation—in an attempt, no doubt, to strengthen its communicative potential—the misnomer itself exposes its shortcomings, since "epistolary discourse is caught up in the impossibility of a dialogue in the present" (Altman, 122). This asynchronicity is for Mistral, as for most correspondents of the past for whom letters were the main means of communication with those afar, a source of considerable frustration. Letters were Mistral's personal and professional lifelines; they were an important venue for alleviating her isolation and solitude; they were a shelter. Mistral is well aware of the structural shortcomings of the epistolary mode: "every day letters seem to become documents that trick me into thinking they are the genuine article. It was something completely different, to converse with you in your home, giving you voice and affectionate gestures." (*Antología,* 84). She is painfully aware that "the unseizability and precariousness of now is constantly reflected in the epistolary seismogram" (Altman, 129). Thus she writes to Victoria Ocampo, "I believe less and less in letters" (6 January 1942). These flaws seem the more meaningful when one considers the amount of time Mistral invested in letter writing, and her dependence on it for personal and professional matters. To Jaime Eyzaguirre she says, "Since I have been writing without the certainty that my letters will reach you, and since I have not received certain letters that I absolutely need at this time, there is in me a great sadness, because always *the best things in my life came from some friends who are dispersed throughout the world*" (20 July 1942; *Antología,* 342; emphasis Mistral's). This explains perhaps why she does not date her letters: to do so would foreground the time elapsed between a letter and a response. By not fixing it in a particular moment, she stresses the flow of the conversation, rather than its interruptions.

The fragmentary nature of the epistolary genre also foregrounds thematic omissions in Mistral's letters, which involve areas of the writer's life and experience about which she chose not to write and which, due to their significance, are conspicuous by their absence. As Sylvia Molloy suggests, such gaps need "to be confronted in their silence itself, as signifiers in themselves." Rarely, for example, does Mistral refer in any detail to her poetic work. Occasionally she alludes to the fact that she is engaged in writing poetry, or that she has enough poems for a book, but there are no recurrent detailed discussions of her work or of the writing process itself. In this respect, Mistral's letters do not neatly fit Saúl Yurkievich's contention that the epistolary genre "is an enigmatic zone between the author's life and his work," revealing of "how life was transposed to the work." Only later in her life, as she is writing *Poema de Chile,* is she more forthcoming. This is mostly motivated, however, by the need for books and materials on Chilean flora and fauna; she does not know or does not remember the names of many indigenous animals and plants, all of which are necessary for her work in progress.

Mistral is more vocal about her prose, which she disliked writing and did not always value. She frequently regretted the time she invested in it. She also thought of herself as an inadequate *"articulista"* and of the articles as utilitarian since they were her main source of income during the years she held various honorary consular posts in Europe: "I wrote columns for newspapers. A lot of articles that 'sustained' me" (to Exequiel de la Barra, 1951; *Antología,* 520).

Striking too, is how little Mistral writes about European cultural and intellectual developments; about individual authors and artists, playwrights and musicians. Were one to judge from her letters only, one could surmise that Mistral rarely visited a museum or a church in Paris, Madrid, Barcelona, Naples, or Rome; that she did not possess in-depth knowledge of the literary, philosophical, and artistic European movements of the time. With noted exceptions—Maritain, for example—she infrequently and then only in passing mentions the books she is consulting. Whose poetry is she reading during her time in Europe? In Brazil? How does Hispanic poetry compare to French or Italian poetry? (We know, for example, that she knows Valery's opus well, as she rejects his translation of her poetry into French, claiming that their poetic projects and aesthetics were very different). Who are her favorite painters? What exhibits did she attend? What about the theatre? Unless she is specifically writing to an author about his or her book, in-depth commentary is often missing. One needs to read her articles in order to access this part of Mistral's thinking. It is as if she had very clearly compartmentalized the topics and functions of her various modes of writing. Perhaps she assumed that her correspondents also read her articles and that it would be best to avoid reiteration. But these gaps also suggest that her prose, poetry, and letters complement each other and that studying one—as I do here—without considering the others will yield only a partial understanding of the total picture.

Another notable silence involves the limited references she makes to Yin Yin (the nephew she adopted) especially during his formative years. When she writes to Alfonso Reyes, one of her closest male friends, whom she frequently addresses as "Mi Alfonso," an unmistakable sign of intimacy, she seldom mentions Yin Yin, even when she is commenting at length about Alfonsito, Reyes's son. Reyes himself writes often about his son's development, yet Mistral is reserved about Yin Yin's. It is only in letters to her family and intimate female friends—Carmela Errázuriz, Victoria Ocampo, and Palma Guillén, who helped her raise the boy—that she writes in more detail about him. This gap is particularly significant considering that the poet herself unequivocally proposed, in her poetry, prose, lectures, letters, and interviews, that motherhood—not only biological but also spiritual—was a woman's central and most fulfilling mission in life. Why wasn't she more forthcoming about her relationship with the boy? Why is she silent about how Yin Yin allowed her to fulfill her own, seemingly natural, maternal instincts? Her reserve on this matter is even more puzzling when considering her words to two former students: "They will give me the illusion that I had daughters, that I did not go through this world in vain" (to Esther Grimberg and María

Baeza, ca. 1917; *Antología,* 63)—a passage that clearly states her belief in motherhood as a unique source of meaning to a woman's life. Five years later she also says, "The complaining mother of my little songs has a great advantage over me: she is an *authentic* mother. Yours truly is a mother in her dreams or in make-believe" (to Bergerac, November 1922; *Antología,* 92; emphasis Mistral's). Moreover, she is aware of the fact that once sent, however private and confidential letters may be, they escape her control. Cognizant that they are historical documents, likely to be printed in an undetermined future, Mistral chose to silence this significant part of her personal life. Faced with innumerable tensions and pressures as a public persona, without a stable home base, and always doubtful of her professional stability as a civil servant, Mistral's reticence may signify her need for privacy, for spaces of retreat and of self-determination, and individual freedom.

Even when it deals with topics and objects that are external to the writer, letter writing is ultimately about self-representation. It allows the writer to create a linguistic persona that rewrites the self, that "contradicts, supersedes or supplements the identity others have assumed" of her (Friedman, 75). This is a particularly important function in Mistral's case, because throughout her life she felt misunderstood and criticized, even persecuted, by groups and individuals, including presidents, as in the case of Arturo Alessandri, Carlos Ibáñez, and Gabriel González Videla, who undermined her career and tarnished her name: "No more than a year ago, my country's press dragged me through the mud in a campaign of insults" (to Aguirre Cerda, December 1936; *Antología,* 261). Letters constitute a means of defense, a way to set the record straight by offering her own version of things. This function of the letter is particularly significant to women whose identities have been defined by the prevalent male culture. Mistral knows that gender status is a central consideration, as the difficulties and discrimination she has had to face have been exacerbated by her gender: "It will be enough that they leave me as an equal to the other consuls, although I am a woman . . . this would be enough" (to Radomiro Tomic, 1951;

Vuestra Gabriela, 162). And three years later: "Many times I have become aware of my dangers as a woman alone" (to the Tomics and Carmela Errázuriz, 1954; *Vuestra Gabriela,* 235). In 1922 she had similarly written to Eduardo Barrios, "I am a poor woman alone" (*Antología,* 98).

From early on she realized that in order to survive, much less succeed in a society governed by the law of the father and its discrimination and antipathy of educated, professional, and outspoken women, she needed the protection of prominent males. Pedro Aguirre Cerda, minister of education and later president, helped her advance in the teaching profession early on, and then supported her diplomatic and literary careers; José Vasconcelos, Mexico's secretary of education under the Obregón regime, enlisted her participation in the educational reform he was spearheading; Carlos Errázuriz, who occupied important posts in the Chilean foreign service, allowed her, as secretary of state, to enjoy professional and financial security for a significant period (though her position was never threatened, since she was by law consulate for life and could choose the location of her assignments); Eduardo Frei, founder of the Falange Nacional—which later became the Christian Democratic Party—then a young lawyer and an up-and-coming politician (he was president between 1964 and 1970), oversaw her interests in Chile. Radomiro Tomic—Carlos Errázuriz's son-in-law—also one of the founders of the Falange Nacional, a senator, and a presidential candidate after Mistral's death, became her confidant during the last ten years of her life.

Her independence abroad, however, always seemed financially insecure, as she constantly reminds her correspondents. Her feelings of vulnerability increased whenever there was a change in the Chilean government: "If Ibáñez achieves power, he will get rid of me and eliminate my teacher's pension (1,000 pesos) because that is what he did before and I do not hide my anti-Ibáñez sentiments" (to Eduardo Frei, 1939; *Antología,* 288). As her biographers have amply recorded, however, this paranoia is not solely grounded in her dependence and political decisions over which she had no control; it is also the result of unfortunate experiences of poverty and exclusion that began in her youth.

The structure of the epistolary mode, its asynchronicity and the fragmented dialog it develops, is an ideal medium to construct and project a multifaceted identity. In her letters Mistral reveals conflicting personal characteristics and objectives: she depicts herself as old even when young; she constantly refers to her ill health even when she is well; she claims to be a misanthrope of sorts, but she wants people's attention and resents exclusion; she wants to remain abroad (in fact she returns to Chile on only two occasions in thirty years), but she seeks to remain influential, and covets the acceptance and respect of Chilean society in general and intellectuals in particular. Epistolary discourse permits her to highlight and manipulate personal weaknesses; it aptly conveys her vulnerability and insecurities, which she reiterates throughout the years, thus eliciting the support and protection of her friends: "I am not a comrade, 'a fighter' . . . ; I am only a poet, half child, half old woman, a truly helpless being who breaks down at the entrance to any battlefield *and does not know how to nor can she fight*" (to Tomic, 1952; *Vuestra Gabriela,* 177; emphasis Mistral's) Despite her fame and recognition Mistral expresses weakness and defenselessness. Even the Nobel prize appeared to her a liability, because in her mind it fed people's resentment against her.

A limited number of letters, however, underscore certain strengths, revealing deep spiritual resources, a need to construct her self-image, and to remind her friends of those personal qualities that warrant their protection. She frequently alludes to her often disconcerting sincerity: "If there is something worthy in me, it is not a bad verse nor bad prose, but rather my almost disconcerting sincerity, my loyalty to my people, my inability to hurt anybody in a cowardly fashion" (to Eugenio Labarca, 1915; *Antología,* 31). Thirty years later she reiterates to Alfonso Reyes: "I am very direct, almost brutal as in these cases. And I am not ashamed" (*Tan de usted,* 160). She also underscores her unwavering commitment to the downtrodden and to social justice: "I went to Mexico when that country was rejected by South America; I defended the indigenous people when no one cared about their problems; I visited very few tropical countries, although I could have taken advantage of the conferences paid for in Argentina" (to Jaime Eyzaguirre, June 1942; *Antología,* 343–44). The self-construction of a multifaceted identity also avails her a means of protecting her privacy, even from trusted friends. By maintaining an elusive identity, she escapes definition and remains opaque to the gaze of others.

The letters reiterate the fact that despite her wishes to remain abroad, particularly in Europe ("I wish to grow old in Europe, peacefully, at the margin of their leisure"; "I am tied to Europe."), she wants to remain influential in Chile's intellectual and cultural development. As Amy Kaminsky indicates, "'presence' suggests the communal sense of the self—the way in which that fallen, disappeared, invisible one is present in the continued action of others" (25). Mistral knows that her writing will insure her presence and influence in Chilean culture and society. Although *Desolación* and *Tala,* her two most important books of poetry, were published abroad, she published poetry and prose in several Chilean magazines and newspapers, the most noted of which is *El Mercurio.* Her letters amply demonstrate a consistent interest in Chile's political and cultural development. She is vocal on educational and social matters, criticizing, for example, Chile's educational programs focusing on the development of abstract thinking to the detriment of practical experience. She is also caustic about the luxury and ostentation of the upper class. Furthermore, she consistently criticizes her colleagues both for ideological and personal reasons, as she not only disagreed with their teaching philosophy but felt they discriminated against her.

Although she was a civil servant, Mistral lived in perpetual exile, as demonstrated by her deep-seated feelings of dislocation and of permanent foreignness: "It is something very sad, and more than that, to grow old in foreign lands, to read strange news, to learn things that are not important for us to experience. That, to me, is more livable *in Europe,* this situation of being a foreign woman, alone" (to Tomic, 1953; *Vuestra Gabriela,* 210; emphasis Mistral's). She also defines herself as errant: "But I leave here like everywhere else. . . . I seem to be acquiring the flesh of a nomadic Jew" (*Antología,* 207). Her wandering is often motivated by circumstances beyond her control. The loss of the consulate in Madrid was caused by the publication of what was a confidential letter to friends she thought she could trust; she had to leave Italy the first time she was appointed consul in that country, after Mussolini refused to grant her exequatur; her leaving Brazil was motivated by her nephew's suicide; she could not settle in the land given to her by President Valdés Alemán in Veracruz because of internal laws limiting land ownership by foreigners; and last but not least, her wandering was also the result of her constant search for climates that would alleviate her many ailments.

In accepting José Vasconcelos's invitation to participate in Mexico's educational postrevolutionary reform, Mistral geographically exiled herself from Chile, particularly from the urban (Santiago) elite that blatantly excluded her. Having grown up in a small town deep in a valley of the northern Andes, she was a stranger to city culture, especially to that of the capital. She felt marginalized and maligned by those who underscored her provinciality, opposed her promotions because she lacked the proper paper credentials, and resented her success: "far from my people because they find me too . . . exotic, those wretched people" (to Alfonso Reyes, 1934; *Tan de usted,* 104) And a decade later: "my people, those of Santiago and the others, never loved me because they saw me as an 'outsider.' And that is what all of us mountain people are. *And it is a little fatal, Ciro; it is hopeless*" (to Ciro Alegría, May 1948; *Antología,* emphasis Mistral's).

The only home Mistral ever recognized was in the Elqui valley. Composed of women only—her mother, her half-sister, Emelina, herself, and later her niece—it was a domestic environment. The father came and went, and one day, when Mistral was still a young child, he never came back. The valley—"I was happy in the Elqui valley and after that I was not happy again" (to Matilde Ladrón de Guevara, 1951; *Antología,* 526)—stands in opposition to Santiago, the locus of cultural, political, and economic power: patriarchal, nondomestic, nonfemale by definition. Mistral knew that the father could not be trusted: he abandoned his daughters and wife in poverty to fend for themselves in a society that discriminates against women, especially provincial, working-class women. Mistral would never overcome a feeling of abandonment and loneliness as she continued to depend on the government—that surrogate father whose discourse is mendacious and therefore unreliable—for professional recognition and material security. Thus the capital, metonym for Chile, was the space of internal exile, the locus she needed to flee ("I always lived locked up in my country"), only to face further exile in foreign countries. Her sense of marginality, both as a memory of the past and as a reality in the present, cut a wound that she would nurse for life: "I do not speak their tongue. On the other hand, it seems I never spoke it. *But only now do I see that clearly*" (to Benjamín Carrión, September 1927; *Antología,* 154; emphasis Mistral's).

Her life abroad, despite the many opportunities it afforded her, was also a constant reminder of her sense of estrangement from "my people." Her resentment and pain, coupled with loneliness and a sense of displacement and vulnerability, translated into paranoia, a condition that Mistral would suffer throughout her life. She made matters worse as she unwittingly gave credence to the malicious gossip regarding her character with the infamous letter to Armando Donoso and María Monvel. In her mind, the document was used to galvanize the opposition against her, to strengthen the hand of those who were envious of her post in Madrid and of her success in Mexico. Even years after winning the Nobel prize—the first Hispanic woman and the first Chilean writer to do so—she continued to mention the "Spanish" letter as one of the reasons for the rumors circulating in Santiago about her. Six years after the prize she wrote to Eduardo Frei, "Defend me there" (1951;

Antología, 507). To be accepted in Chile—and the belated Premio Nacional only confirmed her mistrust—was something she longed for.

Gossip as a form of representation is objectifying: it "plays with reputations, circulating truths and half-truths and falsehoods about the activities, sometimes about the motives and feelings of others" (Spacks, 4). Therefore, she rightly regarded it as an important indicator of her diminished status in Chile. Furthermore, Mistral understood that malicious gossip is a form of aggression, an instrument of attack used by detractors to undermine her position both within and outside Chile. She was almost permanently away, so direct confrontation was impossible; in its stead, gossip became a form of sanction that she could never take lightly: "The worst is coming, Juanita; the people's poison is coming. I have a weakness that I would call a tragic weakness. . . . It hurts me horribly when they mistreat what I hold most dear: within me, not in my verses, which I abandoned a long time ago to their darts" (to Juana de Ibarbourou, March 1925; *Antología,* 129). As Spacks suggests, the gossip's victim is incapable of assessing either the extent of its circulation or its impact. This makes Mistral anxious: "gossip is the dust that flies" she writes to Alfonso Reyes in 1937 (*Tan de usted,* 113). As she had recently experienced, gossip may effect incalculable harm. Constant, unstoppable circulation of gossip then, could only feed her paranoia.

Gossip, however, has its positive side. Patricia Spacks and Gary Fine coincide in defining it as an important form of social interaction and a heuristic resource. More fitting for Mistral's case: gossip "inhabits a space of intimacy, [it] builds on and articulates shared values of intimates" (Spacks, 15). It is therefore not surprising that Mistral's letters abound in gossip. She uses it to reaffirm connections and to foster intimate communication with her friends and supporters. Gossip gave her a sense of belonging, thus alleviating her isolation. In this regard, gossip became a strategy for community building. From a transactional perspective, gossip is an unequivocal sign of belonging, and should have assured her of her centrality to Chilean culture and society. Indeed, in a short note to Teresa Llona she writes, "We arrived well. It is not very hot, but, my God, there are many visitors. How is your stupendous Iñiguez-Pulido-Llona camaraderie? How you must miss the 'crazy' old storytelling woman from Elqui" (1938; *Antología*, 276). The tone of intimacy is obvious, as Mistral characterizes their conversation as wonderful gossip, the nature of their dialog as crazy, and herself as a gossip. This is in marked contrast to the formality of the conversations she held with visitors, with whom there was neither room for gossip nor affectionate intimacy.

Commentary about other people in personal letters also fosters closeness, as certain kinds of gossip presuppose similar thinking among the parties. Gossip constructs a space of coincidence of shared perspectives regarding the characterization of a person or situation. There is no need for much explanation; the writer knows that the correspondent will be able to correctly provide the context and decode the message accurately. To Eduardo Barrios, Mistral writes, "[Pedro Henríquez Ureña] is a sour and mean man who has become corrupted by culture and whose work is well below his great erudition." And in the same letter she later adds, "It was in one of those eternal Central American, effeminate circles, without a literary name, who scribble in two-bit newspapers" (April 1923; *Epistolario*, 60–61). Both comments are slanderous, and presuppose Barrios's receptiveness and his understanding of the context, the players, and Mistral's relationship with them and the intellectual circles to which they belonged. (Such gossip also reflects Mistral's resentment of the intellectual elite in Mexico that, with some exceptions, considered her a foreigner, even an intruder.) In similar fashion, Mistral sent Reyes a copy of the letter she sent to Vasconcelos condemning his philandering. Such exchanges are possible only in the space of well-established trust, and in this particular case, the shared knowledge that Mistral, although critical of her former boss's behavior, remained loyal to him. Thus, gossip exercises a dual objective: to deliver information but especially to underscore shared knowledge, faith, and unwavering trust in the addressee. Gossip, as Spacks has noted, generates and intensifies bonding.

Gossip is also a form of empowerment, and given Mistral's feelings of vulnerability, it became an important discursive practice in her letters. It allows her to counteract the effects of the gossip about her by undermining the credibility of her critics. Amanda Labarca Hubertson, noted Chilean feminist and educator, is a case in point. Although early on Mistral held her in high esteem, circumstances changed when she thought that Labarca's career had been unjustly advanced—to the detriment of her own—on account of her political connections and appropriate credentials: "Keep quiet about everything concerning Mrs. A. L. H., his intimate friend; everything. Do not let this woman gain any power with her tricks. But tell him [Pedro Aquirre Cerda] that my teacher's union will never forgive me for not having a title and that I will live there, pestering him to support me, to give me respect. . . . He knows people have said he is my lover, to justify my nomination. He ignores other things that are just as bad or worse" (to Eduardo Barrios, December 1922; *Antología*, 262). To the outsider, gossip is "an alternative discourse to that of public life" (Spacks, 17), the official public life Mistral feels ostracized from. Gossip fulfills her need to articulate a response that builds an alternative social and intellectual network. To be able to share gossip with noted writers such as Eduardo Barrios, Pedro Prado, Alfonso Reyes, Victoria Ocampo, and Juana de Ibarbourou, or with politicians such as Pedro Aguirre Cerda, Eduardo Frei, and Radomiro Tomic constructs a space of belonging, a "centeredness" of which she frequently felt unjustly deprived. As Elizabeth Horan has demonstrated, however, she also felt proudly independent of the elite, and used her status as an outsider to her advantage. She thus also used gossip about the intellectual and political establishment to distance herself from them and affirm her independence.

Repeatedly, Mistral's correspondence returns to her health. Her letters allow us to explore specific representations of her own body, particularly that of her body as assailed by illness. A more comprehensive study of Mistral's understanding of the body exceeds the limits of this article, as it would need to include not only her personal correspondence but also her poetry and prose. Anyone, however, who has read or written about Mistral's letters has noted her constant, even relentless, references to illness. Vital organs seem to be affected—heart, one kidney, lungs, liver, bones, nerves, and eyes—as she suffers from various debilitating ailments: high blood pressure, bad circulation, diabetes, arthritis, and partial blindness. Since the work of Foucault and an important branch of feminist scholarship on corporeal representation, Mistral's constant preoccupation is significant not only in medical-biographical terms, but also—and mainly—because it sheds light on the construction of her own body image, with its inscriptions of gender, class, social context, and personal experience. As Elizabeth Grosz has stated, "the body image is as much a function of the subject's psychology and socio-historical context as of anatomy. The limits or borders of the body image are not fixed by nature or confined to the anatomical 'container,' the skin" (79). This understanding places the medical-biological construct in a historical context, thus unraveling the duality of mind and body that has until recently dominated Western thought.

Thus Mistral's overriding representation of her body as sick is motivated by physiological dysfunction, but is also both consequence and cause of many of the issues I have discussed thus far: her marginality, her sense of displacement, her isolation, her feelings of vulnerability, her paranoia. In childhood, Mistral had already experienced her body as the locus of extreme pain. In primary school a teacher wrongly accused her of stealing notebooks and prompted her classmates to castigate her physically. In numerous letters, even up to the end of her life, Mistral recounts the trauma of being stoned on the street. This event goes far in explaining her paranoia and feelings of social inadequacy. Given that one relates to others and to the world around by means of one's body, to experience it as a source of both physical and psychological abuse at a young age creates the lasting impression that something is terribly wrong with it and, consequently, with oneself. "Because of my past, I cannot achieve, nor will I ever be, an open soul" (to Eduardo Barrios, April 1915; *Epistolario*, 9).

Debilitating and incurable diseases like those Mistral experienced for years throw an individual's normal life entirely off course. For the Chilean poet, as I have already indicated, there is always—even under normal circumstances—the fear of losing her consular assignment. Her ailments only strengthened her fears, for she was aware that illness and disability are generally stigmatized, and that she may have been judged unfit to fulfill her duties. She therefore hid them from those who could report her ailments to the authorities in Santiago. This in turn increased her isolation: "I experienced almost blinding diabetes in California. I kept quiet about my little tragedy so they would not dismiss me from my post" (to Eduardo Barrios, April 1951; *Antología*, 87). Illness increased her sense of vulnerability as it undermined the established order, coherence, and predictability of her life. Pathographies, writes Anne H. Hawkins, "show us a drastic interruption of a life of meaning and purpose by an illness that often seems arbitrary, cruel, and senseless."

Although Mistral did not rebel against her many afflictions by questioning their justification or invoking injustice, she recognized that they forced her to make decisions she may have otherwise avoided. For example, she continued in the civil service when Ibáñez assumed power for the second time, although she despised him and felt compromised in her principles: "I am disgusted by myself, by the fact that I am serving him again. But, what can I do with this poor body?" (to Alfonso Reyes, 1955[?]; *Tan de usted*, 580). The quote reveals Mistral's recognition of her loss of autonomy and control over her actions; her body overrode her will. From an earlier date, moreover, she was also aware that one of the results of illness is a degree of depersonalization, even of objectification. The individual feels reduced to the ailment, which changes the meaning of her experience and the way in which she relates to her surroundings: "When one gets sick with a serious disease, our people consider us their property, as if we were sad objects" (to Manuel Magallanes Moure, 26 February 1915; *Cartas*).

Organic disorders also cause the ailing individual to magnify the affected area. As Grosz states, "illness engorges specific regions of the body" (76). The affected zone takes over, hindering the individual's command over his or her body and reducing corporeal perception to one area in particular. The ill person will do whatever is necessary to find a cure, to find relief from pain and from the effects of illness as loss of control. In Mistral's case we find evidence of this need in her constant pursuit of better climates, a preoccupation that determined the places she lived and the assignments she accepted: "For the first time in twenty-one years as a consul, I have as subsecretary someone I can talk to about my *clash with certain climates.* None of the others would have ever understood how climate affects the nerves" (to Zenobia Camprubí de Jiménez, 1951; *Antología,* 508; emphasis Mistral's). To Benjamín Carrión she writes: "I am in much better health, happy with the sun, happy with the sea, in good spirits" (1927; *Antología,* 150). And to Adelaida Velasco, who initiated the campaign that led to the Nobel prize: "I will write on the fourteenth to my boss indicating the south of Brazil or California because extreme cold and extreme heat have the same ill effect on me" (1939; *Antología,* 303).

Mistral's illnesses were mostly incurable in her time, so the best she could hope for was containment and relief of symptoms. One form of gaining control over illness, is to participate in the treatment, which like the disease itself, is culturally determined. Firmly grounded in the rural tradition, Mistral pursued alternative therapies to supplement those recommended by her physicians. These she not only determined herself but also recommended to friends with similar health problems. To Alfonso Reyes, who like her suffered from a heart condition, she recommended "the pills made out of pure Yankee wheat, I take three in the morning. When I have a lot of people over during the day, I take one or two before going to bed. . . . Alfonso: *I am very happy to tell you this,* because I think you will feel better with the same remedy" (December 1950; *Tan de usted,* 203; emphasis Mistral's). This is not to say that Mistral rejected traditional medical treatments; on the contrary, she held French and U.S. doctors in high esteem, although she chastised her Brazilian physicians for not recognizing that her partial blindness was a consequence of her diabetes. Departing, however, from the traditional medical paradigm, which expects the patient to relinquish control over his or her body to the physician, Mistral adopted a proactive posture. She fell back on a tradition of folk medicine and homeopathy, widespread in Hispanic America even today.

Writing about one's disease(s) is, as scholars of pathographies have indicated, also an important venue for retaining control over the body, for affirming individual autonomy, and for counteracting invalidism. According to Arthur Frank, "'doing something' about contingency is meta-control. Turning illness into story is a kind of meta-control" (32). It would be inaccurate to contend that Mistral turned any of her illnesses into a story; in fact it is striking, given the preponderance of her references to illness, how little she dwells on them in each letter. This is also evident in the paucity of metaphors—one of the distinguishing features of pathography—she uses to refer to illness. The sheer volume of references to her ailments, however, underscores that writing about her physical condition was an important means for dealing with them.

It is also worth noting that references to illness appear almost exclusively in her epistolary writing. Clearly the personal nature of epistles as a discursive mode is particularly fitting to this kind of intimate disclosure. As with gossip, the discussion of a sickness with a friend deepens and strengthens feelings of intimacy and trust. In her letters to friends who are also ailing—Alfonso Reyes and Juan Ramón Jiménez, for example—she reaches out to them, knowing that they will empathize with her predicament, that they will be able to understand her pain and vulnerability. Once again, then, this intimate sharing becomes an occasion for establishing a community of support. They all needed each other, their sickness setting them apart from those who enjoyed health. This is why her letter to Lydia Cabrera in May 1936, after Teresa de la Parra's death, contains expressions of deep sorrow, as well as a sense of having failed her sick friend because she didn't write to her when she most needed it: "I will never forgive myself this stupid silence" (Mistral et al., 61).

In *Illness as Metaphor,* Susan Sontag distinguishes between the "kingdom of the well" and the "kingdom of the sick." In her rendition, each individual holds dual citizenship, as most everyone moves from one kingdom to another, experiencing illness and recovery multiple times in one's life. Such metaphors of space are almost identical to the ones used by Mistral in her letter "A un Sanatorio-Liceo de California" (To a California high school, 1947), which contains a significant paragraph defining her understanding of the experience of illness: "Pain in general is like a region of a country that we discover, that we enter without noticing, in a silent slide. It is a second home, a hard country since it is not familiar, but whose roads our feet will end up digging up, as we travel with the others. Even she, the illness, once set in habit, becomes bearable. I walk with a couple of ailments as someone who walks between two walls that set me free without limiting the sky and air: that is enough; that which the Lord gives me is enough" (*Antología,* 433).

For Mistral, as for Sontag, sickness is not a condition but a place—a country—inevitable in its existence, unavoidable as one progresses on one's life journey. In Mistral's text, we enter this new place without knowing it, without feeling that we have crossed a border. Individual will and control over the body is therefore illusory, the power of the mind is a mirage, sickness is all-powerful. The only recourse the individual has is to accept the new "homeland"—this metaphor is particularly revealing given her conflicting feelings regarding Chile—however hard and difficult it may be, and to explore it. For Mistral, the harshness of illness lies in its unknown dimensions, in its secret paths, which each individual needs to walk and redraw. Mistral's rendition of sickness is optimistic, since she believes that the individual can conquer it by accepting it and adapting to its demands. As she personalizes her definition, however, the space is reduced to the point of imprisonment: two illnesses—she is clearly exercising poetic license, as her ailments were multiple, not dual—two walls, close together and encroach upon her life, limiting it to the perception of the sky and her ability to breathe. Suddenly the agency of the sick person has disappeared. The individual in the kingdom of the sick has only God to rely upon—Mistral's refuge as she struggled to escape from the imprisonment of physical decay.

Sickness as a place, and the need for each individual to draw his or her map to navigate through this new, unknown land are frequent in pathographies. There is a striking congruence between this representation of sickness and Mistral's life. She suffered from multiple illnesses, which took her to different countries, from one homeland to the next, in perpetual voyage. She sought cures in warm climates only to find herself yet in another place she needed to leave as her exploration of the new land did not bring her the coveted relief. None of these new havens ever afforded the longed-for homeland from which she had been exiled. Her ultimate search for that haven lies in her writing, in this case in the life-writing correspondence that allows her to map out new roads, that does not limit her to seeing the sky and breathing the air, however comforting the belief in God's presence may be.

Note

All translations are mine.

Works Cited

Altman, Janet Gurkin. *Epistolarity.* Columbus: Ohio University Press, 1982.
Fine, Gary A. "Rumors and Gossipping." In *Handbook of Discourse Analysis,* ed. Teun van Dijk. London: Academic Press, 1985.
Frank, Arthur. *The Wounded Storyteller: Body, Illness, and Ethics.* Chicago: University of Chicago Press, 1995.
Friedman, Susan Stanford. "Women's Autobiographical Selves: Theory and Practice." In *Women, Autobiography, Theory,* ed. Sidonie Smith, 72–82. Madison: University of Wisconsin Press, 1998.

Grosz, Elizabeth. *Volatile Bodies: Toward a Corporeal Feminism.* Bloomington: Indiana University Press, 1994.

Guerrero, Pedro Pablo. "Sylvia Molloy: Los silencios del yo." *Revista de Libros* (July 7, 2001): 5.

Horan, Elizabeth. *Gabriela Mistral: An Artist and Her People.* Washington D.C.: Organization of American States Interamer, 1994.

———, and Doris Meyer, ed. and trans. *This America of Ours: The Letters of Gabriela Mistral and Victoria Ocampo.* Austin: University of Texas Press, forthcoming.

Kaminsky, Amy. *Reading the Body Politic: Feminist Criticism and Latin American Women Writers.* Minneapolis: University of Minnesota Press, 1993.

Mistral, Gabriela. *Antología mayor.* 4 vols. Vol. 3, *Cartas.* Comp. Luis Vargas Saavedra. Santiago: Cochrane, 1992.

———. *Cartas de amor de Gabriela Mistral.* Comp. Sergio Fernández Larraín. Santiago: Andrés Bello, 1978.

———. *Epistolario de Gabriela Mistral y Eduardo Barrios.* Comp. Luis Vargas Saavedra. Santiago: Pontificia Universidad Católica de Chile, 1988.

———. *Tan de usted: Epistolario de Gabriela Mistral con Alfonso Reyes.* Comp. Luis Vargas Saavedra. Santiago: Hachette/Ediciones Universidad Católica de Chile, 1990.

— ———. *Vuestra Gabriela: Cartas inéditas de Gabriela Mistral a los Errázuriz Echeñique y Tomic Errázuriz.* Ed. Luis Vargas Saavedra. Santiago: Editora Zig-Zag, 1995.

Mistral, Gabriela, Teresa de la Parra, and Lydia Cabrera. *Cartas a Lydia Cabrera: Correspondencia inédita de Gabriela Mistral y Teresa de la Parra.* Ed. Rosario Hiriart. Madrid: Ediciones Torremozas, 1988.

Sontag, Susan. *Illness as Metaphor.* New York: Vintage Books, 1979.

Spacks, Patricia Meyer. *Gossip.* New York: Knopf, 1985.

Yurkievich, Saúl. "El don epistolar." In *Cartas: 1937–1983* by Julio Cortázar, ed. Aurora Bernárdez, 18–23. Buenos Aires: Alfaguara, 2000.

Chapter 13

Mirror to the Nation
Posthumous Portraits of Gabriela Mistral

Elizabeth Horan

CHILE'S MOURNING OF Gabriela Mistral's death was a climactic moment in her transformation into a national symbol. Her posthumous representations on postage stamps and currency evoke nationalist sentiment in dynastic and religious configurations, depicting a saintly schoolteacher, an absent Nobel queen, and, to a lesser extent, a loyal citizen-peasant. These representations create the impression of a timeless, mythic, noble past for the nation as an imagined fraternal community. Recognizing the political circumstances of her portraiture, including her own ambiguous, often contradictory identifications suggests how women have been used as symbols of nationhood.

La Mistral Memorialized: The Dead Body

To judge from the rapt attention of the press and other national institutions, Mistral's death, wake, funeral, and eventual entombment constituted the most newsworthy aspect of the writer's long, turbulent, productive career.[1] Multiple national institutions, agencies, and associations coordinated the handling of the corpse after her death from pancreatic cancer and her funeral in St. Patrick's Cathedral in New York City. The Ministry of Foreign Relations worked with the military to fly the body to Lima, where the Chilean air force brought it to Santiago, with a full military honor guard. The Ministry of Education (Mistral's employer for much of her life) presided over a wake that celebrated Mistral as a beloved teacher. For the three days of official mourning the corpse lay in state at the University of Chile. The university's rector led the pallbearers, chosen from the trustees of the university. Documentation of the mourning constituted a Who's Who of national citizenship: newspapers recorded the presence of then president Carlos Ibáñez del Campo with his wife, prominent churchmen, bureaucrats, and university officials by the coffin. Recorded with equal care, although on separate pages, are long lines of Chilean citizens, including children (sometimes barefoot, sometimes in school uniforms) lined up for hours in the bright sun and filing past the open casket, which lay in the university's Salon de Honor. With numerous close-ups of the open casket and an inventory of its effects, as well as excerpts from the speeches of dignitaries, the national press embraced the hagiographic discourse that has subsequently dominated Mistral's reputation.

Although present before her death, the use of religious and dynastic terms to describe Gabriela Mistral becomes intense and pervasive in her memorialization, signaling the conditions of her entrance into the public imaginary of national identity. The public pageantry surrounding Mistral, in her life as in her death, builds on the "imagined community" of the nation.[2] Mistral first appealed to that imagined community through print, in the category of the teacher, a public servant with religious overtones, somewhere between guru, spiritual teacher, and living saint.[3]

The ideal of Mistral as teacher combines with textual references and iconography likening Gabriela Mistral to the Virgin, to solve one of modern nationalism's central problems: how to represent, or even to acknowledge, individual historical women within the vast, horizontal fraternity of national citizenship. Pedro Prado's 1922 evocation of the poet on her departure for Mexico, as "the last echo of Mary of Nazareth" was the first to compare her with the Virgin (Prado; in Mistral, *En batalla,* 95). Praise in regal and religious terms emerges with the subject's absence from the national territory, while comparison with the Virgin becomes more pronounced following her death: even otherwise sober chronologies describe the three days of official mourning as an apotheosis.

The "apotheosis" suggests that the body is *the* obstacle to recognizing women as citizens. The university's rector honored this problem of the body in a eulogy that bestowed on her the interesting, anomalous, almost asexual title "angelic doctor." More attuned to the popular imagination was singer-songwriter Violeta Parra's elegiac, "farewell verse," in which heaven prepares a throne for its newest saint, "President and benefactress / of the Spanish language" (208). Parra's memorial typifies subsequent representations, setting Mistral in the Marianic role of strategic intercessor and making Chile a source of shared identity.

Mistral's large, real, female body, with her brown skin, habitual frown, and size-ten shoes, poses a problem for nationalist iconography's inclination to acknowledge the female form only in allegorical representations such as Liberty, Justice, and Republican Motherhood. The Virgin, by contrast, is a figure of victory over both sex and death: in life, alone among her sex; in death, she alone, among all heaven and earth, ascends to heaven in corporeal form. Where portrayal of the poet's youth presents a hagiographic narrative of heroism arising out of the bodily and sexual denial of one who is "more of a mother than mothers," memorials to Gabriela Mistral downplay narrative. Death makes her uncorrupted, incorruptible body a sign for the nation's heroic, remote, and rural past. For the queen, as for the saint, that body is desexualized.[4]

The figures of Mistral as female saint and as queen lead to the land and the body's belonging to the "imagined community" of the nation.[5] Saint and queen reiterate the central concern with death and immortality that is nationalism's greatest source of strength (Anderson, 18). Bodily presence, death, immortality, and the land are closely linked in the saint, whose mortal remains bespeak triumph over death, blessing the land and the environs, providing spiritual mediation as well as pride and revenue to the surrounding, religiously based community. While the saint is most powerful dead, the queen matters most alive, in dynastic continuity for the subjects of her realm, as she represents the nation abroad, beyond physical borders. The saint attends to the interests of her devout followers in heaven, while the queen represents them on earth.

Confirming the religious and dynastic terms employed in creating and maintaining national identity is the fact that critics of the hubbub surrounding Mistral's funeral questioned its management but not the underlying premise of the subject's sanctity. Alfonso Calderón pointed, for instance, to scandal of the corpse, asserting that the North Americans had turned her into a Joan Crawford, a Hollywood nabob, for Mistral's body arrived deodorized, embalmed, touched up with cosmetics, hair neatly coifed. The movie star is false royalty: however heroic her reputation, the star (unlike the saint or the queen) has no direct connection to the land. Calderón went on to further contest the management of Mistral's funeral.[6] Describing the atmosphere of the wake as stultified with the odor of dead flowers and the presence of generals, he asserts a populist Mistral identified with the provincial middle class, more attuned to the appeal of the austere "rural schoolteacher," soberly dressed, in dark colors, wearing no jewels.

Documentation of the nation's solidarity in mourning Mistral cites the outpouring of crowds during her two return visits to Chile (in 1938 and 1954.) Framing the funeral as a third and final return establishes a historical continuity for the nation's attitude toward the subject. That reputation and public viewing create the national memory of Mistral as a saint is evident in the treatment of the body following the funeral: *inventio* (discovery of the body), *translatio* (the transport of the body and relics to a place of veneration) and the subsequent publication of testimony regarding her day-to-day shows of concern for her family, the nation.[7] Although Mistral had real enemies, the corporate interests of the nation kept them at bay so that her body did not suffer the reverse inventio occurring with former first lady Eva Perón, whether in the whisking of Eva's embalmed corpse across countries and continents for twenty-three years, or in the public viewing of glass-encased jewels labeled with their cost to "the people" in order to belie the former first lady's image as humble advocate of the poor.

When Gabriela Mistral stands for the nation's timeless, rural origins, the rural schoolteacher—rather than the diplomat, the writer, or even the school administrator—is her most frequently invoked role. Mistral held that real job from about 1909 to 1918. She had left the schoolroom forty years before her death, but Once a teacher, always a teacher seems to be the rule. The Association of Chilean Primary School Teachers provided temporary shelter for her corpse: a vault in Santiago's General Cemetery, decorated with verses from Mistral's "La oración de la maestra" (The teacher's prayer). The queen is dead, long live the queen, is the subtext of the translatio to Montegrande three years after her death. Emilio Mohor, a physician present at the exhumation, writes as if unaware that the corpse had been embalmed, noting that she appears "regal," the gown untouched, the body uncorrupted (in Gazarian-Gautier, 110). While the Church's interests are honored throughout, the translatio is a public pageant handled by the Ministry of the Interior rather than Education: national interests were at stake in this occasion of closing in on eternity.

Continuity between real body, remembered teacher, and imagined saint or queen converge at the tomb. After a lifetime of vast public homage and diplomatic ceremony, Mistral in writing her will clearly understood that the physical presence of her tomb in Montegrande, in the Elqui valley, would turn the area into a pilgrimage center, bringing clear economic and perhaps moral benefits to the inhabitants, by virtue of their association with the hallowed dead. She could not have anticipated, however, the precise outlines of the struggle between differing versions of historical continuity in Chile, from the opening of the tomb, in 1960, to the present day.

Jesting references to the civic qualities of her beyond-the-grave interventions appear in the comic allusions of Sillie Utternut to how "la adivina Gabriela" caused an earthquake by turning in her grave, in her response to election results (57–58). In a more serious vein, by 1964 the National Writers' Union placed a headstone engraved with a line indicating the artist's social role: What the soul does for its body, the artist does for his people. A group of schoolteachers subsequently organized children in a subscription drive to pay for the bronze bust and plaque now placed on the hillside just below the grave. Then, during the 1970s and 1980s, various police groups marked their presence by affixing plaques to the stone wall facing this bronze. The bronze bust embodies the paradox of the memorial: she is present as a body, yet her gaze is averted. She exists as in life, as the radical embodiment of memory: "I never forget."

The ghostly, illusory presence-and-absence of Mistral dominates memorials to her. Appealing to her memory stamps a sense of historical legitimacy onto a variety of local projects, physic-celestial (a nebula, Ngc3324, found by scientists at Chile's El Tololo observatory in 1995, supposedly bearing her image), mechanistic-aerial (the dispute in 1993 over whether to rename the La Serena airport for her or for Gabriel González Videla), and earthy-cultural (agricultural products).[8] In view of the saint-queen figure's tie to the land, the last is an interesting aspect of the export grape industry that was substantially expanded throughout the 1980s. Promotional literature for this industry depicts the Valle de Elqui as a timeless milieu of rugged individuals (i.e., small-time capitalists) with a long-standing devotion to profitable viniculture. Such pamphlets endow the grape industry with an air of antiquity that belies the objective modernity of that industry's recent domination of the Elqui valley, an area that was agriculturally far more diverse in the poet's childhood than it is today. The pamphlet reproduces the sculpted relief of Mistral's face as it watches over the improvements of the present, blessing the bridge to the remote, humble, antiquated, yet glorious past that the industry promotes.

Where Mistral as an agricultural product is figural, the preservation of the schoolroom associated with Mistral's childhood literally reconstructs the past, tailored to state interests. Five minutes from the tomb one may visit the small, dark room of the primary school where Lucila Godoy Alcayaga was one of some two dozen students of her half-sister, Emelina Molina. The two sisters and their mother lived in a single room adjacent to the schoolroom and postal station. In the schoolroom, only the huge map of Chile and the battered copy of the national shield are recognizably worn, whereas the solid floors of Oregon pine, the room's clean, intact walls, and the back doors always open to a sunny backyard patio ringed with well-established trees all bespeak a past far more pleasant than the rural schools where Mistral worked, from 1905 to 1920, in ramshackle, damp, poorly heated buildings. The only obvious antiquities, in the pamphlets as in the schoolroom, are the symbols of nationhood, the irreducible specifics of Chile: Mistral, map, shield, and nominal allusions to an indigenous past predating Spanish conquest. All else is silently revamped to meet present convenience, predicting a prosperous, albeit bland future in which controversy, discord, and difference are swept to the side and under the rug.

Mistral's Saintly Vita

Narratives of Mistral's origins in the Elqui valley encompass genealogy, childhood, and youth in a nationalist adaptation of hagiographic rhetoric, permeated and shaped by overlapping critical anxieties about sexual and ethnic and racial identity. Just as hagiography suppresses the saint's individuality in the name of conformity, so does the narrative construction of the saintly person's life respond to the eccentricity of a subject whose real life constantly threatened feminine decorum and contradicted the mass of stereotypes about the Chilean. Hagiographic criticism has been ruled by a heterosexist panic that turns Mistral's childlessness and alienation from any traditional family center into charity toward children and reverence for maternity. To support the cliché of the home-loving, sedentary housewife, her lifetime of wandering is ascribed to paternal inheritance. Her suspiciousness bordering on paranoia and her life in exile from a Chile that ostensibly loved her becomes devotion to Latin America. The theological virtues of poverty (she wouldn't handle money, according to Samatán and Ladrón de Guevara), modesty (she had no idea of dressing for public homages and state occasions, no idea of her own importance, according to Ladrón de Guevara and Rodig), and humility (she discarded any and all drafts of her work, according to Rodig) are summoned up to account for her dependence on a series of intelligent, capable, single women who helped her with matters of business, dress, protocol, and editing.

Making up for the absence of the father and of men generally is *the* favored subject in the Mistral vita, producing genealogical speculations that ignore women and concentrate on the paternal line.[9] Only the rhetorical commonplace of Elqui as Golden Age even approximates the imaginative energy thrust onto Jerónimo Godoy as the source of his daughter's wanderlust and her vocations as writer and teacher.[10] The importance ascribed to him is all the more remarkable given that his daughter barely knew him, since her parents separated when she was three, for reasons usually attributed to the father's itch to travel or his ambitions to get ahead, compared to her mother's sedentary nature and (in some more modern versions) silent or active dislike for his "bohemian" lifestyle. Virgilio Figueroa cites the father as the example that inspired her, writing of her determination and clearsightedness as salient aspects of a Horatia Alger–type "[l]ife plan: fight, persevere, win" (49).

Fascination with Jerónimo Godoy works to uphold gender distinctions, to compensate for Mistral's deviance from feminine norms and to reinforce the national myth of the "typical" Chilean fortune seeker: somewhat bohemian, fond of alcohol and music, founder of "accidental" families. This male wanderer of the world shouldn't be judged, it is implied, by the moral criteria evident in the descriptions of Mistral, her mother, and sister, in pious lines about devotion in the face of poverty. The scant detail about these and other specific women who loomed large in Mistral's day-to-day life is striking, given her abundant writing about them as compared to her scarce references to her father.[11]

Accounts of Mistral's life usually feature a childhood conforming to central conventions of feminine sanctity: austerity, obedience, inclination to solitude, a special gift for prayer. The poverty in which she lived with her mother and sister serves for austerity, even though her father knew a similar if not worse poverty, and the three women were better off than many others. For obedience there is her oft-quoted devotion to her mother; for childhood humility, shyness manifest in her stutter and suffering in silence taunts from her schoolmates and unjust accusations from an uncomprehending teacher. The inclination to solitude and special gift for prayer converge in sentimental descriptions of her childhood colloquies with lizards and flowering almond trees, following the poet-saint Francis of Assisi.

For women, overcoming sexuality and the body is central to the drama of the saint's story of confrontation with evil. To identify Mistral with private passion and emotion to the exclusion of intellectuality and reason is central to how hagiography serves nationalist interests. Sainthood flattens women's lives (but not men's) to moral and sexual terms. For females but not males the official classification turns on sexual classification within primary categories—virgin, martyr, confessor—in which no men are described as virgins and no women as confessors. Feminine virtue is embattled virginity: the obliteration of the subject's sexuality provides the foundation of the young poet's fame, in the episode of Romelio Ureta and in the humility of the unostentatious young woman who came to the attention of the Santiago cognoscenti and her anguished "Sonetos de la muerte." While the central figure of the Sonetos is an angry, defiant young woman who has undergone the fire trial and emerged pure—that is, desexed—critics curiously omit that anger, instead stressing love's purifying effect: "When love put zeal in her soul and pain purified its effect, a great poet was revealed" (in Figueroa, 77). "Secret love" becomes self-abnegation: "She consigned her hopeful vow, in which she asked for forgiveness for having suffered and having delivered to men, like Job, the secret of her pain" (Carrión, 27). Finally, the legend about how the poet anonymously attended the ceremony awarding first prize to her Sonetos, listening to her verses declaimed from the balcony, insists on her modesty and lack of proper clothing. The legend suppresses the gender circumstances of the event, in which the winner, as a poet and a woman, was forced into an untenable position as the first-prizewinner charged with composing and reciting verses to honor the girls who made up the beauty contest portion of the "Juegos florales."

The hagiographic imagination of critics more than corrects the poet's discomfort with gender strictures. As an aspect of the Mistral vita, the Ureta episode fulfills multiple requirements for female sanctity. Figueroa, followed by Augusto Iglesias, sets the tone for a long line of critics who elaborate on this supposed longing, a fantasy of heterosexual love: "She gets drunk on the voluptuousness of mutual love, which makes her live in the harem of ineffable pleasures" (83). Making a suffering adolescent of the poet establishes her as "guilt-ridden." Her not marrying and showing no inclinations to marry becomes a "spiritual betrothal" to the beloved. Yet the evidence from her writing evidences a close association of violence and sexual attraction. Mistral's descriptions of sexual intimacy tend to emphasize violence and violation: "I have brutal images in my mind of the physical union between beings, which makes it abhorrent" (in Fernández, 61, 141). For the critics, however, sexual renunciation, the capacity to suffer, a sense of helpless guilt all come together in the hagiographic cornucopia of Mistral as symbolic mother. A "public woman" (and not *una mujer pública*)[12] is acceptable, provided she's a virgin (a male woman) or a virgin mother (uncontaminated by sex). The active sanctity of Mistral's role as symbolic mother legitimates her public presence: "Gabriela Mistral's sanctity is an active sanctity. All those sanctities conjoin to create the epitome of maternity, that which has become her life's profession: the sanctity of the Teacher" (Carrión, 41).[13]

Averted Gaze: The Politics of Portraiture, 1958–1989

The extensive press coverage of the funeral works with Mistral as an icon who helps ensure the continuity of her memory within the national imaginary and who assists in image production long after her demise, in public art, in postage stamps, and in currency. Like the hagiographic vita, which desexed and disembodied her, posthumous portraits present Mistral as an unchanging emblem of the nation's mythic past. More than the funeral, both stamps and money exemplify Mistral's status as an empty signifier, available for a variety of national projects and leaders, for she literally and metaphorically *circulates* within and beyond the boundaries of the nation. While the exact contours of her figure's invocation closely correspond to specifically political exigencies, the national context in which all of them appear requires a codification of the gender relations that ironically she spent so much of her life contesting. The circulation of Mistral's figure on stamps and money necessarily misrepresents her: any abundance of details from the life of the historical woman would undermine the conformity and uniformity of nationhood.

Honoring the first anniversary of Mistral's death, the Chilean government under the presidency of Carlos Ibáñez issued a commemorative postage stamp. It was the first time that a historical woman other than Isabel la Católica had been depicted in Chilean postage, for the portrayal of historical persons on postage stamps is an honor limited to royalty and the dead.[14] The engraving for the 1958 stamp (see fig. 1A) is taken from a photo for which Mistral had posed in about 1923, at about age thirty-four, when she was working in Mexico (Arce and García, 148–49). The sitter's closed eyes suggest inward concentration and ab-

FIGURE 1A. Issued after the poet's death, this 1958 stamp marked the first time that a female historical figure other than Queen Isabella I of Spain (and the Madonna) was depicted on a Chilean postage stamp. Photograph courtesy of the author.

solute detachment from human interaction, utterly refusing the gaze. While taken "from life," the portrait draws from funerary conventions of the profile, a pose reserved for important persons, used in antiquity for coins. Both the original photo and its reproduction on the stamp are highly masculinized: the funerary ledge inscribed *Correos de Chile* replaces the finery of profile portraits of women, more often created as part of a dowry than as representations on coins. The name Gabriela Mistral inscribed above a wreathlike lyre and leafy branch asserts the figure as a laureate, while the printed dates 1889–1957 stress the commemorative intent and reinforce the overall mood of sobriety and restraint. The utter absence of individual characteristics holds to the idea of the coin as an image made for national and possible transnational circulation.

In a 1966 stamp issued under President Eduardo Frei, the ghostly, transparent gray complexion of the death mask representation of Mistral recalls casket shots of her funeral, bringing with it a recall of that moment of national solidarity (see fig. 1B). While the eyes are closed, as in the previous portrait, the full-face representation of Mistral as a death mask can make for more solicitude, even if she's a bodiless wraith, a phantom from the past. Where the 1958 stamp presents an

FIGURE 1B. The ghostly figure in this 1966 stamp promotes a literacy campaign under the center-left regime of Frei. Photograph courtesy of the author.

isolated profile, this figure is depicted in solicitous guidance over two male figures, an adult and a child, seated before an open book, for this version of Mistral appears as a symbol of concern for the nation's progress toward the announced goal of literacy. Here is the solidarity of the national family: the ghostly Mistral, dead spiritual mother become tutelary angel, watches over the solidarity of father and son.

The creation of an eternal type requires flattening specific details that would contradict the subject's standing as a generic representative. Here, the figures represented are male even though Mistral's pedagogical career in Chile took place almost exclusively in the segregated world of girls' high schools. Like most children, she learned to read from a female: in her case, a primary school teacher, her half-sister, Emelina. Stipulating a sacred, unchanging presence, the symbol dismisses such specifics, for it is oriented toward a present and future idea of a nation whose important readers and citizens are de facto male and disembodied.

The death mask invocation recalling the national solidarity of Mistral's funeral reappears amid a range of other significations in an open-air mural that measures ten by five and a half meters (see fig. 2). The mural consists of individually painted ceramic tiles designed by Chil-

FIGURE 2. A mural in downtown Santiago installed in 1971, during the socialist government of Salvador Allende. Photograph courtesy of the author.

ean artist-architect Fernando Daza. Complex, encompassing multiple visual planes, executed in a style both symbolist and abstract, the composition recalls the heyday of Mexican mural paintings in the 1930s. It was commissioned by the municipal government of Santiago, probably following the September elections, and presented in a public ceremony on 22 October 1970.[15] Where *El Mercurio* did not comment on the mural, the leftist *La Nación* indicated that Mistral's association with children merited her a permanent place here, at the omphalos of the city: "the author who always wanted to be near the children, now has a place reserved for eternity, on the foothills that children traverse daily." Located on the side of the Cerro Santa Lucía, the foundational site for what would become the city of Santiago, the mural bears the legend, LA CIUDAD DE SANTIAGO A GABRIELA MISTRAL.

The mural sets Mistral in relation to maternity and labor, where she serves, as women so often do, as a boundary marker visibly upholding the fetishes of national difference. Here, those realms include the time-less, rural past, associated with the land and indigenous purity; em-bodied motherhood, associated with the Andes and children, the nation's prime material; and the world of industry, associated with ho-mogenous citizen-workers. The robed figure of Mistral isolates the Andean world of enthroned maternity to the far right. The train of her gown frames the world of labor, close to the center, raised up and cele-brated as key to the nation's progressive future. Mistral is the door for these citizens and the wall of socialization toward which a line of naked children marches away from their equally naked, but static, mother. Her stance of receiving the children resembles that of Jesus, while the quasi-religious status of the educator is evidenced in the book that she holds in her left hand and in the dark, flowing robes that completely desexualize her flat-chested body.

With tireless modern industry and timeless seasonal agriculture be-hind her, facing the realm of children and the mother, the flat, isolated figure of Gabriela Mistral belongs to neither realm. She is the asexual conduit through which the naked children must pass. Of the fifteen figures in the mural, only Mistral bears no gender markings, and only the mother is engaged in no visible activity whatsoever. Mistral also exists, in the mural, in agriculture—another aspect of the nation's time-less rural past associated with Indians and the land—as two disem-bodied death masks amid the roots.

After 1973

Government-sponsored versions of Gabriela Mistral from 1973 through at least the mid-1980s appear within a campaign of repudiat-ing the preceding socialist regime's cultural program. Within this cam-paign of repudiation, the official celebration of Mistral as quasi-regal Nobel laureate contrasts with the absence of official celebrations for Pablo Neruda, Chile's "other" Nobel laureate, associated with the previous socialist regime. Where the previous regime used representations such as the mural to note the presence of indigenous peoples in the remote past, the post-1973 Mistral stipulates a single, homogeneous national identity in which non-European racial identification becomes socially unacceptable: within the post-1973 formulation, "Somos Chilenos," describing oneself as Indian or mestizo, amounts to saying "I am poorly adapted." At times, "Gabriela Mistral" presents a middle ground: the state-subsidized Editorial Quimantú was renamed Editorial Gabriela Mistral before being closed down entirely.

Another facet of the program of reshaping the nation's history and identity was the new national currency issued in 1981, which honored on banknotes two pre-twentieth-century figures, the military hero Arturo Prat and the conservative jurist Diego Portales, in addition to Mistral, the only twentieth-century figure in the series. The profile portrait of Mistral on the five-thousand-peso note (the second-highest denomination, worth about $40 when first issued) is a realistic engraving based on a photograph taken in her later life, somewhere between 1950 and 1954 (see fig. 3A). This representation of a stoic Mistral approaching old age perhaps reifies the regime's image of its constituency as mature, stability-seeking citizens. The portrait of Mistral on the front of the note bears the legend "Gabriela Mistral" just above the nape of her neck, and on the back of the note is, "Nobel Prize 1945." The reference would not be to the Swedish academy, for Sweden was not especially friendly to the seventeen-year dictatorship. Rather, the reference to the Nobel suggests the vaguer quality of "international esteem," which the military government constantly asserted and relentlessly sought.

The old-age Mistral of the banknote abandons both the death mask image, associated with the mass public solidarity of the funeral, and the religious symbolism of earlier representation. To legitimate the nation's origins as dating from the remote past, the reverse of the note depicts scenes from an antiquity that is vaguely classical—that is, Greco-Roman, or more precisely, Augustan, as in Augusto Pinochet—promoting family values (see fig. 3B). The antiquity celebrated is not antique, Indian,

FIGURE 3A. A 1981 bank note issued under the Pinochet military regime depicts a visibly older and distanced Mistral. Photograph courtesy of the author.

mestizo, or even specifically Latin American, for the image on the reverse of the note is drawn directly from the scene on the modern Nobel medallion. A man, nude but for the laurel wreath of the poet, writes while a decorously robed woman holds the lyre aloft: she is the Muse, the inspiration, not herself a producer of poetry. When the banknote is raised to the light, a watermark appears, a foregrounded profile of Mistral that faces but does not see the seated male.

The banknote, issued under Pinochet, concurs with the 1970 socialist-realist mural in placing woman, and Mistral, outside of politics. The front of the banknote presents a family grouped much as in the 1970 mural: a woman enthroned with a small boy on her lap. As before, Mistral is juxtaposed to active citizens and a frozen family, embodied as "enthroned motherhood," with the state supplying the place of the father. The females on the banknote, be they allegorical or historical, are passive, decorously robed watchers in a clearly male-centered representation of the state, which only nominally honors Mistral as Nobel

FIGURE 3B. The reverse of the 1981 bank note, invoking the Nobel prize, represents a male artist and a female muse. Photograph courtesy of the author.

laureate and which presents women only as figures of Charity and the Muse, attending to boys and men. The great inconsistency of this appropriation of Mistral is that a note ostensibly honoring a woman writer represents male figures—the seated male writer, the doubly enthroned boy—as the only active, writing, speaking subjects.

A set of four multicolored stamps was issued in April 1989 for the centenary of Mistral's birth (see fig. 4). The stamps appeared in a period of political transition, amid the first presidential and parliamentary campaigns in over seventeen years. No previous version of Mistral in public art so extensively incorporates text into the images. The theme of Latin America is omnipresent in depictions of Mistral outside Chile by way of quotations on the stamps themselves and by two lengthier quotations printed on a border around the set, usually discarded when the stamps are used for postage or sold to collectors. This combination of text and imagery creates a narrative more specific than previous representations, attending to locale, to precise stages in the poet's life, and to her publications. Each stamp portrays a distinct

FIGURE 4. Postage stamps commemorating the 1989 centenary of Mistral's birth. Photograph courtesy of the author.

epoch or aspect of the subject's life, with the issue of national identity threading throughout, throwing a very wide net of quotes demonstrating the inconsistency and subjectivity of how "the nation" is experienced: in the first stamp, as a chosen condition (the return to Elqui); in the second, as an essence ("the beauty of the lesson"); in the third, as inescapable ("a 'knot' of identity"), and in the fourth, as transcendent ("at this time . . . the direct voice").

In registering "Gabriela of Montegrande" as a kind of genius loci, the centenary stamps reiterate and absorb the preexisting categories of Mistral teacher and Nobel queen, adding a new, more palpably masculine one, faithful citizen. That category is implicit in the first stamp's specific reference to Montegrande in the Elqui valley, as represented by the mountain slopes and distinctive steeple of the village church. Mistral's head as she appeared in her twenties is a disembodied visage lightly sketched against Montegrande, under the legend, *Chile, o la voluntad de ser,* that is, the nation is not a given but conscious effort, "to make a homeland," with the irreducibly specific Montegrande and the ghost of the young Mistral invoked to inspire that action. This youthful ghost is both a genius loci and a revamped version of the death mask, tutelary spirit.

The second stamp of the series, more openly didactic than the first, represents the now familiar scene of the poet, wearing her schoolmistress cape, a triangulated figure towering over the faithful: a round of schoolgirls. She recalls the Madonna of the Misericordia (of fifteenth-century painter Piero della Francesca, for example), the Intercessor, who intercedes for those too weak or awed to deal with God directly. This portrait is probably not taken from a photo: Mistral did not smile for photos taken in her capacity as a schoolteacher. The scene's location emerges from a quote from *Desolación:* "All lessons are susceptible to beauty." National identity, too, is a lesson to be learned, while the schoolteacher-madonna is the most readily recognized aspect of beauty in her public figure.

The third stamp presents the poet in profile, isolated, seated at a desk, writing, in the most masculinized version of her body in the centenary set. Her gray-streaked hair, the progression beyond the schoolteacher phase, the absence of any backdrop identifiably Chilean, even the three books on the desk suggest Mistral during the second half of her life, living in exile. Above the desk are printed the words "I emerged from a labyrinth of hills and something of that impossible, unsolveable knot remains in what I do, be it verse or prose." The narrative of the four stamps contextualizes this statement as an expression of loyalty to Chile, a delicate subject after nearly two decades when one in fourteen Chileans saw fit, or was forced, to live abroad. Yet in Mistral's writings generally, loyalty is rooted not in Chile but in Elqui and Montegrande: the latter, more than Chile, are the topoi to which the writer perpetually returns.

The fourth and last stamp of the series depicts Mistral regally attired in the famous black-velvet gown, shaking hands with King Gustav of Sweden as he hands her a small box and some papers. A gigantic drawing of the golden Nobel medallion forms the backdrop. Inscribed down the right-hand margin is a phrase from her acceptance speech: "I am at this moment the direct voice of the poets of my race." In the narrative of the four scenes, it is a transcendent moment in which the country schoolteacher makes good: summoned by the king, her individual effort recognized and rewarded, she recalls, at the height of her success, her origins and remains true to them. What those origins or "race" may be, is open to interpretation, but the printed text has been guiding us along: it is "Chile, the will to be, a lesion susceptible to beauty, a labyrinth of hills, a knot without solution . . . remains in everything that I do." Yet in the larger context of her Nobel prize speech, the ideal *race* that Mistral honors is not specifically Chilean but generally Latin American, for she accepts the prize on behalf of a fictively unified Latin America.

As a whole, the state's recognition of Mistral gestures toward the symbolic inclusion of one woman even as it silences her, and women generally, as speaking, active, historical subjects. In general her writing and presence are subordinated to a ghostly ideal. In all cases the message is that a woman may exist in the public sphere so long as she is isolated and desexed, for the conditions on woman's entry into the public sphere require that she be identified with the nation's secular school system and that her private life be full of Christlike suffering. She becomes the exception that proves the rule: "The figure of Gabriela Mistral condenses all feminine characteristics, if we except those, often charming, but contained in the possible word *frivolous*" (Enrique Díaz Canedo; in Figueroa, 157–58).

Palimpsest of Identity: The Return of the Erased

Until recently, the hagiographic tradition of unchanging, exemplary heroic virtue has dominated Mistral's reputation. Mistral's 1989 centenary epitomized the dehistoricized aspect of her canonization, with more recent writers indicating an awareness of how the construction of sanctity often entails the exclusion of complexity, accuracy, or specificity. As we become more aware of historical specifics, we find that Mistral is not alone: other writer-educators—Sor Juana, in Mexico; Carmen Lyra, in Costa Rica—have been similarly canonized, with narratives of their work and intellectual background subordinated to a personal life rendered along the lines of hagiography. Sanctity is at once an enabling fiction that apparently creates a space for women within history and a set of conditions that tend to limit women as speaking, historical subjects. The biography of the saint matters less for the individual than for the community. In this context, Mistral is a figure that expresses, establishes, and negotiates some aspect of the social order, teaching us "something about the group which selected them" (Delooz, 189). "Gabriela Mistral" is a message variously emptied or filled with meanings depending on who receives the message from whom. Just as we may get, from one generation to the next, an Augustine who struggles with chastity, rival schools of philosophy, or monotheism, so has Gabriela Mistral varied: descendant of conquistadores or mestiza; rural teacher, socialist saint, Nobel queen, loyal pioneer; Horatia Alger. The sum of these representations appears as a mirror for ghosts, an always shifting memory of what the nation would like to consider its past.

Notes

This chapter is a condensation of an earlier essay that appeared in *Taller de letras* 26 (1996). All translations are mine.

1. Coverage of the funeral, circulating first in the national press and then in *Revista de educación nacional, Orfeo,* and the University of Chile's *Homenaje a Gabriela Mistral* recalled and surpassed the ample attention to the poet's two previous visits to Chile, in September 1954 under Carlos Ibáñez and in September 1938, during the contentious presidential election campaign leading to the victory of Frente Popular (Popular Front) candidate Pedro Aguirre Cerda. By contrast, far less attention went to the Nobel prize ceremony in 1945.

2. See Anderson's book on the nation as "imagined community."
3. On how the teacher constructs an audience of women, and on Mistral's conscious desexualization of herself, see Horan (*Gabriela Mistral,* "Sor Juana," and "Gabriel[a]") and Fiol-Matta.
4. Descriptions of Mistral's body desex her, avoiding mention of her limbs but instead lingering over her eyes, which Torres Rioseco has described as green, Gazarian-Gautier as blue-green, and Sepúlveda as blue. Torres echoes advertisements for beauty crème in descriptions of Mistral's hands as "aristocratic" and "not at all like a peasant's."
5. Beyond *saint* and *queen,* Mistral identified as *campesina* likewise supports the nation conceived as a vast, horizontal comradeship, yet the campesina is a mortal figure, exposed to the unpredictability of the land, heir only to the body's frailties in a lack or powerlessness that ideology uses to define the community of the dispossessed. Where *the queen* exists on a separate plane from the community, bringing prestige to it, *la campesina* would represent the base of the community, and the struggle for land and resources, leading to widely divergent interpretations of Mistral's public actions, for example, her speech from the presidental palace of La Moneda, in Santiago, in 1954, congratulating the assembled populace on a land reform program that existed only in her own mind: while Díaz Arrieta suggests that she was verging on senility in this speech, Concha and Teitelboim follow Fernando Alegría in suggesting that Mistral was deliberating trying to embarrass the government into action.
6. Calderón here follows Ladrón de Guevara and María Urzúa.
7. The saint's relation involves personal relations and local power: thus, "Santa Gabriela" identified with Elqui. Nationhood involves formal relations: "Presidenta Mistral" identified with Chile.
8. Jaime Quezada, "Gabriela Mistral y las estrellas," *El Mercurio,* 9 April 1995, E12; Rosa Markmann de González Videla to editor of *El Mercurio;* published as "Cambio de nombre," in *El Mercurio.*
9. Genealogies "function as a legitimation of power and also as versions of history" (Williams, 37). Díaz Arrieta bestows Mistral with a white, European background: "descendants of the conquistadores"; "the true aristocracy" (9). Peruvian writer Ciro Alegría, by contrast, furnishes her with Inca antecedents. Vicuña specifies *mestizaje* not as essence but disguise and performance: "She disguises it [the Andean] setting it free and allowing it to blossom among the raiment of her Christianity. The mestiza is like a popular religious feast, where the ancestral indigenous people adopt the Judeo-Christian language to speak" (97).

10. Most descriptions of the poet's childhood milieu in the Elqui valley are written by urbanites and they reiterate conventions of the nation's past as forming a golden age in which race and class privileges do not exist.

11. Concha notes that Mistral always lived with a household of women, while Fernando Alegría notes the omnipresence of secretaries. Most reconstructions of Mistral's early life follow nineteenth-century biographical conventions, which "have privileged the subject's father and ignored the mother," in a bias that becomes "an outright denigration of the mother" (Bell and Yalom, 7–8).

12. A "public man" in English as in Spanish, is understood to be a statesmen, while *"una mujer pública,"* in Spanish, is a prostitute.

13. Regarding "active sanctity": in the vitae of "public" women canonized as abbesses or foundresses, "extreme private penitence combined with vigorous public activity" appears more than with their male counterparts (Weinstein and Bell, 35). The vitae of Latin American saints emphasize a balance of active with contemplative practices and on ministering to "the underdogs." This emphasis is manifest in the vitae of Martín de Porres and Rosa de Lima, and in the quasi-hagiography of Eva Perón as "the Madonna of the poor" (Taylor). J. M. Taylor and William Sater both regard sanctity as a pattern for national heroism in Latin America.

14. By 1945 schools and libraries in Argentina, Chile, Colombia, Guatemala, Mexico, and El Salvador were named after her, and her statue had been carved several times (Gazarian-Gautier, 109).

15. The mural, not mentioned in *El Mercurio*, is discussed in *La Nación*, 11 October 1970, 3. The inaugural ceremony is described in *La Nación*, 22 October 1970, 6. I thank Amalia Pereira for locating and sending me these commentaries.

Works Cited

Alegría, Ciro. *Gabriela Mistral Intima.* Cali: Oveja Negra, 1980.

Alegría, Fernando. *Genio y figura de Gabriela Mistral.* Buenos Aires: Universitaria, 1966.

Anderson, Benedict. *Imagined Communities: Reflections on the Origin and Spread of Nationalism.* Rev. ed. London: Verso, 1991.

Arce, Magda, and Eugenio García Carrillo. *Gabriela Mistral y Joaquín García Monge: Una correspondencia inédita.* Santiago: Andrés Bello, 1989.

Bell, Susan Groag, and Marilyn Yalom, eds. *Revealing Lives: Autobiography, Biography, and Gender.* Foreword by Lillian S. Robinson. Albany: SUNY Press, 1990.

Calderón, Alfonso. "Esa vez que la Mistral volvió a Chile." *Ateneo* 459-60 (1989): 179-91.

Carrión, Benjamín. *Santa Gabriela Mistral.* Quito: Casa de la Cultura Ecuatoriana, 1958.

Clissold, Stephen. *The Saints of South America.* London: Charles Knight, 1972.

Concha, Jaime. *Gabriela Mistral.* Madrid: Júcar, 1986.

Delooz, Pierre. "Towards a Sociological Study of Canonized Sainthood in the Catholic Church." In *Saints and Their Cults: Studies in Religious Sociology, Folklore, and History,* ed. Stephen Wilson, 189-216. Cambridge: Cambridge University Press, 1983.

Díaz Arrieta, Hernán [Alone, pseud.]. *Gabriela Mistral: Premio Nobel 1945.* Santiago: Nascimento, 1946.

Fernández Larraín, Sergio. *Cartas de amor de Gabriela Mistral.* Santiago: Andrés Bello, 1978.

Figueroa, Virgilio. *La divina Gabriela.* Santiago: Impreso el Esfuerzo, 1933.

Fiol-Matta, Licia. "The 'Schoolteacher of America': Gender, Sexuality, and Nation in Gabriela Mistral." In *Entiendes,* ed. Paul Julian Smith and Emilie L. Bergmann. Durham: Duke University Press, 1996.

Gazarian-Gautier, Marie-Lise. *Gabriela Mistral: The Teacher from the Valley of Elqui.* Chicago: Franciscan World Herald Press, 1975.

Horan, Elizabeth. *Gabriela Mistral: An Artist and Her People.* Washington D.C.: OAS, 1994.

———. "Gabriel(a) Mistral's Alternative Identities, 1906-1920." In *Reading and Writing the Ambiente: Queer Sexualities in Latino, Latin American, and Spanish Culture,* ed. Susana Chávez Silverman and Librada Hernández, 147-77. Madison: University of Wisconsin Press, 2000.

———. "Sor Juana and Gabriela Mistral: Locations and Locutions of the Saintly Woman." *Chasqui: Revista de literatura latinoamericana* 25, 2 (1996): 89-103.

———. *The Subversive Voice of Carmen Lyra.* Gainesville: University Press of Florida, 2000.

Iglesías, Augusto. *El Modernismo en Chile.* Santiago: Univesitaria, 1949.

Ladrón de Guevara, Matilde. *Gabriela Mistral: Rebelde magnífica.* Santiago: Araucaria, 1984.

Mistral, Gabriela. *En batalla de sencillez: Epistolario de Gabriela Mistral a*

Pedro Prado. Ed. Luis Vargas Saavedra, María Ester Martínez Sanz, and Regina Valdés Browen. Santiago: Ediciones Dolmen, 1993.

———. *Homenaje a Gabriela Mistral*. Santiago: Anales de la Universidad de Chile, 1957.

Mistral, Gabriela, and "Orfeo." *Antología general de Gabriela Mistral*. Homenaje de Orfeo, 23, 24, 25, 26, 27. Santiago: Editorial Roble, 1967.

Parra, Violeta. *Décimas: Autobiografía en versos*. Barcelona: Pomaire, 1976.

Rodig, Laura. "Gabriela Mistral." *Homenage a Gabriela Mistral*. Santiago: Anales de la Universidad de Chile, 1958.

Samatán, Marta Elena. *Gabriela Mistral, campesina del Valle de Elqui*. Buenos Aires: Instituto Amigos del Libro Argentino, 1969.

Sater, William F. *The Heroic Image in Chile: Arturo Prat, Secular Saint*. Berkeley: University of California Press, 1973.

Sepúlveda, Elías. *La niña del Valle de Elqui*. La Serena, Chile: Círculo de Escritores, 1989.

Taylor, J. M. *Eva Perón: The Myths of a Woman*. Chicago: University of Chicago Press, 1979.

Teitelboim, Volodia. *Gabriela Mistral pública y secreta*. Santiago: BAT, 1992.

Torres Rioseco, Arturo. *Gabriela Mistral*. Valencia: Castalia, 1962.

Utternut, Sillie [Guillermo Blanco and Carlos Ruiz-Tagle]. *Revolución en Chile*. Santiago: Editorial del Pacífico, 1962.

Vicuña, Cecilia. "Andina Gabriela." In *Una palabra cómplice: Encuentro con Gabriela Mistral*, ed. Casa de la Mujer La Morada, 95–102. Santiago: Colectivo Isis Internacional/Casa de la Mujer La Morada, 1990.

Weinstein, Donald, and R. M. Bell. *Saints and Society: The Two Worlds of Western Christendom, 1000–1700*. Chicago: University of Chicago Press, 1982.

Williams, Raymond. *The Sociology of Culture*. New York: Schocken Books, 1982.

Chapter 14

Gabriela Mistral's Political Commentaries

Emma Sepúlveda
Translated by Darrell B. Lockhart

I STARTED READING GABRIELA MISTRAL when I was eight years old. I did not read her works because I had an interest in them but because I had to. All of Chile's children at that time had to memorize some of her poems and recite them during school events or in our Spanish class. We spent hours repeating, "Children's little feet blue with cold, how can He see them and not cover them, my God." Not only did we memorize her poems, but our teachers interpreted for us what Mistral supposedly meant in her poems. Mistral was a poet who loved children. She was the rural teacher who had dedicated her life to children. She was Catholic and conservative. She had never married and was not interested in politics. Based on those statements we evaluated her poetry and thus we had to understand her and her literature.

The vision I had of the award-winning poet did not change much during my years in high school, but at that time different dimensions were added to the study of Mistral's writings. We had to read her books in their entirety, not just a couple of poems. She was still that historical-literary myth we all loved but whom no one dared judge. Saying during those years that we did not like Mistral's poems would have been blasphemy. Among my high school friends in Spanish classes with professor Lidia Cuadra, Mistral was a combination of the tragic heroine (the great love of her life had committed suicide) and the wonderful sweet woman who never realized the quintessential dream of becoming a mother. She was stoic and romantic. She was sweet and strong. She was a good example of what all women should hope to be. The fact that my school was run by nuns and was attended only by girls certainly had a lot to do with the interpretation and divine respect we had for Gabriela Mistral, not only as a woman but as a writer and Nobel laureate.

At the University of Chile in Santiago things changed. Or did we change? We reread Gabriela Mistral, but this time we read more than just her poetry. For the first time we read her essays, newspaper articles, and speeches. We discovered another facet to her literature and with that we could, I believe, start to discern between the myth and the reality surrounding Mistral. She went from being the admirable elementary school teacher to the woman whose sexual orientation we questioned; from conservative in politics to a staunch advocate of women's rights. In the 1970s, for my generation, Mistral was more than the illustrious daughter of Elqui who wrote poetry about children.

Many years went by and the history of Chile surprised many of us with its drastic and unexpected changes. Some of us left Chile and some stayed behind. Among all those people, maybe we reread more carefully the messages of Chile's writers and thinkers that we needed to reinterpret in order to find a more sensible explanation for our history. Far away from Chile and in the middle of my doctoral studies, I again took up Mistral's writings, and I found a new sense in her works, different from the one I had been given decades before. I found what I liked about the real Gabriela Mistral and I left behind what I had been inculcated or taught based on myth.

Here I review some of the political commentaries I have followed throughout Mistral's writings. These commentaries have led me to reread and reinterpret many times what I learned about writers during my academic career and to reevaluate Mistral's ideas.

Mistral was perhaps not, as many have affirmed (and she herself repeated), a devout political activist, but she did show throughout her speeches, public presentations, newspaper articles, and various essays, that she had a clear idea of what she supported, rejected, or was willing to defend insistently in the political arena.

One of the topics that I believe has been silenced, but is of great importance when we evaluate Mistral's political opinion, is her absolute rejection of U.S. intervention in Latin America. Her critique can be seen in her unconditional support for Augusto César Sandino. Mistral joined the international critics and publicly supported Sandino, recognizing him as one of the greatest fighters against power, not only during the U.S. intervention in Nicaragua but also against the national military forces that safeguarded the country's political and financial power. The overwhelming and self-serving intervention of the United States was criticized around the world for many years, but the critique escalated when the intervention reached the extremes of creating, supporting, and maintaining the Nicaraguan National Guard, a military force that served to protect U.S. interests in Nicaragua. The guard underhandedly tried to protect foreign interests and was attacked when it became the strongest force in Nicaragua's internal politics. Mistral severely criticized the U.S. intervention in Nicaragua:

> How far doth the North American cruelty, daughter of the lust for possessing, reach. The French and English press show—and even they [the United States] boasts about—esteem and stimulus toward the Nicaraguan liberal party, as well as repugnance toward U.S. extortion. If the North Americans did not possess that invulnerability to the world's opinion and its expressions of sympathy or revulsion, they would take into account this censoring chorus of the great European countries. But its [North America's] lack of sensibility, which is part of its strength, leaves it deaf to such reactions, which would not go unheeded by any other country. (in Quezada, 229)

Mistral followed the activities of Sandino and his small army, which at one point had more than three thousand members, among them blue-collar workers, peasants, and students. She called upon the youth of Latin America to join Sandino's army and form an alliance—"the Hispanic Legion of Nicaragua"—for strength in battle that "only youth can give." In various articles written in Europe and the United States, she asked that the Latin American countries unite and join or financially back the groups that fought with Sandino in order to achieve changes in Nicaragua:

> The Hispanic politicians that help Nicaragua from behind their desks or in their student clubs could do more honest deeds by going to help this heroic man, a legitimate hero, the likes of whom they may never see again, by becoming his soldiers. (Alas, Nicaragua has two not-so-small borders that can be breached.) At least, if, despite your verbal support, you do not want to lend your bodies to the cause, you should gather a continental collection to bear tangible witness to the fact that you care about the future of this small army. Never would the dollars, [Ecuadorian] sucres, and South American bolívars, which are so frivolously spent on urban sensualities, be better spent. (230)

While supporting Sandino's activities in Nicaragua, Mistral also denounces, prophetically, the imminent danger that the North American intervention may expand to the rest of Latin America: "On the vigorous shoulders of a rustic man, on the virile back of a smithy, Sandino carries the honor of us all. Thanks to him, when the larger-than-life steps taken by North America travel south, the South will remember 'Sandino's two thousand' and do the same" (231).

In another article written that same month, Mistral quotes the words of an American, without revealing his name publicly, to criticize the position that U.S. leaders had with regard to intervention: "Our industry, which is on the road to becoming the largest in the world, needs Mexico's oil, Cuba's sugar cane, and Central America's coffee. If we allow strife to thrive in these countries, they will not exploit their goods or they will be in the way of our exploitation. Our intervention is prudent and will be for the good of these countries" (234).

Republican Herbert Clark Hoover governed the United States from 1928 until 1932 and he declared Augusto Sandino an outlaw because of his revolutionary activities against U.S. intervention in Nicaragua. Mistral strongly criticized Hoover and that which she called the "search," or the "hunt," for the leader, because the Nicaraguan army and the U.S. navy had united in the search for Sandino and his followers. Her commentaries in the articles from that period severely denounce the internal military politics of Nicaragua, which practically sold the country to the North American forces: "The damned Nicaraguan politicians—when they asked for the United States' help against Sandino, maybe they could not imagine what they were doing and maybe today they will be scared by the chains of rights they have created for the strangers and the performance of concessions through which they gave away their country" (*El Mercurio,* 7 June 1931).

For Mistral, Sandino was a hero and not a bandit, as the U.S. press and government described him. During those years, Mistral wrote from Europe and the United States and her opinion about the two continents is diametrically opposite. She admired how the European journalists covered the news of the Sandinista movement and how they joined in glorifying the struggle of a "born hero, a creature of providence" while the newspapers in the United States spoke of a "malignant armed criminal." Europe followed Sandino's journey and wished to inform the public that "Sandino was still alive" while the New York papers hoped that the bandit, who already had a price on his head, would be captured with the help of "five thousand men and dozens of airplanes."

In the newspaper articles and essays she published during that period, Mistral often commented that not since the struggle for independence in 1810, a movement that extended from Mexico and Venezuela to Chile, had Latin America lived so long united under the immeasurable expectations of triumph or defeat, for a cause that would affect the political, financial, and social destiny of the rest of Hispanic America for decades.

Mistral saw Sandino as another Simón Bolívar and she thought that his struggle was Latin America's struggle. Mistral believed that if Sandino's movement triumphed the continent would then be free from the oppression and intervention of the United States, but if Sandino's cause were to die, the hope for a better future for the continent would die with his cause (and with him).

Mistral was wrong perhaps in her prediction of the impact the United States' persecution of Sandino would have, particularly on the future unity of Latin America; "Mr. Hoover, you will make us experience a feeling of continental unity that we have not felt since 1810, during the war for independence; that you will, but this hero is not a local hero, although he works from a square mile of rural territory, rather he is an ethnic hero. Mr. Hoover, you will achieve, without searching too hard, something which we had not achieved ourselves: to feel as one from end to end" (*El Mercurio,* 7 June 1931).

In 1923 *El Mercurio* published an article that Mistral wrote about Mexican president Alvaro Obregón. The article highlighted the positive changes that had occurred in Mexico: the agrarian and educational reform. In the same article, Mistral took advantage of the opportunity to criticize the power of the U.S. oil companies over the Mexican economy. She noted that the United States, "that country that after a brief struggle annexed a third of its territory [Texas] in the midst of cowardly silence from other countries and with the ease that one adds a few hundred square feet," did not have the right to reject or protest against Mexican nationalization laws imposed on U.S. companies. Mistral emphasized that the United States had already imposed severe laws to force foreign companies to respect its national laws: "The financial policies of this country [Mexico] are neither more nor less nationalistic than those of the United States. The Northern neighbor has just dictated laws that are so rigorous they become prohibitive with regard to foreign businesses. Since it achieved its independence, the United States traced an absolute line of industrial protectionism" (in Quezada, 244).

The nationalization of the subsoil, as Mistral called it, was the reform that caused conflicts with the government of the United States. The exploitation of oil was crucial for the financial development of Mexico and the North American companies did not want to accept the principles of nationalization imposed by Obregón's government. In the same article, Mistral wrote, "The [Mexican] people have every right to defend those things that have become the source of their financial life." Mistral added that not only was Obregón responsible for Mexico's financial destiny but that his position on the negotiations with the United States would affect the future of other Latin American nations: "The president speaks about the conflict between the United States and Mexico not with words of hatred but with a great sense of not only national but racial dignity. He sees clearly that the breakup of his country due to the economic actions of the United States, which has already happened in Central America and the Antilles, would be fatal for the Southern countries" (245).

A few years later, during a speech to the women of Puerto Rico, in San Juan, Mistral reiterated the ideas of economic control by the United States in Latin America. She presented the problems of selling and acquiring land as another way in which the United States would have control of the continent:

Each of our countries, whether Peru or Cuba, has at this moment the sword of Damocles hanging above it: the problem of alienation of the land, its slow and silent loss. Poor countries lacking the means and backed by underdeveloped industry, ask foreigners to visit them and list for them—like a list of selling points—their mines, oil, and rubber trees. The North Americans come to visit us, take the biggest possible liberties to guarantee their investment; they make themselves at home and take their stance as definitive owners. (289)

Granting lands and handing over the control of the exploitation of Latin American natural resources to the foreign interests was for Mistral the worst mistake committed by the governments and people of Latin America. The liberation from Spain achieved by the Latin American countries could not, and should not, be lost to the new threat of colonization presented by the United States in its attempt to extend its financial power to the limits of the Southern countries. One of the greatest dangers Mistral warned of was that help from the United States carried a commitment that would only extend U.S. imperialist power but would not begin to understand the reality of the Latin American countries: "We ask that you [the U.S.] not only help us with your dollars and equipment, but also that you understand us, particularly that you understand us" (157). Democracy must be the same in Latin America and the United States: "Our men, entrusted with our luck: we want to defend the freedom in the same way that the United States does; we want to ensure a peace married to social justice as much as the United States wants it" (158).

As in the other topics she defends in her political writings, Mistral shows solidarity with the Latin American people—the peasants, the miners and the blue-collar workers—when she speaks of the North American intervention and the financial control of that country over the rest of the world: "In a way I speak for the masses, to which I belong in terms of being a person without land who is part of the land; in the name of the masses that have the bad luck of waking up one day knowing that their province stopped being Cuban, Chilean, or Venezuelan, without knowing the how or when of its misfortune" (290).

Possibly one of the strongest commentaries against the acquisition of lands and the entry of foreign capital to exploit the natural resources in Latin America was the one Mistral formed in her speech to the women of Puerto Rico in 1931. She explained that any problem Latin American countries might face with regard to internal politics, their laws, or social and economic programs, could be resolved, but if the foreign interests controlled them and owned the national territories and resources, the underdeveloped nations would be condemned to live under the control of the great foreign empires:

> While the land is ours, there are all kinds of possibilities, because creation has a place to stand. If the administration is bad during a certain period, it does not matter, it will be better. If education is uncertain, that is more serious, but it can quickly be strengthened. If social services are inadequate, it is not a matter of life and death; they will slowly become adequate. But once we lose the land, the mine that sustains the city changes ownership; the coffee plantation inevitably changes hands; the salt deposit is outside our power; in other words, once we take away the land from the plants, as if yanking a tray out from underneath them, we have lost all possibility of making our land perfect. (291)

Gabriela Mistral wrote about other aspects of the United States' intervention in Latin America and the contradictions of the foreign policies that the United States maintained with regard to the Southern countries. She criticized and defended the use of Spanish in Puerto Rico and also highlighted the irony of the name and the meaning that Rio Grande had as a divider between Mexico and the United States and for the relations between the two countries. Her words, although she continuously defended them when they were deemed to be "political," now have in this new century as much or more validity than they did when they were written (1920s–40s). The years went by, the intervention continued, and Nicaragua was involved in a bloody civil war, like that of many Latin American countries, in which the United States intervened. Puerto Rico today is still a colony of the United States; South America gave away more mines, oil, and other natural resources to multinational companies that later, when these resources were nationalized, instigated military coups in these countries; and the citizens watched democracy die before their own eyes. And as Mistral also foresaw, the Rio Grande of the North—or the Río Bravo, as Mexicans know it—became the "river of tears," a name she gave it when she traveled to its banks in 1931: "It is a sad body of water with a conscious and painful limit." Mistral's words continue to define the relationship between the United States and Mexico that separates and unites, distances and brings closer, without being able to determine if they are close friends or distant enemies.

Work Cited

Quezada, Jaime. "Sandino: Contestación a una escritura." In *Gabriela Mistral: Escritos politicos.* Mexico City: Fondo Monetario de Cultura, 1995.

Chapter 15

Gabriela Mistral and the United States of America

Luis Vargas Saavedra

A MULTIDIMENSIONAL WRITER, capable of both praise and censure, Gabriela Mistral, using a level hand and a keen sense of observation, challenged and criticized the United States. Influenced by her own experiences, current literature, and the views of José Rodó, José Martí, and Vargas Vila, her claims continue to be viewed as theoretical and free from prejudice.

In 1905, Mistral declared that the writings of Vargas Vila had revealed to her the meaning of art. Mistral had an intense passion for literature and often satiated herself by immersing herself in the prophets of the Old Testament or the work of Dante (as evident in her poem "Mis libros," *Desolación*). She had the remarkable ability to write with bombastic, exacerbated, and Lear-like prose.

Vargas Vila, whose work spurred much of the growing "anti-Yankee" sentiment, raged not against Babylon, but against North America. His most significant work, *El yanqui he ahí el enemigo* (The Yankee that is the enemy), paralleled the critical views presented in José Rodó's *Ariel*. Mistral was strongly influenced by Vila's and Rodó's depiction of the United States as a monster. But the writer who probably influenced her the most concerning elements of thought, style, and sincerity of life, José Martí, wrote the famous phrase that would continue to resound in her mind: "New York: I know the monster, I have lived in its entrails."

These writers were reacting to the increasing power and influence of the United States that emerged after its triumph over Spain in 1898. With these apprehensions in mind, Mistral made her first visit to the United States in 1924.

In a 1922 article titled "El grito" (The yell), written while living in Mexico and working on a pedagogic collaboration with José Vasconcelos, she calls for the spiritual and economic construction of Latin America. However, the essay does not reflect any of the anti-American sentiments common in Mexico but instead urges Northern America to recognize its social responsibility to its southern neighbors:

> Industrialist: help us to overcome, perhaps even stop, that so-called harmless invasion that is actually fatal, of the blond America that wants to sell us everything; we fill our fields and cities with their machines, their cloth, even what we already have and do not know how to exploit. Teach your workers, teach your chemists and your engineers. Industrialist: you should be the boss of this crusade that you leave to the idealists.
>
> Do I hate the Yankee? No! He is beating us, he is crushing us, but it is our fault, it is due to our torrid languidness, our indigenous fatalism. It is breaking us down through some of its virtues and all of our racial vices. Why would we hate him? Let us hate that within us that makes us vulnerable to his steel and golden nail: to his will and opulence.
>
> Let us direct all our activities as an arrow toward the unavoidable future: Latin America, unified by two wonderful things: the language given to us by God and the pain given to us by the North.
>
> We made the North haughty with our inertia; with our laziness, we are creating its opulence; with our petty hatreds, we are making it appear serene and even just.
>
> We argue endlessly, while the North *does*, executes; destroys us, while it squeezes itself like fresh meat, it becomes hard and formidable,

the North solders the links with its states from sea to sea; we talk, allege, while it sows, founds, saws, labors, multiplies, forges; it creates with fire, earth, air, water; the North creates every minute, educated in its own faith and through that faith becomes divine and invincible.

America and only America! What rapture for such a future, what beauty, what a vast kingdom for liberty and the greatest good! ("El grito," *Desolación,* 69; emphasis Mistral's)[1]

Rodó's previous publications focused on extolling the Ariel-like "spirituality" of Latin America, in contrast to the Caliban-like "materialism" of North America. However, Mistral transcends this convenient cliché. Rather than support the "virtues" of Latin America, she denounces them as "racial vices." While many had recognized that the Latin spirit wasted itself in the pursuit of chimeras, none before had ever had the intellectual courage or lucidity to vocalize this observation. In Mistral we find a woman and poet who, through practical advice and lyrical language, is capable of instructing the world concerning matters such as overcoming underdevelopment.

In 1930 she published her first article for the Spanish newspaper *ABC,* titled "Antillas" (Antilles), in which she first expresses her concern regarding the U.S. presence in Puerto Rico—a topic that later became a prevalent theme in her writings: "Puerto Rico knows the experience of seeing its blood blended with an American spatula—an experience that should interest us very much, because the blender, in its attempt, is keeping one eye on the island and the other on the continent [South America]."

In her 1931 article "Voto de la juventud escolar en el día de las Américas," she continued to lay the foundation of core beliefs that she would reiterate and subsequently modulate in successive articles. She believed that Latin Americans must understand the cultural idiosyncrasies of North America and of South America, as much as those of Asia; they cannot destroy ancient civilizations or their "interior landscape [collective sensibility]"; they must acknowledge the "potential richness, real democracy, and fulfilled freedom" that is evident in the heritage and history of both continents. According to Mistral, geography, civil rights, and ethnicity, whether accounted for or assimilated, ought to inspire collective well-being before the creation "of a spiritual costume, worthy of our racial heritages and of our geographic fortune."

One month before the publication of "Voto de la juventud" Mistral was living in New York and was so inspired by her experiences there that she wrote "La Estatua de la Libertad" (The Statue of Liberty). In this article she semantically decodes the statue while also examining her own vantage point. In later articles she executed similar analyses of the Cathedral of Saint John the Divine and the New York subway system. In "La Estatua" the reader witnesses an original reading that compares and contrasts the exterior with its interior, its parts with the whole, intentions with results, and dissonances with discrepancies. In these extremely personal interpretations, where self-censorship is attenuated, certain pricks of irony and humor surface, making these articles livelier, more surprising, and perhaps more genuine, than her political texts.

Pedro Labarthe accompanied Mistral during her sojourn in New York. Her political suspicion spurs a commentary from the characterization of the two visitors: "Labarthe, whose island remains under HER circumscription, and a Chilean whose country is at a convenient distance that allows her to be considered a stranger" ("Estatua," n.p.; emphasis Mistral's).

In an effort to find a suitable object, symbol, or entity to compare to the Statue of Liberty, Mistral tries the image of the muse: "The Muse of institutions, a kind of lover of the Jeffersons of yesterday and of the Borahs of today, who might inspire constitutional articles." However, this image is discarded because "In this country, devoid of intimacy, without one secret wrinkle of life, the idea of a muse, which corresponds with the hollowness of the ear, falls, cut off from thought, as soon as one conceives it." The core of her criticism is that it "is called the Liberty of the United States and no longer liberty itself, which was a sword-word, rotund and definitive."

A living statue is the theme of her next article, "Charles August Lindbergh." Hero and country interact in her appraisal:

> Charles Lindbergh articulates with the American people through four aspects: beautiful physical agility (I do not know if there is a more beautiful race than the American); a childlike simplicity; the passion of the one hundred percent capacity of his [air]craft; and that high patriotic climate that, in spite of the mixture of bloods, the United States manages to preserve.

Touchingly, the article concludes with a description of the hero's wife, Anne Morrow Lindbergh:

> Cultivated and sensitive, she looks tenderly and speaks tenderly; I had not yet encountered this feminine tone in a country so full of loose Dianas and Junes. . . . So Latin in culture she seems to me that in the common French language I forget "place" and "circumstances." With a courtesy that resembles charity, she makes me forget that I am living for months in a land that does not belong to my body or my soul.

Mistral was still in the United States when her article "En defensa de la honra italiana" (In defense of Italian honor) appeared in a Caribbean newspaper in June 1931. Here she compares the richness and dignity of the ancient Italian culture to that of the "new" American society. She sarcastically describes the North American as a "lucky child" with a "budding mentality." That October, in "Clemencia Isaura en Nueva York," the same reproach appears: "pure medieval emotion is impossible for a race that has not, nor will not experience the Middle Ages."

On the same page as "En defense de la honra italiana" was an obituary Mistral had written in honor of Khalil Gibran, whom she had visited a few months earlier. In it New York is depicted as a baroque chaos of mysticism that she holds responsible for the corruption of the purity of creative spirit that Gibran was noted for. She describes New

York art as a series of "bad-taste transcendentalist allegories that balanced between a Rodinesque paganism and naive spirituality in the manner of Miss [Mary Baker] Eddy of 'Christian Science.'"

In July, Mistral attacked the United States politically. In "La cacería de Sandino" (The hunt for Sandino) she compares Sandino to President Hoover. She accuses Hoover of being either so badly informed or so impervious that he does not realize that the death of Sandino will serve only to unite Latin America against the imperialistic North: "Mr. Hoover will accomplish, without trying to do so, something that we ourselves have not accomplished: the continent feeling united from head to toe, because of the death of Augusto Sandino."

One year earlier, Mistral evaluated the importance of the media, namely the newspapers, and its influence on U.S. policy and public opinion, particularly regarding Latin America, in her article "Información de la América Española en Estados Unidos" (Information on Spanish America in the U.S.). According to Mistral, the media provides a steady stream of indoctrination of ideas. She also contends that the media is more influential than universities, colleges, churches, or clubs. Consequently, aliens, outsiders, or whoever else wants to be heard in such a country, must take a "seat in the daily assembly of publicity or he will not obtain anything." In order to be heard one must successfully deliver two things, information and explanation. Information, according to Mistral, is given via hard news, while explanation is delivered best through an article written by a professional capable of mollifying and of "magnify[ing] the brutality and limitation of daily events."

She assumes that Americans want to know about South America, and that this interest constitutes "a physical and spiritual research." She feels that the American looks to South America for the assurance that "the Indian was useful and that the mestizo reenacted in the Indian, is useful as a cultural cell." She also believes that "modern progress in the South is somehow near that of North America and certainly allows relations to be on equal terms, as we have asked for."

"We want to deliver our answer to the North American majority, to the country or democracy in which the masses account for much, although they do not make the decisions." As a writer, Mistral feels not only a calling but a social responsibility to provide such an answer. She writes, "The most legitimate interpreters of the sensibility of a race are its writers and, in the case of information, its social writers."

The differences between the United States and Latin America are more those of sensibility (due to racial mixture) than of ideology (they share similar ideas on democracy). However, although "both [were] fecundated by the French Revolution, North and South have understood and served the idea of democracy with a spirit and with norms that are absolutely different."

Twenty-three years after the publication of "El grito," Mistral published "Coincidencias y disidencias entre las Américas" as a reflection on the progress of Latin America. She recognizes certain improvements, some more considerable than others. She points out Latin America's "courage to legislate, the decision to rectify errors and start the delayed march [of progress]." However, courage and initiative are not enough to solve the many remaining problems. Once again she asks for help from a North America that has, according to Mistral, been "achieved without tragedy" and has not had to unify "three bloods and three souls that serve, in a very diverse way, Good and Evil [Indians, mestizos, Caucasians]" (34). To further her argument for the unification of and mutual aid among the Americas, she outlines four "areas of coincidence": freedom, territory, youthfulness, and Christianity. In each are sufficient similarities to unite the Americas. The text of her article deserves to be quoted extensively.

Coincidences and Dissidences between the Americas

At first glance, we see an abyss between the North and the South of the American continents with regard to people. We all feel the shock of these differences: some are hurt by them and others are disappointed.

If instead of looking for the foci of dissidence with an entomologists' eye we looked for the nuclei of similarities, things would go much better, for there are many surprises.

Maybe among us Americans there are four common soils, four zones of immediate friendship, or if you prefer, four known languages that we subconsciously possess in common [Spanish, Portuguese, English, French]. These are moral languages and the outlines of old forgotten rendezvous.

. . .

Of the four coincidental areas that could be more a foundation, not mere bridges—love for liberty, territory, beliefs, and a young spirit—two of them are now speaking up strongly and two have taken the wool from our eyes: the risk of losing our land, which feeds us, and of losing our soul as well as the land. The continent has to defend itself with a united effort and in an instant it happened. . . . There is an America that is rich, that worked more and with better luck; there is another that has struggled to unite three opposing bloods, carrying out a very delicate operation, a vital or mortal graft. The North did not waste time nor did it mask its strength in the immense experiment that has been going on for four centuries in the South: the North did not want to work with the soul of the Indo-American inhabitants; the North took nature merely as a battlefield: it opened, destroyed, and grabbed the land, and all of this it did with great speed as it left behind the conquered and dead indigenous peoples. Once the land had been cleansed and validated to the point of becoming an agrarian archetype for the world, the North plunged head on into industrialism with the impetus of a champion who does not accept defeat in any area.

In the meantime we, the Indo-Spanish people in the South, pursued a heroic endeavor that was both violent and lazy: that of building a democracy based on merchants and with civility replacing local tribal leaders. That is difficult and it had to last for four centuries. No one has expressed well the heroic task of unifying three bloods and three souls that serve both Good and Evil in diverse ways and three consciences that follow such contradictory rhythms that they do not seem to stem from the same natural law.

The North, established through its melting pot, without tragic actions, must see and acknowledge the reality of the South and give us help in the final strokes.

What we offer is loyalty, a chivalrous virtue but one that is still thriving and in use; what we need is a generosity that goes beyond the commercial and even the political and becomes moderate cooperation and true Christian help, which the Old World either ignored or could not achieve.

We want to be understood and then helped; but above all we want to be understood, since that is the only way we can be helped efficiently and without an aftertaste of superiority and servility.

The continent must not become a dominion managed by hands that are adept at games. Europe has already employed ingenuity and malice, shady deals and fallacies, and it lost because of this painful business and despite its diplomatic claims. We, the witnesses of that lost game, have the obligation of creating a more honorable and durable creation, working the forged iron rather than the fragile tin of the annual "agreements" that result only in prolonged waiting.[2]

Mistral's preoccupation with understanding the cultural phenomena in both Americas can easily be traced throughout her various writings. She uses the press as a way of reaching the masses in a way devoid of elitism. Continually searching for social progress, she never forgets her spiritual values. Thus the empirical, mixed with the religious, saves her from a romantic utopia.

Unfortunately, while Mistral recognized and declared the need to publish in the forum of the U.S. media, she herself never was able to do it. Thus, none of her translated articles were ever published in the United States. Consequently, all her thoughts remain confined among the elites of a Spanish-speaking world.

Notes

Unless otherwise noted, all translations are mine.

1. Translated by Monica Bruno Galmozzi.
2. Translated by Monica Bruno Galmozzi and Luis Vargas Saavedra.

Works Cited

Mistral, Gabriela. "Antillas." *ABC*, 24 January 1930.

———. "La cacería de Sandino." *Repertorio americano*, 11 July 1931.

———. "Clemencia Isaura en Nueva York." *El Mercurio*, 18 October 1931.

———. "Coincidencias y disidencias entre las Américas." *Revista de América*, no. 2 (February 1945).

———. "En defensa de la honra italiana." *Puerto Rico ilustrado*, 13 June 1931.

———. *Desolación*. Santiago de Chile: Editorial Nascimento, 1923.

———. "La Estatua de la Libertad." *Puerto Rico ilustrado*, 5 April 1931.

———. "El grito." *El maestro rural: Revista de cultura nacional* 2, 4–5 (1922).

———. "Información de la América Española en Estados Unidos." *El Mercurio*, 30 November 1930.

———. "Voto de la juventud escolar en el día de las Américas." *Repertorio americano* 22 (4 April 1931): 199.

Chapter 16

The Walking Geography of Gabriela Mistral

Marie-Lise Gazarian-Gautier

> *I am a wandering Chilean who has partaken of the bread of brotherhood from three continents, receiving from each of them, day after day, the bountiful richness of their cultures.*
> —Gabriela Mistral

BORN IN VICUÑA, CHILE, on 7 April 1889, Gabriela Mistral, the 1945 winner of the Nobel prize for literature, died in Roslyn Harbor, New York, on 10 January 1957 after a long struggle with cancer. A poet and a diplomat versed in world affairs, with a fascination for folklore and an ecumenical sense of religion, she remained all her life true to her first love—that of being a teacher, in particular, a geography teacher.

A rural schoolteacher at the age of fifteen, a title she held with the highest pride and dedication, along with that of poet, she journeyed first through the elongated geography of her native land from north to south. Pablo Neruda, the 1971 Nobel laureate, recalling his first encounter with her in Temuco, when he was a young boy and she was the principal of a girls school, was struck by the magic of her smile: "When

I was introduced to her I found her a good-looking woman. Her tanned face showed her predominant Indian blood, like a beautiful Araucan pitcher, her translucent white teeth stood out in a full generous smile that lit the room" (31). In "The Human Geography of Chile," a speech given at the Pan-American Union in Washington in April 1939, Mistral spoke of the main characteristics of her country and the bravery of its inhabitants: "Chile was created, as any other nation, under a warlike spirit. It was better to give it the shape of an oar, wide as it nears Antofagasta, narrow toward the southern tip. We are good sailors because we enjoy an immense coastline" ("Breve descripción," 5). Like a sailor, leaving behind scenes from the homeland, Mistral, too, felt the urgent call of other shores.

In 1922, when José Vasconcelos, the Mexican minister of education, invited her to join him in his country's educational reforms, she left Chile for the first time. Thereafter she returned to it only for brief intervals. She traveled throughout Mexico on horseback to towns and remote villages to bring education to the people and, inspired by this first encounter with the Mexican people, she wrote some of her most vivid poems and poetic prose. In 1924 she was sent to Europe to serve as Chilean representative to the International Institute of Intellectual Cooperation (an organization connected with the League of Nations and precursor of UNESCO), at the Palais Royal in Paris. In 1927, together with the Peruvian diplomat Víctor Andrés Belaúnde, then technical adviser to the institute, she founded the Collection of Ibero-American Classics (in French translation). Although she knew nothing about the management of money in her private life, she was active in finding the necessary subsidies for the collection, so that works that best reflected Latin America, its folklore, and its culture would become known in Europe.

In 1932, Mistral entered the diplomatic career. A special law passed in 1935 by the Chilean government assigned her the title of consul per vita and assured her of much-needed economic security. She served as consul in Madrid from 1933 to 1935; in Lisbon in 1936; in Niterói and

Petrópolis, Brazil, from 1940 to 1945; in Santa Barbara, California, in 1947; in Veracruz, Mexico, from 1948 to 1950; in Rapallo and Naples, Italy, from 1951 to 1952; and in New York from 1953 to 1957. She also represented her country in the United Nations Commission on Human Rights. She greatly contributed to the creation of UNICEF and is considered its spiritual godmother. She also assumed the role of mother for her young nephew, Yin Yin, who was like a son to her, "the soul of my home, my reading and travel companion, my conversation partner, my all," as she confided in a letter to Eduardo Frei in 1943 (Frei, Mistral, and Maritain, 150), shortly after the young boy was forced by a gang of young xenophobes to commit suicide. Yin Yin, whose full name was Juan Miguel Godoy Mendoza, was the son of Carlos Godoy, Mistral's half-brother (born out of wedlock), and Martha Mendoza, a Catalan.

Just as Christopher Columbus introduced the New World to Europeans through his letters to the Catholic kings, "la chilena errante" (the wandering Chilean), as she referred to herself in a letter she addressed to me in December 1954, bridged the gap between the New and the Old Worlds through her writings and her conversations. She was a constant contributor to such newspapers and journals as *El Tiempo* of Bogotá, *La Nación* of Buenos Aires, *El Universal* of Mexico City, *El Repertorio Americano* of San José, Costa Rica, *El Mercurio* of Santiago, *ABC* of Madrid, and *La Nueva Democracia* of New York.

Through her travel chronicles and her poetry, we come to know the places where she lived or merely passed by, attracted by their people and their climate: Provence, in southern France, the country of Frédéric Mistral (1904 Nobel laureate in literature) and of the mistral wind, from which she borrowed the second half of her name; Florence, Genoa, Naples, Rapallo, in Italy, the native land of Gabriele D'Annunzio, along with the Archangel Gabriel the origin of her first name; Castile, in Spain; and, within her own hemisphere, Argentina, Brazil, the length of Chile (with special emphasis on the Elqui valley), Cuba, the Dominican Republic, Ecuador, El Salvador, Mexico, Peru, Puerto Rico, and the United States (in particular Santa Barbara, California), and Uruguay.

Like Don Quixote, the routes she took never led to large urban centers but rather to parts of the world that had something in common: the gentleness of their climate, the beauty of their animals, the profusion of their flowers or, on the contrary, the austerity of their landscapes. Her "Estampas" (Vignettes), "Siluetas" (Silhouettes), "Elogios" (Praises), "Retratos" (Portraits), "Motivos" (Motives), and "Recados" (Messages) are a lasting testimonial to the places she traveled to, the people she met, and the works she read.

She adopted the *recado,* an ancient mode of popular oral expression, and adapted it to the written form, whether in poetry or in prose. It possessed the spontaneity of the popular voice, the warmth and vitality of a conversation, and the familiarity of a letter between friends. Her own definition of this genre is quite revealing: "The recado is an expression that is most authentic in me; it is the tone most often used by me and that reflects the rural world in which I lived and in which I am going to die" (*Tala,* 158).

In a conversation I had with Luis Alberto Sánchez when he was my mentor at Columbia University (he later became rector of the University of San Marcos in Lima and vice president of the Republic of Peru), he acknowledged that Mistral's recados represented the best prose ever written in Latin America (in Gazarian-Gautier, *Mistral,* 54). Victoria Kent, director general of prisons at the time of the Spanish Republic and a writer and founder of a journal, while in exile, wrote of the sparkle that sprang from Mistral's conversations: "a creative luminosity that can never be reproduced" (in Gazarian-Gautier, *Mistral,* 54). Victoria Ocampo, the grande dame of Argentinean letters and founder of the publishing firm Sur, wrote of her, "To hear her speak was like a miracle; through her voice we listened to America. Words have a new flavor when they are selected and pronounced by her" (178).

Like her beloved Saint Francis of Assisi, who knew the many paths of Umbria by heart (Mistral belonged to the Third Order of Saint Francis, a religious lay order), she walked upon the earth and left her imprint on each of the routes she depicted in detail in both her chronicles and her poetry. "In geography, as in love," Mistral wrote in 1934, "he who does not love minutely, one virtue and one feature at a time, the scatter-brained who is vain, who measures kilometers and does not know how to savor details, is also incapable of seeing, understanding, and loving" ("Breve descripción," 10).

The map she elaborated, piece by piece, forged with words, as if they were colors placed on a canvas, reflects a rich variety of shades. Bent over her writings like a cartographer, she traced with utmost precision rivers, mountains, flowers, and gestures. Ahead of her time, her map is audiovisual as well as tactile. Multidimensional, it is endowed with sounds, images, movement, and depth—all of which reflect some of the qualities displayed in today's educational materials: "We poets, my friends, are not only collectors of wide imagery, we also collect minute gestures" (Mistral, *Prosa,* 590). In "Beber" (Drinking), for example, she knits together the many regions of Latin America, where, at different stages of her life, she was offered a sip of water to quench her thirst: in the Elqui valley, with her mother; at the foot of Aconcagua, as the crystalline water gushed from a waterfall; in Puerto Rico, as she tasted the sweet juice from a coconut; in Mitla, near Oaxaca, where an Indian held her as she bent over a well. In this poem, she evokes her spiritual baptism and oneness with the Mexican Indian and finds in him a bond that reminds her of the face of her own father:

> In the countryside of Mitla,
> by a scorching sun, with locusts and fatigue,
> I bent over a well
> and an Indian came to hold me over the water,
> and my head, like a fruit,
> was between his palms.
> I was drinking what he drank,
> which was his face with mine,
> and in a flash I knew
> that his race and mine were one. (in Gazarian-Gautier, *Mistral,* 36)

As readers of her work, we are pressed into caressing the tips of mountains, climbing hills, walking through valleys, bathing in lakes and rivers, feeling the salty sea breeze on our lips, smelling the scent of flowers and trees, tasting delicate, juicy tropical fruits, hearing the breathing of the roots within the bosom of the earth, and feeling its heartbeat. We come to truly know the people, their traditions, their folklore, their inner thoughts. In an article in which she quotes the mayor of Grasse, in Provence, Mistral says, "'We honor the Earth.' Well said. . . . One begins honoring it. And one ends up loving it" (*Prosa*, 584).

Oblivious of man-made boundaries, her cosmic vision is not confined to our planet, it also includes the hereafter: "You shall love beauty, which is the shadow of God upon the Universe" (*Selected Poems*, 36). She sees God's presence in every particle of life and elevates it to the Divine, just as she lowers the Divine to a human scale to bring it within the reach of all people:

> God comes down to take us
> on a cloud of dust;
> He falls in the starry sky
> like a waterfall overflowing.
> He descends, He descends in the Heavenly Chariot;
> He is coming, yet never comes . . .
>
> And one day the chariot does not stop,
> it's coming down, it's coming closer,
> and you feel the chariot wheel alive and fresh
> touching your heart.
> In a fearless leap it lifts you up
> and carries you, and carries you
> as you burst with joy, in songs and tears! (*Poesía*, 246)

For Mistral the act of writing was in itself a voyage into other dimensions, a mystical experience, an ascent toward an unattainable perfection. Very demanding of herself, she stood like the Holy Inquisition in front of her own work. As she wrote in "Decalogue of the Artist,"

"From each act of creation you shall leave with a sense of shame, because it was inferior to your dream, and inferior to that marvelous dream of God, which is nature" (*Selected Poems,* 36). Poetry was a queen and she yielded to her every demand:

> And she said to me: "Go up the mountain,
> I never leave the prairie,
> Cut me flowers white as snow,
> hardy and soft."
>
> They were not growing on branches,
> nor did they open between rocks.
> I cut them from the sweet air,
> I cut them with gentle shears.
>
> I cut them as if I were
> A blind cutter.
> I cut them from one air and another,
> turning the air into my forest . . .
>
> When I came down the mountain
> and went looking for my queen,
> she was by then walking,
> no longer white, no longer strained;
>
> she was walking, somnambulant,
> abandoning the prairie,
> and I followed her, followed her
> through pasture and poplar grove,
>
> laden thus with so many flowers,
> shoulders and hands covered with air,
> ever cutting the flowers from the air,
> reaping a harvest from the air . . . (in Gazarian-Gautier,
>   "Teacher," 288–89)

Like Saint Teresa of Avila, Mistral was a relentless traveler. In a trip through Castile in 1925, she imagined a conversation in which the saint confided to her: "Capitals ruin us all. I'll take you with me through small towns. . . . I measured my Castile while treading upon it. I carry its map under my feet, O daughter. I never tire of founding [convents]. You, woman of Chile, without founding you are already tired" (*Prosa de Gabriela Mistral,* 18).

Mistral spent most of her adult life away from Chile, yet her thoughts were always with her native land, the *patria chiquita* (little fatherland), which served as a point of comparison. As she commented on more than one occasion, "We believe that the Almighty is present in one's region as in the host; we serve this tiny wafer because it encompasses everything. That yearly wheat may bring a smile to some, others will pass by without seeing it; it makes us fall on our knees" ("Breve descripción," 10). "Despite my wandering spirit, I am a traditionalist at heart and I continue living in my childhood valley of Elqui" (*Prosa,* 586). "Since I became a wandering creature, in voluntary exile, it feels as if I am writing surrounded by a mist of ghosts. The American soil and my people, dead or alive, have become a melancholic procession that encircles me. Most loyal, they press against me, cover me to such a point that they rarely let me see foreign landscapes and their people" (*Prosa,* 553). The following confession shows her personalized way of viewing nature: "I am in the habit of greeting the day, awakening by the first ray of sun that comes through the window, by saying, 'Good morning, Valley of Elqui'" (*Prosa,* 163).

She was always attracted by small countries. She wrote of El Salvador: "This small country has been carved out like a jewel, forged by its volcanoes, polished here and there by landslides and explosions, manipulated by Pluto like no other soil in the world. The geography of this country, unlike that of others, is like a continuous Genesis that does not heal like that of other terrestrial lands" (Mistral, *Prosa,* 92). She also reserved a special place to Uruguay: "Here, the word *friendship* means complete understanding, rapid trust, and a lasting memory, in other words, loyalty" (in Pereira, 86). She called Puerto Rico "her island" and was deeply moved by the natural beauty of its scenery: "The sea is everywhere. A few steps and you leave it behind; a few steps and you find it again. This is the magic of Puerto Rico and of all islands. . . . On an island the taste of salt is constantly in your mouth, like a grain of salt that clings to the corners of your lips. If the sea is like a father because of its appearance, it is also like a mother because of its soft taste" (*El Mercurio,* 10 January 1932). The other Caribbean island she loved dearly was Cuba:

> The palm trees of Siboney
> look for me, take me, carry me.
> The palm rocks my spirit,
> my slow gait is made of palms.
> A passing flight of palm trees,
> slow ecstasies of the earth. (*Poesía,* 697)

But Cuba was to her, perhaps above everything else, the birthplace of José Martí, the person she admired both as a man and as a writer. "A beam of light transcends from his work to descend directly upon me," she wrote in her preface to his book *Versos sencillos* (Mistral, "Versos," 11).

Mistral did not build convents, as Saint Teresa of Avila had done long ago, but wherever her duties took her and whatever role she performed—whether as an educator sharing her knowledge with the less privileged, as a delegate and consul representing her country abroad, or as a poet and a writer—she devoted her time to promoting the works of others, especially those whose writings reflected spiritual beauty, and to defending the cause of social justice and peace. She considered that writers should take upon themselves the loving task of devoting pages of their works to describing their homelands. From an early age she gathered her impressions of the Chilean flora and fauna in a notebook, a habit she maintained throughout her life and that came to include landscapes and figures from other latitudes. She felt it was up to teachers and writers to turn geography into something alive: "We still need to cultivate another form of patriotism in which we depict with fraternal tenderness sierra by sierra, river by river, this miraculous ground we walk upon" (*Lecturas para mujeres,* 11). She pointed out, as a model to follow, Alfonso Reyes's *Visión de Anáhuac,* a narration she compared to "a Chinese lacquer" (*Prosa,* 190).

What she perhaps admired most in people was a capacity for telling stories, to be able to awaken in others a sense of awe, something she accused herself of lacking. And yet she was a unique storyteller. She had a gift for discovering in the most insignificant things a spark of magic. She endowed nature with human and sometimes divine characteristics and, like the mystics, enjoyed giving names to the elements. The mountain was to her a "Temperamental Creature," "the Saint of Saints of our Continent," "the Tremendous One," "the Centaur of Stone," "the Original Matriarch," "the Walking Mother," "the Reclining Mother," "the Kneeless Mother," "the Geological Dragon," "the Granite Beast," "the August Mother." The sea, which she came to know when she was twelve, embodied the qualities of "Father/Mother," according to whether she referred to the Pacific, the Atlantic, or the Mediterranean. The sea was "the Master," "the Bossy One," "the Great Triton," "the Main Vagabond," "the Tremendous Fickle One," "Our Lord," "Gentle Water," "Marvelous Mother." The mountain and the sea were two parental forces that exercised control over her.

Mistral drew a lived-in geography of all countries she visited and got to love as her own. She juxtaposed scenes she had discovered in her own continent with those in European countries and the United States. She describes, for example, the Chilean copihue (Chile-bells, the national flower), the Cuban palm, the Puerto Rican coconut, the Uruguayan tassel, the Ecuadorian ceiba, the Mexican maguey, the okote pine of Arizona, the Californian poppy, the flowers of Grasse. And she writes, "Castile is not a land, it is a norm: one cannot feel its aroma, like that of the plantain fields in the tropics, nor is it palpable to the eye, as is the North American prairie: it is all thought. Many concepts are born from it rather than fragrance, instead of productive humus, the bones of the dead create their own feverish fertility" (*Prosa de Gabriela Mistral,*

15). Florence was for her "the prettiest city in the world" (in Gazarian-Gautier, *Mistral,* 49). She compares the hills that surround the city to young girls encircling it with their arms. Ecstatic before the beauty of Naples, she exclaims: "Like a masterpiece, the Gulf of Naples leaves our eyes sated with praise. I have traveled over many of our archipelagoes, entered who knows how many fjords and bays, large and small, but, until now, I did not know what it was to behold a gulf" (*Prosa de Gabriela Mistral,* 39). In Cavi, on the Ligurian coast, she recalled memories and gestures from her native land: "My mouth recovers a series of expressions sunk deep inside me, sweet and happy, that I thought I would never re-utter. . . . And I am once again a *comadre* [a woman who, like the Yiddish *yenta,* has a say in what happens to the people of her town] with a face like a good almond-shaped bread, a good woman who greets lovingly, truly wishing a good day to her neighbor and instinctively raising her hand to bless a child passing by" (*Prosa,* 249).

However, Mistral's sense of geography was also founded on the books she read, especially those that accompanied her in her travels and were like close relatives with whom she could never part: the Bible, the lives of saints, in particular Saint Francis of Assisi, to whom she wrote some of her most beautiful pages, Saint Teresa of Avila, Saint Thérèse of the Child Jesus, Saint Catherine of Siena, Saint Vincent de Paul. She also read works by Dante, Gorky, Jacques Maritain, Frédéric Mistral, Romain Rolland, Tagore, Tolstoy, as well as the books she acquired on her trips or that friends gave her. On the blank pages of her Bible, which she donated to Liceo N° 6 de Niñas (Girls' high school) in Santiago, where she was the first principal, she wrote in 1919 a description of what the Holy Book meant to her: "Book of mine, book at any time, any given hour, good friend to my heart, strong powerful companion. . . . My best friends are not my contemporaries, but the ones you gave me: David, Ruth, Job, Rachel, and Mary" (in Pinilla, 65). In 1923 she defined her attitude toward life in an autobiographical note: "I am a Christian of democratic beliefs. I believe that Christianity, with a deep social commitment, can save our nations. I have written as one who speaks in loneliness because I have lived in solitude in every place" ("Nota biográfica," 5–6).

Mistral learned a great deal from her travels: "I see landscapes as never before. It is as if someone had lifted my eyelids and opened my eyes. I have come out of my unilateral perspective, so as to gently enrich myself with other people's tastes, reasoning, and interests" (*Prosa,* 555). She savored people's generosity and friendship in every part of the world: "I slept over in so many houses that I have lost count; I ate many varieties of stew at the most disparate tables; I ate from Tarasco to Zapotecas, from Yaqui to Otomi. . . . I was a woman from the cold, slow, opaque southern tip [of Latin America]" (*Prosa de Gabriela Mistral,* 56–57).

She traveled the earth by foot, by car, by ship, and "in two thousand trips by train" (*Prosa,* 97–98), even on horseback and, much to her distress, by plane. When she boarded a plane for the first time, in August 1931, flying over the Antilles, she felt frustrated when she contemplated her beloved earth from high above: it had shrunk, it had lost its stature, it was like a small child in kindergarten. Looking down on Puerto Rico, where she had spent sweet moments among her friends, she said, "My island, my graceful island, so pretty to see when you travel over it by foot, or on horseback or even by car, although cars pollute the landscape." And she added: "I've been a geography teacher for a few years, always walking on green soil, having lived for thirty years within the inner skirts of the Cordillera; how this flight has discredited my idol by turning it into something so small" (*Prosa,* 98). "Romantics we are," she clamored (*Prosa,* 99), echoing Rubén Darío's verse in "La canción de los pinos," in an outburst of passion and compassion for the earth. An advocate of nature, she stands as a precursor of today's ecologists, who fight for the preservation of the environment against hazardous pollution.

Her familiarity with and respect for nature and her passion for traveling began when, as a child, she took her first steps in the tiny village of Montegrande, in the Elqui valley, steadied by the loving hand of her mother, Petronila:

My mother was very tiny,
like mint or herbs,
she hardly cast a shadow
upon things, hardly,
and the earth loved her
because of her being so light
and because she smiled at it
when happy and when sad. (in Gazarian-Gautier, *Mistral,* 47)

I visited Montegrande for the first time in 1974, in the company of my good friend Francisca Santa Cruz. A bronze bust of the Chilean poet stands on the top of a hill and a monument, carved in stone, bears the inscription, "What the soul does for the body, artists do for their people." Had I believed in reincarnation, as Mistral did at one time, I would have said that I had come back to my native place. I felt I knew every inch of that village ensconced in the majestic Cordillera. It was 10 January, the anniversary of her death. We felt her presence everywhere—in the air we breathed, in the eyes of small children playing, in the smiles of the elderly, in the fruits we tasted. Every pleat of the Andes surrounded us in a single embrace:

The Valley of Elqui has mountains
that search for God upon awakening,
that seek God at night
and find Him at dawn
and praise Him at daybreak.
They are high and beautiful;
they praise Him the whole day
and keep vigil with Him as night falls.
When I was small they awoke me
with their soft and fervent sun;
their psalms of light still
recall their eternal prayer. (in Gazarian-Gautier, *Mistral,* 10)

The sun moved and cast shadows that covered the flanks of the mountains. It was as if a divine brush had been painting the mountains one by one with green, yellow, white, pink, gray, and black. I was over-whelmed by the stones of Chile, which have been praised by its poets. I could not help thinking of "Balada de mi nombre" (Ballad to my name), a soul-searching poem in which Mistral evokes her baptismal name, Lucila, left behind in her valley:

> The name I have lost,
> where does it live, where does it prosper?
> Name of my childhood, drop of milk,
> a myrtle twig so light.
>
> But they tell me it roams
> by the ravine of my mountain
> in the late afternoon, silent,
> without a body, turned into my soul. (*Prosa*, 825)

Time had stopped for me. I was overhearing voices of another period: that of a little girl named Lucila, of Petronila, her mother, of Emelina, her sister and first teacher, guiding me through the valley, telling me the names of flowers and trees.

The map Gabriela Mistral has left us through her poetry and her prose has little to do with the true scale of the cities and villages she visited. Her recollections of the landscapes she came to know in her childhood, and those she later discovered in foreign lands, have little in common with rigid textbooks or a world atlas. They are testimonies that only a poet can conceive. Her poem "País de la ausencia" (Land of absence), a mythical land of things gone by, erases boundaries and distances between the dead and the living. It connects places and faces from different times, different nations, and foretells the poet's own death. Strangely enough, she died in the United States, a country "without a name" that carries as a sign of identity the name of two continents:

> It does not bear pomegranate,
> nor grow jasmine,

neither has it a sky
nor indigo seas.
Its name, I have
never heard it,
and in a country without name
I shall die. (*Tala,* 89)

I recall Gabriela Mistral in the last years of her life, surrounded by books with illustrations of animals and flowers, while she was working on *Poema de Chile.* She never forgot that she had once been a geography teacher. "I am finishing a long narrative poem about Chile," she wrote to me. "Don't forget that I am an old geography teacher."

Poema de Chile, written during the last two decades of her life and published posthumously in 1967, is a poetic interpretation of Mistral's last journey on earth. She transcends all human bondage and imagines herself in an astral body returning to Chile, after her death, visible only to an Indian boy from Atacama and a deer, the *huemul,* represented in the Chilean national coat of arms. Holding the child by the hand, she takes him on a poetic journey of his homeland, describing for him the magic of its geography.

Written in two voices, this dialogue between the mother/guide (Gabriela Mistral) and the young boy/girl (Lucila Godoy Alcayaga) when she was a child stands as a testament she left to her people. With the poem, she brings to a close her pilgrimage on earth. Her "walking geography" comes to an end where it all began. The tiny village of her childhood dreams is to her the heart that nurtured her poetry, the lungs that purified the air she breathed, and an axis around which revolved regions and countries that attracted her attention. Well-known Spanish writer Salvador de Madariaga said of her, "Universal in spirit, a world traveler, Gabriela Mistral lived and died with her heart in Chile" (3). Along with Pablo Neruda, she forms an alliance with the Chilean landscape and has become a vital part of its geography. The hill next to her tomb in Montegrande, formerly known as the Friar, has been renamed Gabriela Mistral. A galaxy was also named after her, because of the resemblance it bears to her effigy.

But her ultimate voyage, left undescribed, is her ascent to and union with the Divine Master:

> I take leave of you now,
> I hear the voice of my Master.
> He calls me with a sharp thrust
> that strikes like lightening:
> Sweet and bitter is the call
> that bids us to depart.
>
> I came back to save
> my little Indian boy
> and to tread the earth
> that nursed me upon its breast
> and to remember as I walked upon it
> the trinity of its elements.
> I felt the air, I touched the water
> and the earth. And now I must leave. (*Poema de Chile*, 243)

Note

All translations are mine.

Works Cited

Frei Montalva, Eduardo, Gabriela Mistral, and Jacques Maritain. *Memorias y correspondencias con Gabriela Mistral y Jacques Maritain*. Santiago: Editorial Planeta, 1989.

Gazarian-Gautier, Marie-Lise. *Gabriela Mistral, the Teacher from the Valley of Elqui*. Chicago: Franciscan Herald Press, 1975.

———. "Teacher from the Elqui." *The World and I*, a publication of the Washington Times Corporation (October 1999): 288–89.

Madariaga, Salvador de. *Homenaje a Gabriela Mistral.* London: Hispanic and Luso-Brazilian Councils, 1958.

Mistral, Gabriela. "Breve descripción de Chile." Lecture delivered in Málaga. Santiago: Prensas de la Universidad de Chile, 1934.

————. *Lecturas para mujeres.* Mexico City: Secretaría de Educación Pública, 1923.

————. "Nota biográfica." In *Gabriela Mistral: Poesías.* Barcelona: Editorial Cervantes, 1923.

————. *Poema de Chile.* Santiago: Editorial Pomaire, 1967.

————. *Poesía.* Santiago: Lord Cochrane, 1992.

————. *Prosa.* Santiago: Lord Cochrane, 1992.

————. *Prosa de Gabriela Mistral.* Comp. Alfonso Calderón. Santiago: Editorial Universitaria, 1989.

————. *Selected Poems of Gabriela Mistral.* Ed. Doris Dana. Baltimore: Johns Hopkins Press, 1971.

————. *Tala.* Buenos Aires: Editorial Losada, 1946.

————. "Los 'Versos sencillos' de José Martí." *Cuadernos de cultura,* series 5 (1939).

Neruda, Pablo. *Confieso que he vivido: Memorias.* Buenos Aires: Editorial Losada, 1974.

Ocampo, Victoria. "Gabriela Mistral y el Premio Nobel." In *Testimonios.* Buenos Aires: Editorial Sudamericana, 1956.

Pereira Rodríguez, José. *Páginas en prosa.* Buenos Aires: Kapelusz Editores, 1962.

Pinilla, Norberto. *Biografía de Gabriela Mistral.* Santiago: Editorial Tegualda, 1946.

Contributors

DIANA ANHALT

Diana Anhalt is the author of *A Gathering of Fugitives: Voices of American Political Expatriates in Mexico, 1948–1965.* Her essays have appeared or are forthcoming in, among others: the *Southwest Review, Grand Tour, Jewish Currents, Midstream, Voices of Mexico, Under the Sun, Passager, Colere,* and in over half a dozen anthologies. She is currently a literary reviewer for the *Texas Observer.*

JONATHAN COHEN

Jonathan Cohen is a specialist in the Pan-American literary tradition. He has published studies of it in journals such as *American Voice, Romance Notes, Missouri Review,* and *Translation Review.* Among the awards for his work in this field, he has received grants from the American Council of Learned Societies, the New York Foundation for the Arts, and the National Endowment for the Humanities. He is a widely published translator of contemporary Latin American poets such as Ernesto Cardenal, Roque Dalton, Enrique Lihn, and Pedro Mir.

RANDALL COUCH

Randall Couch is a poet, translator, and critic working in Philadelphia. A recent graduate of the Warren Wilson College M.F.A. program for writers, he received a Pennsylvania Council of the Arts fellowship in poetry for 2000.

287

VERÓNICA DARER

Verónica Darer has a doctoral degree in multilingual and multicultural education from the University of Florida. She teaches Spanish, multicultural education, and second-language teaching at Wellesley College and at the Harvard Graduate School of Education. Her research has focused on the social and pedagogical processes in second-language classrooms.

SANTIAGO DAYDÍ-TOLSON

Santiago Daydí-Tolson teaches at the University of Texas, San Antonio. He has written extensively on Mistral and has authored a detailed study of Mistral's *Poema de Chile*. He is also the author of several books and articles on contemporary Spanish and Latin American literature.

MARIE-LISE GAZARIAN-GAUTIER

Marie-Lise Gazarian-Gautier is professor of Spanish and Latin American literature and coordinator of the graduate program in Spanish at St. John's University in Queens, where the Gabriela Mistral Scholarship/Beca Gabriela Mistral has been established. She is the author of *Gabriela Mistral, la maestra de Elqui, Gabriela Mistral, the Teacher from the Valley of Elqui*, and countless articles on the Chilean poet. She is also the director-editor of *Entre rascacielos*, a student literary journal founded at St. John's University as part of Epsilon Kappa, St. John's chapter of Sigma Delta Pi, the National Hispanic Honor Society, to promote poetry on and off campus. Gazarian-Gautier is the U.S. representative of the Fundación Premio Nobel Gabriela Mistral. In 2003, she received the Civil Order of Alfonso X, El Sabio, from the Spanish government. She is also known for her collage "Recado a Gabriela Mistral."

ELIZABETH HORAN

Elizabeth Horan teaches at Arizona State University. She earned the Ph.D. in literature from the University of California, Santa Cruz, and received additional training from the School of Information, University of Michigan. She has held Fulbright Fellowships to Chile (1985–86) and to Costa Rica (1996). Her first book, *Gabriela Mistral, an Artist and Her People,* was awarded first prize in an international contest convened by the Organization of American States and the Chilean government. Her most recent book is *This America of Ours: The Letters of Gabriela Mistral and Victoria Ocampo 1926–1956,* coedited with Doris Meyer.

DARRELL B. LOCKHART

Darrell B. Lockhart, who received his Ph.D. from Arizona State University, is assistant professor of Spanish at the University of Nevada, Reno. He specializes in Latin American Jewish literature and cultural production and has published a variety of essays on that topic. He is editor of *Jewish Writers of Latin America: A Dictionary* and coauthor of *Culture and Customs of Argentina.*

EUGENIA MUÑOZ

Eugenia Muñoz, who received her Ph.D. from the University of Virginia, is associate professor of Spanish at Virginia Commonwealth University. Her teaching and research interests include feminist studies and literature, cultural studies, and creative writing. She has published numerous articles on both female and male Latin American writers. She also has published a book of literary criticism, *Novelización y parodia del mundo femenino en cuatro autores colombianos,* and a book of poetry, *Voces y razones.* Currently she is working on two bilingual collections of poems.

ANA PIZARRO

Ana Pizarro is professor of Latin American literature at the Universidad de Santiago, Chile. She is the author of various books on the culture and history of Latin America as well as numerous studies on the poetry of contemporary Chileans, such as Vicente Huidobro and the avant-gardes. Among her most recent books are *De ostras y caníbales: Reflexiones sobre la cultura latinoamericana* and *Marta Traba y la cultura en América Latina*. Pizarro was recently awarded a Guggenheim fellowship to complete a book on the culture of the Amazon.

PATRICIA RUBIO

Patricia Rubio is professor of Spanish at Skidmore College. Her publications include *Escritoras chilenas: Novella y cuento, Gabriela Mistral ante la crítica: Bibliografía anotada,* "Elisa Serrana," "Sobre el indigenismo y el mestizaje en la prosa de Gabriela Mistral," and "Carmen Naranjo, from Poet to Minister." She is presently writing, with María Claudia Andre, a book on friendships and influences among Spanish American artists and writers.

EMMA SEPÚLVEDA

Emma Sepúlveda was born in Argentina and raised in Chile. She attended the University of Santiago until the coup d'état in 1973. She immigrated to the United States in 1974 and completed her B.A. and M.A. at the University of Nevada, Reno, and eventually earned her Ph.D. from the University of California, Davis. She is the author or coauthor of seventeen books, including works of poetry, nonfiction, photography, literary criticism, and textbooks for teaching Spanish. In 1995 she founded Latinos for Political Education, a nonprofit entity in northern Nevada dedicated to the empowerment of the Latino community through voter registration. In 1994, Emma was the first Latina to run for the state senate in Nevada. She is currently professor at the

University of Nevada and is a columnist for the *Reno Gazette Journal* and the newspaper *Ahora*.

JOSEPH R. SLAUGHTER

Joseph R. Slaughter received his Ph.D. in the Ethnic and Third World specialization from the Department of English at the University of Texas, Austin, in 1998. He has been a visiting professor of postcolonial studies at the University of Montana and is currently an assistant professor in the Department of English and Comparative Literature at Columbia University. He teaches and has published on Latin American and African literature, as well as writing articles on human rights and literature. He is currently coediting an anthology of short stories on international human rights and is completing a book, *Becoming Plots, Unbecoming Acts,* that looks at the collateral development of international human rights and the novel.

IVONNE GORDON VAILAKIS

Ivonne Gordon Vailakis is a native of Ecuador. She is professor of Latin American literature at the University of Redlands in Redlands, California. She has written three volumes of poetry, numerous studies on women writers, translated some of Mistral's poems into English, and is currently finishing a book on Gabriela Mistral. In 1999 she was awarded a Fulbright scholarship, which led to the publication of *Manzanilla del insomnio,* her latest volume of poetry.

PATRICIA VARAS

Patricia Varas was born in Guayaquil, Ecuador. She has a Ph.D. in Latin American literature from the University of Toronto and is associate professor in Spanish and chair of the Latin American Studies department at Willamette University in Salem, Oregon. Her works include *Narrativa y cultura nacional* and *Las máscaras de Delmira Agustini*. She has published extensively on cinema, women's literature, and modernity.

LUIS VARGAS SAAVEDRA

Luis Vargas Saavedra is a professor of Latin American literature at the Universidad Católica de Chile and of European literature at the Universidad Adolfo Ibáñez, both in Santiago. He has published extensively on Gabriela Mistral, including essays and anthologies. His publications include his own poetry; the most recent is *A la luz del ojo*.

Index

Note: Page numbers in italics indicate illustrations.

working classes, 257
World War I, 3, 41
World War II, 19, 169, 204; plight of the
Jews, 109

Xavier, Joaquim José da Silva, 174
xenophobia, 154–55

"Yanqui he ahí el enemigo, El" (The
Yankee that is the enemy), 260
Yin Yin. *See* Godoy Mendoza, Juan
Miguel (Yin Yin)
Yurkievich, Saúl, 206

Zweig, Stefan, xv, xvii, xix, 105, 170

DATE

DEMCO, INC. 38-2931